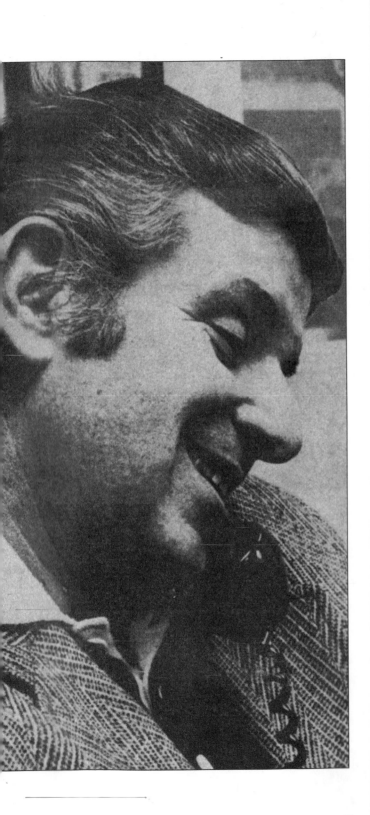

"It's
SID BER
Callir

"It's SID BERNSTEIN Calling..."

The Amazing Story of the Promoter Who Made Entertainment History

by SID BERNSTEIN

as told to Arthur Aaron

JD

JONATHAN DAVID PUBLISHERS, INC.
Middle Village, New York 11379

"It's SID BERNSTEIN Calling . . ."

Library of Congress Cataloging-in-Publication Data

Bernstein, Sid, 1918-
  "It's Sid Bernstein calling . . .", the amazing story of the promoter who made entertainment history / as told to Arthur Aaron.
    p. cm.
  Includes index.
  ISBN 0-8246-0444-X
  1. Bernstein, Sid, 1918- . 2. Impresarios—United States—Biography. 3. Popular music—United States—History and criticism. I. Title: Sid Bernstein, the amazing story of the promoter who made entertainment history. II. Aaron, Arthur. III Title.
  ML429.B36 A3 2001
  791'.092—dc21   2001042113
                                                          CIP

Book design and composition by John Reinhardt Book Design

Printed in the United States of America

For my wife, Gerry,
and my loving kids,
Adam, Denise, Dylan, Beau, Casey and Etienne

A very special thanks to
Dick Roemer,
esteemed entertainment attorney and close family friend,
for his encouragement and wisdom

Words of Love, Gratitude, Respect and Affection

from Sid Bernstein

To egg creams, éclairs and napoleons—for making life sweeter and more delectable!

To David Ippolito, the guitar player on the hill near Strawberry Fields in Central Park—for providing endless hours of music, song and a sense of tranquility.

To the Apollo Theatre—my university of musical knowledge.

To Harlem—the home of my birth.

To the City of Liverpool—my home away from home.

To Daytop Village—Brian Madden, Monsignor William O'Brien and Stan Satlin—my deep respect.

To Nightfall—Did I serve Him well today? Did I do enough?

To Dawn—For another chance to do something for my fellow man.

To Bill Bradley—for keeping hope alive.

To Dr. Maureen Nelligan—my gratitude and respect.

To David Fisher, VP of Bloomingdales—for our first book party! Can never forget you!

To Joel Gutterman, CPA—how very special you are. You're absolutely indispensable!

To Ken Roberts and Don King—thank you for all your support and confidence.

To Gary Smith—for the world of *Hullabaloo* and everything you taught me.

To Ida Langsam—thanks for your friendship and business savvy.

To Joey Reynolds, the incomparable radio talk-show host—for opening your microphones to me.

To Buddy Clark, Nat King Cole, Perry Como, Bing Crosby and Tony Bennett—for endless musical pleasures!

To Eddie, Felix, Gene and Dino of the Rascals—for five great years and an education in music.

To John, Paul, George, Ringo and Brian Epstein—thanks for the memories!

To John Lennon—eternal thanks for "Imagine" and "Beautiful Boy."

To Alfred J. Kolatch, David Kolatch, Robin Klein, Marvin Sekler and the entire staff of Jonathan David Publishers—for making this book a beautiful reality.

To Howard & Richard Rubenstein—you are very, very special friends.

To Arthur Aaron—for walking down memory lane with me and putting my words to paper.

To our dog, Mimi—for her everlasting affection.

To Abe Margolies—all my love, gratitude, respect and affection.

To my son Beau—I can't wait to tell the world that my son and I are both "published" authors.

To my two daughters, Casey and Denise—for their love. Mine in return.

To my four sons, Adam, Dylan, Beau and Etienne—how proud I am of all of you.

To Gerry Bernstein, my wife—for thirty-eight years of partnership.

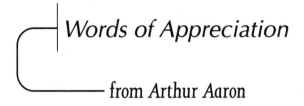

Words of Appreciation

from Arthur Aaron

Without the contributions and support of many people, I would not have been able to complete this project. My thanks to:

Antoinette Sconamilio, for her tenacity in deciphering my scratchings.

Marilyn Kaskel, for her support and her overwhelming knowledge of "the biz."

Vicki Beer, for her insight, friendship, spirit, and editorial expertise.

Ida S. Langsam, for her quick wit and nimble brain.

Jim Kaufogiens, for the pens. (Yes, I wrote this book by hand.)

Stan Satlin, who knows the difference between being a warrior and a worrier and for his ability to focus.

Robert Cohen, for his insights and suggestions.

Mark and Miriam Aron, Judith Barzilay, David Fisher, Ken Jacobson, Arthur Levy, and Charlotte Waldman, for reading the manuscript and offering constructive comments.

Mark Lapidus, for the "facts"; Dick Lopez, for his dedication; Steven Kuhn, for being a mensch's mensch.

And to Sid Bernstein, for spending countless hours sharing his rich and wonderful past.

Special thanks are due my children: Ariella Ives for her perceptiveness and advice; Avrum and Eliana Aaron, for offering invaluable help and support; and Ahava Leibtag for her steadfast belief that, in the end, all would be well.

And to my wife, Julia, without whose advice, encouragement, support and love, this book would not have been possible.

To all of you I say thank you, thank you, thank you.

Contents

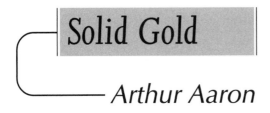

Solid Gold

Arthur Aaron

ONE DAY, AS I WAS WALKING down Broadway, I saw him—Sid Bernstein, the man who brought the Beatles to America—strolling toward me. He had that ever-youthful smile on his face.

"Sid, how are you? It's good to see you!" We greeted each other with hugs, as old rockers do.

Seeing Sid always brings back memories of the good old days. The Beatles, the Rolling Stones, the Moody Blues . . . the list goes on and on. Sid was a direct pipeline to the entertainment world, and we had met over thirty years ago when he managed the Young Rascals. I was a huge fan, and whenever Sid would see me at one of their shows, he'd refer to me as "kid." He still does.

"How're you doing, kid?" Sid asked as he beamed up at me. "What have you been up to?"

I looked down at his earnest face. He really wanted to know. That's Sid. Always interested and involved.

"Working hard," I answered. "You know, I think of you often. Remember that desk you gave me, the one you had during the time you were bringing the Beatles to the U.S.? It's in my home office. I'm constantly reminded of all the music history attached to it—and you."

"It's amazing, isn't it? Christie's or Sotheby's would love to get that desk for auction!" he said. "Beatles memorabilia is very hot!"

"Well, I can't sell that desk. You gave it to me."

"I don't blame you, kid."

As Sid recalled some of the show-business greats who had sat across that desk over the years, I stood there mesmerized by all he had achieved. He had presented the first rock concerts at Carnegie Hall and Madison Square Garden, revitalized the careers of Judy Garland and Tony Bennett, knew everyone from Frank Sinatra and Shirley MacLaine to Elvis Presley. This was a man who helped make the dreams of others come true. As he continued to reminisce, I was struck by his unusual warmth and civility—how he never failed to remember what was truly important—family, friends, treating people with respect.

It dawned on me that Sid Bernstein has led an extraordinary life and that his is an extraordinary story. His career has been full of color and excitement and yet—in a business populated with outsized egos—he's as down-to-earth as a man can be. When I approached Sid about doing this book, he was reluctant. His humility got in the way of the long-overdue telling of his story. But I pressed him, and he finally agreed. We worked on this manuscript for the better part of a year, and I came to understand how he gets things done and why people respond to him as they do. Sid abides by an honor system that people often abandon in their push to the top. His journey makes one realize that people who truly aspire to succeed can— and that all things are possible.

Sid Bernstein has a gentle manner. If your phone rings one day and the voice on the other end says, "Hello, it's Sid Bernstein calling," consider yourself fortunate. You will be speaking to solid gold.

The Top of the Mountain

Sid Bernstein

A GOOD PORTION OF MY LIFE has been spent on the telephone—making deals, cementing old friendships and forming new ones. But one particular conversation stands out in my mind. It took place in 1971 as the family was gathered around the dinner table.

"Hello, this is Sid Bernstein." I heard that unmistakable Liverpool accent on the other end.

"Sid, this is John."

"John, how are you?"

"Good, mate, thanks. Sidney, I have a big favor to ask of you."

"Name it."

"I need tickets for the Jimmy Cliff concert you're putting on tomorrow night at Carnegie Hall. A good friend of mine who loves reggae is coming from Liverpool, and I promised to take him to the concert. I tried everywhere, but there are no tickets to be had. Any possibility that you could come up with three?"

"John, the concert's sold out and I don't have a single extra ticket, but let me see what I can do. I'll call you back in a little while."

"Okay, I really appreciate it."

It was ironic. I always put aside a few extra tickets to cover just this type of last-minute request, but on this occasion even the emergency reserve was gone. Luckily, as a matter of habit, I always saved a ticket for myself, my wife and our three oldest kids. Unlike most other promoters, I didn't enjoy being backstage during the show. I preferred to sit out front and gauge audience reaction.

I decided to ask the children if they would mind giving up their tickets to John Lennon. Being pretty young, they didn't really know who Jimmy Cliff was. "Sure, Dad," they said, "but you have to tell John that we gave up our tickets for him!" They definitely knew who *he* was.

I called John back to tell him I had the tickets.

"Great, Sid! I knew you'd come through for me."

"Just go to the box office and ask for them. They'll be in your name."

"Thank you so much, Sid. That's smashing. See you tomorrow."

CARNEGIE HALL WAS PACKED the next night. There was a buzz of excitement in the air. Just moments before the show was to begin, John Lennon walked into Carnegie with a date and his friend from Liverpool. The noisy, bustling crowd grew hushed when they noticed John take his seat next to me. In the silence, the concert began.

At intermission, John chose to stay in his seat, which gave us a chance to talk. He told me about his current musical direction and a little about his personal life, which at that time was in turmoil. I told him about the concerts I was promoting and the acts I was managing. It was an easy conversation between two friends.

Right before the end of the intermission, John gazed at me with a distant look in his eyes.

"You know, Sid, that concert in 1965 at Shea Stadium . . . I saw the top of the mountain on that unforgettable night."

I looked at him for a moment and thought to myself what a truly unbelievable night that had been.

"I know what you mean, John. I saw the top of the mountain, too."

PART ONE

Opening Acts

1

To Be "Somebody"

PEOPLE SAY I AM A SOFT-SPOKEN MAN. That's probably so. In our home, no one shouted. My mother, Ida, was ill, so everything was done in a quiet, calm manner. I can remember hearing my father, Israel, raise his voice in anger only once. A fine tailor, he told a customer in his thick Yiddish accent, "Go a-vey! I don't vant you for a customer!"

All in all, my childhood memories are of peace and harmony. My grandmother, or bubba, Rachel had a gentle way. She and I shared one of the two bedrooms in our Manhattan apartment, and I loved her with all my heart. Bubba spoke only Yiddish, so I had no choice but to learn to speak that flavorful language while memorizing my abc's.

Our home was filled with the soaring voices of Caruso and a sweet-singing Jewish cantor named Yosele Rosenblatt, coming to us by way of a hand-cranked phonograph. It was in those early days of my life that I began to develop an unbridled appreciation for music.

We had what you could call a traditional Jewish home. Mama and Papa, out of respect for my grandmother, kept a kosher kitchen. That means that we bought all our meat from a kosher butcher, didn't serve shellfish or other forbidden foods and kept two sets of dishes, one for meat and one for milk.

Our home was traditional in other ways as well. My parents had recently emigrated from the small Russian *shtetl*, or town, of Lukshivka, and our extended family, also immigrants to America, would often join us for Friday night and holiday meals. Bubba would light the Friday night candles, and the entire family would then sit down to a heavenly dinner of chopped liver, gefilte fish, roast chicken with brown potatoes, kasha varnishkas . . . and the best apple strudel in New York City. Mama and Bubba stretched the dough on a kitchen tablecloth specially reserved for the occasion, then they filled it with cinnamon-scented apples, moist golden raisins . . . I could go on and on. My mother and grandmother were great cooks. They made some of the best food I have ever eaten . . . and, believe me, I have tasted some good food in my life!

As a matter of fact, food and I have had a lifelong love affair. So I hope you will indulge my occasional whim to describe for you some of my favorite delicacies or take you to some of the restaurants I have enjoyed over the years. . . . I guess you could say that food has been my muse.

I WAS BORN ON AUGUST 12, 1918, and as the only child of the Bernstein household, I received lavish attention and boundless love. My parents and grandmother called me Simcha, which in Hebrew and Yiddish means "happiness" or "party" or "celebration." Considering that I have spent most of my life in the music and entertainment business, I would say that my Hebrew name was prophetic.

When I was three years old, my parents and I vacationed at Zissel-man's Farm, in the Catskill Mountains. Some of my aunts, uncles and other relatives, including my favorite cousin, Maxie Goldberg, came along. At one time, "The Mountains" was one of the major New York resort areas, with glorious hotels like Grossinger's, The Concord and Brown's.

As my father grew more successful, we began to go to the bigger and better places, and it was at these resorts that I saw my first singers, comedians and other performers. There they were—onstage, basking in the limelight. That made a lasting impression on me. The performers were "somebody," and I wanted to be somebody, too. I particularly remember Napoleon Reid, a black performer who sang in fluent

Yiddish to the delight of his 100 percent Yiddish-speaking audience. Napoleon was a sensation.

WHEN I WAS FIVE, my father decided to go into business for himself. He bought a tailor and dry cleaning shop on 116th Street in Harlem. The premises had an apartment attached, so we moved from Madison and Ninety-ninth to the back of the shop. Shortly thereafter, I was enrolled in P. S. 10, just a block from our new home.

School was never my place of choice. I never did my homework, hated the regimentation and resented being told what to do. I didn't have many friends, preferring my folks' company to anyone else's. . . . Truthfully, I was alone most of the day. My father worked twelve to fourteen hours, my mother was either in bed or in the hospital, and Bubba spent a lot of time caring for her.

My parents never pressured me about school, never asked me about homework. I attended P. S. 10 for two years, and my most vivid memory of that experience is a snowball fight we seven-year-olds had across 116th Street. I'm sure I couldn't possibly have thrown a snowball from one side of that street to the other, yet when a window was broken, the black kids banded together to blame me: "Jew Boy did it! Jew Boy did it!" For a while, I thought that was my real name. My father had to pay to repair the window; he knew I didn't do it, but he paid anyhow.

During this time, I discovered Cushman's Bakery a block and a half from my father's shop. I would venture there to eat the marvelous jelly doughnuts, and many times I would bring home crullers to share with my grandmother. Soon, I began wandering farther north and found a German bakery that made the most mouthwatering napoleons for five cents. I went farther north still and discovered 125th Street, which was teeming with crowds, huge stores, movie theaters and the now-legendary Apollo Theatre.

I checked out the Apollo, which was across the street from Woolworth's. I clearly remember the large posters out front, featuring the performers' photographs. I knew instantly that the acts pictured on the posters were somehow connected to those I had seen at Zisselman's Farm. I remembered that they weren't the same performers, but I sensed that the posters had something to do with being on a stage, being applauded and being "somebody."

The sign above the box-office window said that anyone under twelve could be admitted for ten cents if accompanied by an adult, so I would get a dime, find someone who would take me in, and enter the magic world of the Apollo Theatre. Onstage there would be an orchestra, colorfully dressed dancing girls and, of course, the featured acts. I loved the whole scene: music, dancers, singers, comedians. Those afternoons were complete fun. Aside from the fact that the entertainers were very attractive and beautifully dressed, it was evident that the audience was having a good time. The shows would change every week or two, and I tried to see the new ones as soon as they debuted.

The first time I saw the Jimmie Lunceford Band at the Apollo, I began to understand what elements were needed for a band to be successful. There were fourteen pieces in the Lunceford group, and I could tell—even at such a young age—that they were cohesive. In fact, they were just fabulous.

DURING MY CHILDHOOD, our family moved several more times, and eventually my father sold his shop and bought a store in the Bronx. Mama continued to be hospitalized frequently, and Papa still worked extremely long hours, so I had to fend for myself much of the time. This nurtured my spirit of independence.

When I was nine, I began delivering suits and dresses for the tailor shop. That provided me with enough extra money to buy goodies and to frequent restaurants on my own. I had become a real nosher—malted milks, doughnuts, hot dogs with mustard and sauerkraut. Constant noshing meant constant love.

I loved eating out, particularly at the M&F restaurant, west of Tremont Avenue and Southern Boulevard in the Bronx, and the G&R Café, two blocks from Yankee Stadium. You could buy a complete lunch for twenty-five cents. I was a big tipper and a favorite of the waiters. I also would take the subway to Manhattan to eat at the Ruppiner Bar, a German place on East Eighty-sixth Street that had a big pot of beans in the window. For ten cents, you could get a large roast beef sandwich, and for an additional five cents, a great side dish of baked beans!

Talk of the Depression was everywhere, but it had little direct effect on the Bernstein household because my father's income was steady. And since I was earning money by delivering the dry cleaning, I always had the wherewithal to attend movies. There, watching Movie-Tone newsreels, I became informed about what was going on in the world beyond my own. I knew that the Market had crashed, although I didn't really understand the significance, and I knew that desperate people were jumping out of windows. The Bernsteins were among the lucky ones.

AT AGE TWELVE, I landed a job as an office boy at the Bronx Coliseum, a seven-thousand-seat arena that featured wrestling and boxing matches and a pretty decent Canadian ice-hockey team. I loved the wrestling matches—I even entertained thoughts of one day becoming a wrestler myself—and for many years thereafter followed the sport. When I worked in the Bronx Coliseum selling programs, I began to notice a very boisterous young man who attended the fights regularly. His flaming red hair was so bright it was almost orange, and one night I saw him screaming for a fighter named Kid Tracy. Everyone else was cheering for the favorite, but the redhead was rooting for Tracy, the underdog.

Soon after, I saw this distinctive-looking fellow in the neighborhood and approached him: "Aren't you the guy I saw cheering and screaming for Kid Tracy the other night?"

"Yeah, yeah. He's my favorite lightweight fighter."

"Do you live around here?"

"Right around the corner."

The redhead lived with his parents, and he and I became friendly. He was a very funny guy, and over the years I watched as his comedy career grew: from burlesque to vaudeville to stand-up to Broadway to television and, finally, to Hollywood, where he won an Academy Award for *Sayonara*. Success notwithstanding, he remained the same engaging person he had been in the neighborhood. The only thing different was his name: Red Buttons.

While working at the Coliseum, I got a second job at the soccer stadium adjoining it. There, I sold programs for fifteen cents each, so I was good for another dollar fifty a week during soccer season. Clearly, I was more interested in making money than in attending school.

During this time, a little man who kept smoking the same wet cigar began to come to our home to prepare me for my bar mitzvah. He taught me the prayers and, on the appointed day, about twenty to thirty family members assembled at the storefront synagogue that my father frequented on the High Holidays. There, we celebrated my "becoming a man." Unlike today, when people throw huge parties, no gala event followed—no food, no flowers, no music. I remember receiving only one gift, a fountain pen, and that was the extent of my formal religious experience.

Immediately following my bar mitzvah, I went directly from the synagogue to the Saturday craps game that was held in the schoolyard of P. S. 47. For some reason, it was protected, as no police ever showed up there. But on that morning, with me standing there holding my only gift, a cop broke up the game. For a minute, I thought that I was about to be arrested. How would that have looked, getting arrested for shooting craps in the schoolyard on the day of my bar mitzvah?

MY PARENTS CONTINUED to take their summer vacations in the Catskills, and they left me in the city in charge of the store. They knew that Phil, my father's presser, would keep an eye out as I collected cash, took in cleaning and gave people receipts. The store was underneath Lefty's Pool Hall, a hangout for my neighborhood friends. When they weren't playing pool, my friends would come downstairs to play knock rummy for money. As my card-playing skills improved, I won more than I lost, and that meant more money for dining out and going to the cinema, passions that would be with me always.

2

That First Contract

NOT LONG AFTER MY BAR MITZVAH, I began to travel more frequently to Manhattan to watch movie, stage and vaudeville shows at various theaters. The performances were great and the chorus girls dazzling, so I would play hooky from school to arrive at the theater early enough to get the best seat I could afford.

At that time, radio was a popular form of entertainment, one of America's favorite programs being *The Eddie Cantor Show*. Eddie had been a vaudevillian who made it big in the Ziegfeld Follies and was rewarded with a radio program that aired in front of a live audience every Sunday night. I enjoyed taking the subway downtown to see Cantor's shows, and somehow I always found a way to get in and enjoy entertainers who would later become famous: Deanna Durbin, Bobby Breen and the lovely Dinah Shore. When the shows were over, I would hang around and observe the producers, public relations men, agents, writers and managers to the acts. I found it all very exciting.

Another program I loved watching was NBC's *Fred Allen Show*. For all intents and purposes, the *Eddie Cantor* and *Fred Allen* shows became my university. I was absorbing and learning. Show business was evidently very much in my blood.

Nicknamed "Banjo Eyes," Eddie Cantor had a unique blend of energy and boyish charm that earned him enormous popularity as a comic actor and singer on stage and screen.

AS A TEENAGER, I was an avid reader of the best-selling magazine *Popular Mechanics*. The mail-order offerings particularly intrigued me, and one day I noticed an ad for a closeout on Eddie Cantor song books. The price quoted was two cents apiece, so I bought five hundred and lugged them to the opening night of Eddie Cantor's new stage show—unrelated to the radio program—at the Palace Theater on Broadway and Forty-seventh Street. I priced the songbooks at ten cents each and sold every one. I placed a reorder and had just about sold those out when the theater management asked me to pick up and leave. It seems that the entrepreneurship of a thirteen-year-old was less than appreciated.

AT THE BEGINNING of my first term at James Monroe High School, as I sat in an assembly, I heard a beautiful rendition of "Star Spangled Banner." The singer—a huge, swarthy fellow—was unfamiliar. I waited for the class to file out of the auditorium, and the first thing I noticed was that this young man looked older than everyone else.

I stopped him.

"Excuse me, what's your name?"

"Sol Strausser," he replied with a trace of an accent.

"You sing beautifully, Sol. I'd like to talk to you."

"Okay," he said. "But I have to go to another class."

We talked as we walked. There were only a few minutes, so I asked if we could speak at greater length after school.

"I can't," he explained. "My mother is at home waiting for me. She's all alone."

"Well, I'll be glad to come to your home if that's okay with you."

He shook his head yes, and we walked the twelve blocks to Bathgate Avenue, in a poor section of the Bronx. When we reached his apartment building, I said, "Sol, I would like to manage you."

He was stunned. "What do you mean?"

"Well, you have a great voice and I would like to manage you."

"I must tell this to my mother."

I learned that Sol and his mom were newly-arrived immigrants from Poland, and while Sol's English was quite good, his mother's was not. Sol said that in his homeland he had taken opera lessons. I asked if he knew "Vesti La Giubba," the well-known aria from *Pagliacci*, which I remembered hearing Caruso sing on my parents' crank-up Victrola. Sol proceeded to sing it so beautifully that I said, "My God, I think you sing better than Caruso. I would like to make a contract with you."

I remember writing an agreement stating that I would get 10 percent of Sol's earnings in exchange for getting him work. Sol signed the contract, and at age fourteen I had my first act. Now I had to find him some work.

A popular weekly radio program of the day was *The Major Bowes Amateur Hour*, for which aspiring entertainers would audition, and if accepted, appear on the show in front of a live audience. The magnitude of the audience's applause for a given act would determine the weekly winner, and that act would be invited to join the Major Bowes twenty-city bus tour. The value of this exposure was immeasurable, and many successful performers actually began their careers this way.

"I would like to get you on *The Major Bowes Amateur Hour*," I said to Sol and his mother. They listened to the show, so they knew what I was talking about. Both nodded in agreement.

The following Saturday, Sol and I took the Lexington Avenue line to Fiftieth Street and walked to the Capitol Theatre building, from which the Major broadcast his show.

"Where is Major Bowes's office?" we asked the guard.

"Back there, two floors up."

"Wait for me here," I instructed Sol, and proceeded to Major Bowes's office. I rang the bell and was admitted to find a rather large lady by the name of Bessy Mack seated behind a desk. A longtime associate of the Major, Bessy was the sister of Ted Mack, who later hosted television's very popular *Ted Mack Amateur Hour*.

"May I help you?" she asked.

"My name is Sid Bernstein, and I go to James Monroe High School.

Last week in our auditorium class, I heard a great singer. This young man is from Italy and he is returning next week," I concocted. "He sings only in Italian. I would hate to see him go back to Italy before he has a chance to sing "Vesti la Giubba" for you and Major Bowes. I'm sure that once you both hear him sing, Major Bowes will want to put him on the show."

Miss Mack broke up. "Where is this young man?"

"He's in the Bronx, but I can get him here quickly."

"Why don't you call him? Major Bowes is here now. Do you think your friend will sing for us?"

"Sure!" I said. "I'll ask him!"

I shot down the stairs to find Sol.

"Listen. Here's what I told them, Sol: You're a young man from Italy and you're going back on a boat next week. I heard you sing at school. They want you to come upstairs now and sing 'Vesti la Giubba' for them."

"Yeah?" he questioned, a look of awe on his face.

"Yes! Now remember, you're supposed to be Italian and I don't want them to think I'm lying, so try not to speak. Just answer me by nodding yes or no. If necessary, talk to me with as few Yiddish words as possible, okay?"

"Sure, Sid!"

We waited several minutes and then walked upstairs.

"Sol, this is Miss Mack."

"What key do you sing in?" she asked. "I have a piano player here."

I interrupted: "Sol, *vus far a key zingst du?*"

Sol answered with one letter: "C."

"All right," Miss Mack said, ushering in the accompanist.

"Okay. Sol, *in das key in C, zing* 'Vesti La Giubba' *far Miss Mack.*"

As the music started, Sol began to sing even more beautifully than he had in the school auditorium. Bessy Mack and the piano player were enthralled.

"When is he going back to Italy?" she asked. "Will he be here next Monday night?"

"*Vilst du zein du montag nacht?*" I asked Sol. "*Zug, yah,*" I added, instructing him to say yes.

"*Yah,*" Sol nodded.

"I want the Major to hear him." She left the room and returned a moment later with a courtly, elderly gentleman in a beautiful smoking jacket. The Major was a man of great bearing and charm.

"Hello, how are you, young man?" He extended his hand with a warm smile.

"Fine, Major Bowes, and permit me to introduce Sol Strausser, who is visiting here in New York but is going back to Italy next week. I was hoping that maybe you or someone on your staff would listen to him sing. He has a beautiful voice!"

"So I hear," said the Major, "Miss Mack told me that he is quite a young talent."

He turned to Sol. "How old are you, young man?"

Sol didn't answer. I translated into Yiddish: "Sol, *zug tzu de Major vie alt du bist.*"

"*Fuftzen,*" Sol said.

"He's fifteen years old."

"Fine, fine. Would you like to sing 'Vesti la Giubba' for me?"

I translated the Major's question.

"*Yah, yah,*" Sol answered.

"Good," said Major Bowes. "Do we have his key?"

The piano player nodded and began to play. As Sol started to sing, you could see how thrilled the Major was at the magnificent sound.

"When did you say he was leaving?" Major Bowes asked me.

"Next week, Major."

"Do you think he might be able to stay so that he can be in our next show?"

"Well, I could ask his mother. I think it could be arranged."

"Good," said the very pleased Major Bowes.

The Major and Miss Mack spoke in hushed tones, then the Major turned to me. "Young man, I would like you to bring Sol to our studio early Monday morning for rehearsal. You know how our show works, don't you?"

"Of course, Major. My parents and I have been listening to it for years."

"Okay," he said. Then he gave me a time to bring Sol back on Monday and bid goodbye to us both.

"*Nem sein handt un zug goodbye,*" I coached Sol.

Sol shook the Major's hand, then off we went.

Upon our departure, Bessy Mack must have surely laughed so hard that she fell off her chair. Both she and the Major understood that Sol was not Italian, but they didn't care. All that mattered was that Sol's voice was incredible.

In the alley, Sol and I hugged, congratulating each other on our good fortune. We were on cloud nine!

The following Monday, I brought Sol to the rehearsal. He was spectacular. Orchestra members, stagehands, engineers, staff—all were in awe of Sol's musical gift. That night, Major Bowes introduced his new find to the live audience and millions of radio listeners: "Ladies and gentlemen, here's a young man that I had the privilege of hearing who's on his way back home to Italy, and I asked him to spend another few days in New York so that you could hear his magnificent voice."

Sol's performance of "Vesti la Giubba" sent the applause meter off the charts, breaking all records for audience reaction. Letters, cards and phone calls flooded *The Major Bowes Amateur Hour.* The response was stupendous. When Sol and I left the show that night, people were waiting outside the stage door to greet him and ask for his autograph. "Just nod and shake hands," I kept telling him. He was literally an overnight sensation.

A few days later, I got word to go back to see Miss Mack. There I was—a fourteen-year-old manager in knickers—at Major Bowes's office in the Capitol Theatre, renegotiating with Bessy Mack.

The Major Bowes Traveling Amateur Show offered Sol two hundred dollars a week for a sixteen-week bus tour. Sol would join other winning acts appearing in major cities across the U.S. Hotels, food and other expenses would be covered, and since Sol was only fifteen years old, the show would provide him with a tutor.

I accepted the offer on Sol's behalf. When he joined the tour, Sol sent his weekly salary to his mother, and I would visit the Bathgate Avenue apartment every week to collect my twenty-dollar commission. I was in the chips.

THAT TWENTY DOLLARS a week enabled me to move up a notch in lifestyle. I had read about the Brass Rail, a first-class restaurant where wealthy and influential people dined, and I was now able to afford an occasional meal there and at Lindy's, another premier eatery. Lindy's was right next door to *The Eddie Cantor Show*, so many entertainers frequented it, including Milton Berle, whose star was rapidly rising, and John Garfield, already a major movie personality.

One day about three months after Sol had signed with the Major, an elderly gentleman visited me and flashed his business card. He had offices in the Palace Theater building and was a theatrical agent, the card said.

"Did you write this?" he asked, holding up the one-paragraph contract that I had drawn between Sol and me. *Where could the agent have obtained the contract but from Sol's mother?*

"Yes, I wrote it."

"Well, I could report you to the authorities, young man, and you'd be in a lot of hot water. You are only fourteen years old and you are not permitted to write or sign contracts. A heap of trouble awaits you, young man!"

More than frightened, I felt betrayed, so later that day I paid Sol's mother a visit to plead my case. But to no avail. She just pretended not to understand. It was a moment of great disappointment.

I sought advice from my folks and grandmother, but neither they nor I had the experience to deal with a situation like this in a professional manner. "Forget about it," they reassured me. "You will go on to do other things in life."

The older man became Sol's manager, and Sol never returned to James Monroe High School. I didn't see him again until a few years later when our family was vacationing in the Catskill Mountains and he was performing at our hotel. Sol was impeccably dressed, had lost weight and had a polished act. The audience adored him. After the performance, he greeted me as if nothing had happened. We spoke briefly, but the hurt remained.

Years later, I learned that Sol had changed his name to Jan Bart and was performing nationally on behalf of Israel bonds. I saw him once more at the Young's Gap Hotel in the Catskills, and he told me he had gotten married and was the father of a young son. By then my ill feelings toward him were a memory. Sol had become just another chapter in my life.

FOLLOWING THE DISAPPOINTMENT with Sol, I immersed myself in the social life and extracurricular activities of James Monroe High School. The girls were pretty and I had delusions of being an actor, so I tried the drama club for a while, losing interest when I realized that I didn't have the necessary talent. And though I couldn't play a musical instrument, I was also attracted to the school orchestra. They had a fine teacher and were quite good, and I would often go to their rehearsals and just sit, watch and listen. I also attended their concerts. I loved the music.

AT AGE SIXTEEN, I had an experience so traumatic that I believe I still have not recovered. One night as I lay sleeping, I felt something strange pressing against the back of my head. An object was projecting from the pillow, and as I groped, I felt a folded document. I picked up the pillow and tiptoed into the living room so as not to awaken Bubba.

I sat and opened the seam. Reaching through the feathers, I extracted the document and unfolded it. There was my name: Sidney Bernstein. It was an adoption paper, and written there was the name Rae Popkin, who I assumed had given me away. No man was mentioned.

I remember shaking as tears fell onto the paper. I realized then that I had not been born to Ida and Israel Bernstein. When the shock subsided, I buried the document back into the feathers and sewed the seam back up. Remember, I was a tailor's son, so needles and thread were always at arm's reach.

I never slept on that pillow again. And I never talked to anyone about what I had discovered. I so loved Mama, Papa and Bubba, and was so happy to be a part of their family, that silence seemed like the most prudent choice. Nonetheless, not having spoken about it bothers me to this day. *Who, I wonder, were my birth parents?*

3

A Beautiful Friendship Begins

A S I APPROACHED HIGH-SCHOOL GRADUATION, I started thinking
about the future. Like most immigrants, my parents hoped
that I would become a lawyer or a doctor, professions that
promised financial security. Since it took me five years to get out of
high school (algebra and geometry were my nemeses, causing me
to spend an extra year at Monroe), I wasn't about to subject myself
to four years of college. I figured that something of interest would
come along. I had always been entrepreneurial and able to generate
cash, so I reasoned that I would be able to fend for myself.

Toward the end of high school, I met someone who was to become a lifelong friend and a major influence in my life. Abe Margolies
was a star basketball player at James Monroe. Although he had trouble
with his eyes and wore thick glasses, that didn't stop him from
being a fabulously accurate shooter on the court.

Abe hung out at Lefty's Pool Hall, above my father's shop. At
Lefty's you could bet on all kinds of sporting events, and since I
liked to place a wager once in a while, I would sometimes spend

time upstairs. Abe was charismatic and respected, and he and I became nodding acquaintances.

In 1936, at the age of eighteen and still in high school, I had the opportunity to go to Madison Square Garden to hear Franklin D. Roosevelt speak in support of his own reelection. This was the first political rally I ever attended, so I got to the Garden early and secured a seat near the front. Unaware that the president was a victim of polio, I was shocked to see him wheeled in and helped to the podium. Heavy leg braces made the simple act of walking an extreme challenge, and I was touched and moved at the sight of President Franklin Delano Roosevelt in a wheelchair. I thought of my mother, an amputee early in life, who had to cope with a heavy, cumbersome wooden leg.

To see FDR in person, to hear his mellifluous voice, gave me goosebumps. Although the Garden was packed, it seemed as if the president was talking to me alone. I had seen him on the Movie-Tone newsreels, but here he was in the flesh.

The president's words that day helped crystallize emotions that had been running through me during my frequent wanderings in the city. When I left the Garden that evening, I had the fervent desire to think and believe as this great man did. FDR had ignited in me a political consciousness that would burn forever.

POP WANTED TO OPEN another tailor and dry cleaning store, and for a while after graduation, he tried to persuade me to run it. But I preferred to continue my adventures around the city. Frequently I would run into high-school acquaintances, and I began to appreciate how big the school truly was. Luckily, I had a good memory for names and faces, and people were often amazed that I remembered them.

About a year later, it occurred to me that it would be nice to have a James Monroe reunion dance. I negotiated with the school and cleared a Friday night to use the gym for a rental fee of $10.00. Then, I sent postcards to all the graduates and hired a deejay to play records. The weather was beautiful on the night of the dance, and the turnout was tremendous. I charged 15¢ for the girls and 25¢ for the guys. It was a huge success, and I netted $18.00, a goodly sum in those days.

A year later, I held another reunion dance, this time at a larger hall. Many who had attended the previous year's event attended this one as well, so again I had a success. My confidence soared. In actuality, these were my first promotions.

As much as I enjoyed arranging the reunion dances, I really needed to find serious employment. I registered with several agencies downtown and went on as many interviews as I could get, but when I wasn't looking for a job, I was hanging out with the neighborhood kids. The country was still recovering from the Depression, Europe was in turmoil, and to us young adults politics had become a major topic.

Some of my friends had become Young Communists. They were called Y.C.L.ers (the Young Communist League), and a few had become Norman Thomas socialists. I enjoyed listening to the debates, which were spirited and sometimes heated, but I was basically a loner, not a joiner. So I didn't get caught up with the Y.C.L. or the Y.P.S.L. (the Young People's Socialist League). My friends and I had the same concerns as President Roosevelt about how to help the poor and oppressed recover from the Depression.

I had begun hearing Father Coughlin, an Irish Catholic cleric, on the radio. Coughlin, a rabid anti-Semite, broadcast his popular Sunday radio programs from Royal Oaks, Michigan. He was a great orator, and although his message was frightening to the Jewish population, my usually nonpolitical father felt that we should listen. It was a case of "know thy enemy."

Father Coughlin issued a weekly thirty-two-page tabloid called *Social Justice* that reminded me of Hitler's *Mein Kampf*, which I had bought at the age of sixteen at a German bookshop. One day, while walking west on Forty-second Street from yet another employment agency, I passed Stern's department store. At the entrance, a burly young man with a canvas magazine pouch slung over his shoulder was selling *Social Justice* for ten cents a copy. An elderly lady passed by and scolded him in her heavily Yiddish-accented English: "You should be ashamed of yourself, selling that awful magazine. Shame on you!"

He shoved her. "Get out of here, you kike!"

Blinded by rage, I rushed over and pushed the man as hard as I could, causing him to fall off the narrow curb and his magazines to spill from the canvas bag onto the street. As I was about to kick the magazines in every which direction, a policeman approached me from behind.

"Hey, you, come here!" he screamed, his face crimson. "Follow me!"

We walked into Stern's, he ushered me to the mezzanine where two other policemen were hanging out, and in his slight Irish brogue said, "You were wrong, absolutely wrong! I saw the whole thing!"

"Yeah? What about what he did to the old lady?"

"Don't say another word," he admonished, not wanting the other two cops to hear how the fascist had pushed the old woman. "You should be ashamed of yourself. And you should also pay for those magazines in the gutter."

"What? Why?" I could not believe my ears.

"You pushed him, you hit him, you created a disturbance and you ruined his merchandise, that's why! Now, just keep your mouth closed. Shut up!"

I was incensed, but I took a look at the other two cops and thought better than to protest. After a while, they gave me a warning and sent me on my way. As I left, I was seething. This bully who had pushed the old lady was a manifestation of Hitler and his repulsive ideas, yet the authorities protected him. It was quite sobering indeed. My sensitivity to being a Jew was heightened. I was born a Jew, and I would always be a Jew.

Not long after this incident, outside a restaurant on East 149th Street in the Bronx, I saw about a hundred people milling about being addressed by a man perched on a stepladder. My curiosity drew me closer to the speaker, who turned out to be Joe McWilliams, a handsome fellow with a beautiful head of prematurely gray hair. McWilliams was an extremely gifted orator capable of mesmerizing the crowd. Since I had happened upon this event, I didn't quite understand what was going on. I heard McWilliams invite the crowd to two similar events at which he would be speaking later in the week—one in the Bronx and the other in Washington Heights, in Upper Manhattan. Then I heard him mutter, "And Roosevelt's real name is not Roosevelt; it's Rosenfeld."

"You're a liar!" I blurted out foolishly. Had I been thinking, I would have realized that the crowd was in complete agreement with McWilliams. I was attacked from all sides. Women scratched me; men screamed at me. The cops, who were there supposedly to keep order, surrounded me, and several began poking at me with their nightsticks. The hatred was palpable.

I fled the rally as fast as I could and, not wanting my blood-stained shirt to alarm my parents, delayed my return home. I waited to make sure that Mom and Pop were asleep. As soon as I entered the apartment, I removed the bloody shirt and tossed it in the garbage.

My curiosity led me to McWilliams's next two rallies, and although I didn't stay long at either, it was evident that the thrust was the same: Jew-hating and calling Roosevelt "Rosenfeld." But having learned my lesson from the first rally, I didn't utter a word of protest. It was clear that anti-Semitism was becoming pervasive. I had now seen it in three different neighborhoods. This was not happening on a movie screen but in New York City. These events so disturbed me that I felt I had to respond.

I went to Lefty's Pool Hall, upstairs from our tailor shop, to speak to Abe Margolies.

"Abe, could I possibly talk to you privately?"

"Sure," he said.

We went off to a corner, and I told him what I had discovered—that I thought McWilliams was a growing menace and that something needed to be done to curtail his activities.

"I wonder, Abe, could you get a few of the guys to go to McWilliams's next rally? I don't want to fight them, because there will be a lot of cops around, but I'd like to interrupt McWilliams's speech by singing the 'Star-Spangled Banner.'"

"Let me talk to a few of the guys up here," he said. "I'll get back to you."

Later, Abe came down to the shop. He had lined up Red Ryan and

Don Daley and some of their Irish friends, and George Manze and a few of the Italian boys.

"Sid, we're gonna meet at one o'clock on the day of the rally and go up to Fordham Road and Valentine Avenue as a group. And in the middle of the speech, we're going to sing the national anthem."

I was elated. I was going to get revenge for what had been done to me. Now I had allies.

Precisely as promised, Abe and his group met me at Lefty's, and we proceeded to walk to the McWilliams rally. There he was—up on his ladder, spouting venom at the huge crowd. We were a mixed group of guys: Jews, Italians, Irishmen. Abe had done a fine job of organizing us. We easily infiltrated the crowd, and at a signal from Abe we began to sing the "Star-Spangled Banner." Abe couldn't carry a tune if his life depended on it, but there we all were, singing in unison.

The police were at a loss for what to do. The crowd grew restless, but there was no scuffling. McWilliams was shocked. He was momentarily speechless, then tried to shout over the singing: "Ignore them, ignore them! They're all kikes trying to break up this meeting, but no one is going to break up this meeting! This is what America is really about! This is what we Americans stand for!"

From nowhere came the sound of fire engines, which promptly pulled up to the gathering. Out came hoses but we kept singing. The firemen directed water at the crowd, which quickly dispersed, and McWilliams lost his permit to hold rallies on that Bronx site from then on. We had peacefully, and I thought cleverly, thwarted that venomous creature.

Word got out about what we had accomplished, and we learned that the Jewish War Veterans, who had fought in World War I, were interested in doing the same thing in Manhattan, where McWilliams was scheduled to hold still another rally. We met the veterans and descended on the gathering together. There, Joe McWilliams was standing on the back end of a covered wagon, holding a lantern.

"I'm looking to find one patriotic Jew." He squinted and dramatically lit the wick of the lantern. And as soon as he did, we started singing the national anthem. Now it was the poolroom boys and the Jewish War Veterans, wearing their Army caps. The crowd dispersed.

When we returned to the Bronx, we learned that McWilliams had lost his permit to hold rallies on East Eighty-sixth Street, the heart of Manhattan's Germantown. I presume the authorities felt that he was a riot waiting to happen. For our part, we felt that we had rendered the community at large an important service.

The relief was temporary, however. It was 1939, and now Hitler was menacing everyone: the Jews, the Europeans, the British, the entire world. War was in the air. I was twenty-one years old. I was doing clerical work at Bronx Hospital and the YMHA in the Bronx on alternate days and continuing my meanderings throughout the city. Although I had been a disinterested student, my reading and study of Tom Paine, the American patriot who published pamphlets supporting the Revolutionary War, had intrigued me. Paine became my hero.

FOR YEARS, ON THE BACK COVER of every telephone book in New York City the Eveready Label Corporation advertised that for only two bucks you could get five thousand labels imprinted with any message. I decided that instead of Tom Paine-style pamphleteering, I was going to do stickering. My success in exposing Joe McWilliams encouraged me to broaden my political horizons.

The first sticker I produced was directed at Henry Ford, the great American industrialist who had been given the Iron Cross, the highest honor that Germany could bestow on anyone. Ford was known as a Jew-hater who had paid for the printing and distribution of a vicious anti-Semitic pamphlet entitled *The Protocols of the Learned Elders of Zion*. I placed thousands of anti-Ford stickers, which read, "Henry Ford, Give Your Iron Cross Back to Hitler," on Wrigley gum machines on every subway platform in New York City. And I signed them "Buddy Burnside." (I liked the sound of that.) Even though I had to lick each and every sticker, I did it gladly because I knew that hundreds of thousands of people who rode the subways daily would read the message.

My next target was Charles Lindbergh, the renowned aviator who was first to fly solo across the Atlantic. A notorious anti-Semite, Lindbergh also had accepted an Iron Cross from the German government. As with Ford, the Lindbergh stickers encouraged him to return his cross. So bold was I in these sticker campaigns that I even pasted one on the door of Fritz Kuhn's office at the German-American Bund, in reality a Nazi organization.

I became a full-time activist. I got a post-office box and began to imprint in tiny letters at the bottom of my stickers: "If you would like to help spread the word, send a self-addressed, stamped envelope to Buddy Burnside at P. O. Box 38, and we'll send you a supply of stickers." I started to get stamped envelopes, and since the stickers were so cheap, I could fulfill all the requests. It was no longer only me licking and pasting those stickers around the city; others were doing it, too. Now, millions of New Yorkers who rode the subways would be able to read the message.

One day, two young men showed up at my parents' door and showed me their IDs. They were FBI agents. They looked around my room, spotted the piles of reading material I had collected and interrogated me about my reading habits. I told them that I was just staying abreast of what the fascists were writing and had also gotten interested in liberal publications. Some of the material had been characterized as Communist, but my sole objective was to educate myself about the emerging political forces. The agents focused on a leftist magazine entitled *The New Masses*. They asked me if I was a member of the Communist Party.

"No," I responded.

"Then why are you reading this stuff?"

"Because I want to gather information about the people I am opposed to and also gather as much information as I can on the people who are opposed to them. My reading covers a wide gamut." I held up several of the fascist magazines. "My reading doesn't make me a Communist, now does it?"

"No, it doesn't. Sorry to bother you." And with that, they left.

The sticker campaigns became so well-known that *Life* actually reprinted one of the stickers. Also, John Wilson, of the liberal tabloid P.M., tracked me down, either through the post-office box or the Eveready Label Corporation, and interviewed me. "Buddy Burnside is really someone named Sid Bernstein," he reported in the magazine. My secret was out!

IN 1940, THERE WAS A BATTLE within the Republican Party over who would be named its presidential nominee. Although I wholeheartedly supported President Roosevelt, the Democrat, I so abhorred the conservative Republicans who were opposing the more moderate Wendell Wilkie for the Republican nomination that I decided to do whatever I could to help Wilkie.

To that end, I placed forty or fifty thousand "Win With Wilkie" stickers around the city. And to broaden my geographic reach, I enlisted some of the fellows from Lefty's Pool Hall to accompany me to Philadelphia, where the Republicans were holding their convention.

Somehow, we gained admittance to the convention floor. Surreptitiously and cleverly, we placed "Win With Wilkie" stickers on every seat and at every microphone. Amazing that we weren't caught or, still worse, arrested.

Wilkie won the Republican nomination. FDR won the national election. I was delighted. The conservatives did not carry the day, as I had feared.

Chalk up another one to Buddy Burnside!

PART TWO

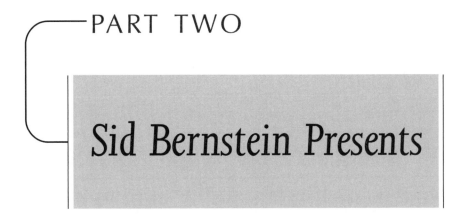

Sid Bernstein Presents

4

Over There

O N SUNDAY MORNING, December 7, 1941, I was sitting in the kitchen with my father. We were listening to the lib-eral radio commentator Drew Pearson when a bulletin interrupted the program: The Japanese had attacked Pearl Harbor.

Although no one could be happy at the thought of war, my view of the situation was different from most others. To me, the attack on Pearl Harbor signaled the end of isolationism. America would become involved, and the Nazis would finally be stopped.

I wanted to enlist, but my mother's health was still quite poor. Bubba was getting on in years, and my father had to spend most of his time at the tailor shop. It was up to me to take up the slack. Eventually I would be drafted, but until then I helped out around home . . . and waited.

In January 1943, at twenty-five years old, I received my induction notice. Of course, Mama, Pop and Bubba hated to see me go, and I hated leaving them. *Who knew when or if I would return?*

At Camp Upton, on Long Island, I was sworn into the Army. From there, I was ordered to Verona, New Jersey, for eight weeks of basic training, and then was issued a temporary assignment in Prospect

Park, Brooklyn. The Army had taken over this large and beautiful park right in the middle of New York's most populous borough. They fenced it in, built some barracks and made it a stopover before transferring soldiers to advanced training elsewhere. There I was, a member of Battery A, of the 602nd AAA Gun Battalion, stationed in Prospect Park to defend the local citizens against air attacks. I didn't know from whom and I didn't know why, but there we were defending Brooklyn.

The food in the Army was so lousy that every once in a while I would climb the fence after bed-check and go to Garfield's Cafeteria, Dubrow's, and Nathan's Famous, the hot-dog place in Coney Island. I was usually back in a few hours and, thank God, I never got caught. How could my parents possibly have coped with the news that their son was being court-martialed for going AWOL for a piece of kishke or a corned beef sandwich!

After eight weeks of basic training, we were in the best shape of our lives. The girls from the neighborhood took notice and came looking for us. I became friendly with a very pretty twenty-one-year-old blonde I'll never forget. One night, she and I went to a little place called "Blanket Hill," and I lost my virginity. Though I had been brought up to respect women and the sanctity of marriage, what happened, happened, and I didn't complain about it afterward!

Upon completing our assignment in Prospect Park, we were sent to Fort Totten to learn the workings of an artillery battery—how to sight the big 90-millimeter cannon, how to be a loader. Finally, we were moved to Riverhead, Long Island, to gain experience actually firing those massive weapons. We shot directly into the ocean, which was safe enough, but the cannons made so much noise that they permanently impaired my hearing. To this day, I have trouble with certain registers, but not so much as to diminish my love for music.

LATE IN 1943, I was shipped with my Army buddies to Gurock, Scotland, in anticipation of the invasion of Europe. After a brief stay there, we were sent by rail to Nottingham, England, made famous by the *Tales of Robin Hood*.

I had thought that the food at basic training was bad, but Army food overseas was indescribable. Fortunately, Pop heeded the slogan made famous by Katz's Deli on New York's Lower East Side: "Send a salami to your boy in the Army." And, in addition to those welcome salamis, he would send one-pound blocks of Nestlés chocolate and copies of a few New York newspapers, like P.M. and *The Daily Mirror.*

GI Sid's U.S. Army headshot.

My unit was stationed near a huge airfield, and one morning the earth literally shook from the noise coming from the air base. It seemed as if every plane had its engine running; the sound was deafening. That turned out to be D-Day. Five days later, our company crossed the English Channel to Normandy. We landed on Omaha Beach, which we later learned had seen some of the fiercest fighting during the initial hours of the invasion. Had we been there on Day One of the offensive, most of us would have been killed. Omaha Beach had been cleared, but at night we could hear gunfire, the sound of Allied Field Marshal Montgomery's troops engaging the enemy.

Countless truck convoys moved men and equipment. Most of the vehicles were driven by black men. It bothered me that we weren't integrated as an army. I thought that it somehow made us less of a nation.

Our unit moved farther into France and bivouacked on an abandoned farm. We were going to set up camp there for a while, so Frank Diano, my buddy and fellow machine gunner, and I got ambitious and decided to build a little hut. We found some lumber, which we used to erect sides, used our pup tent as the floor and made mattresses out of straw. Frank and I made the hut as cozy as we could.

During our free time, we would walk into the local town to see what was going on. I remembered some of my high-school French and was able to converse with the girls, notably a buxom French farm girl named Madeleine. We got chummy, and she would visit our camp at the farm, often bringing us fresh eggs and cow's milk. Given the powdered milk and horrendous Army food we were accustomed to, that was a real treat.

One pitch-black, moonless night, Diano and I were asleep in our makeshift hut. Suddenly, I was awakened from a deep sleep by hands groping my body.

"Frank," I said. "Cut it out! Stop kidding around!"

I reached down and grabbed his hand, which I then realized was a woman's. I opened my eyes and there, at the foot of the bed, was Madeleine, her silhouette barely recognizable in the darkness. She moved up, lay beside me and started hugging and kissing me. Diano was now in a deep sleep.

I longed to touch Madeleine's hair, but first had to remove the turban she was wearing. Slowly, I eased back the bandana, and to my astonishment her hair came off as well. Madeleine was bald! She must have been disciplined by the French for collaborating or dating the German invaders. They were known to shave a girl's head and make her parade through the center of town. Apparently, Madeleine liked soldiers, no matter which side they were on.

"Go away! Go away!" I yelled at Madeleine, and she did. I never saw her again.

Not long after that hair-raising event, we were transported farther inland; our troops moved toward the border of France and Germany. The mission was to shoot down the V-1 rockets that the Germans were directing toward Great Britain. The V-1's, which we could see taking off, made the most frightful noise. Diano and I were manning a machine gun one day when we heard and then spotted a low-flying rocket. I started firing, and Diano kept feeding the gun. Luck was a lady that day: I blasted the V-1 right out of the sky. Knocking down a V-1 was highly uncommon, so I was a big hero for a day or two. The reward: promotion to private first class.

Shortly thereafter, we saw heavy action in the Battle of the Bulge, one of the most famous confrontations of World War II. The overwhelming German forces pushed our front-line troops back so far that we in the rear were ordered to move even farther back. Ambulances and wounded soldiers were everywhere. Captain McCarthy asked Diano and me to be the rear guard for the company as we retreated.

We were positioned with our machine gun covering the guys as they fell back, and McCarthy told us to hold that position until all our men had passed. He would return for us when everyone was in the clear. Diano and I were terrified, but we stayed until the captain came back and got us.

I remember taking the firing pin out of the machine gun we were about to abandon, thereby rendering it useless. En route to the rear, we saw all the guns and ammo that the American forces left behind. A memorable sight indeed.

Soon, the tide turned. The American army regrouped, and we were ordered to a town called Epinal, where we were to stay a few months, until V-E Day (Victory in Europe), May 8, 1945. We were overjoyed. The war in Europe was over!

5

Welcome to the Club

OUR STAY IN EPINAL, a quiet town that had been spared the devastation of war, was uneventful. From there we were ordered to Dijon, a city of one hundred thousand or so made famous by its tasty mustard. Dijon was also the place from which we embarked for home.

The process of being shipped back to the States was based on a point system. A soldier who had been wounded or had received the Purple Heart was awarded a certain number of points; one who had fought in a battle earned other points; and so on. The troops with the most points went home first, and since we had gotten to Europe rather late in the war and had seen relatively little action, our point totals were comparatively low. So we stayed in Dijon longer than we would have liked—but that worked to my advantage.

Most of our activity in Dijon consisted of guarding German POWs. One day early in our stay, the captain, who took a shine to me, presented an option: "Bernie, do you want to keep guarding these German prisoners or do you want to drive one of the provision trucks or do something else?"

"Well, to tell the truth, Captain, I'd just like any job where I wouldn't have to carry a heavy rifle."

"You know what, Bernie?" he countered. "The battalion needs a newspaper, or at least a newsletter."

"A newsletter?"

"Yeah, a daily one-sheet with some news that we can get out to our boys and to the other battalions. Something to let everyone know what's going on with us."

"Okay, Captain, I'll take a shot at it."

We called the newsletter the Comeback Diary, since we now knew for sure that we would soon be coming home. The captain gave me two German POWs as assistants. The one who spoke fluent English was my typist; the other did the mimeographing. Even though a few months earlier we had been hell-bent on killing each other, we came to realize that we were just human beings who had been put in this position by the fortunes of war. The POWs were just as eager to get home to their families as I. We quickly became friends.

Every day for the Comeback Diary, I wrote an article filled with battalion news and information that I got from the States via the newspapers that my father included in his food shipments. We wanted the Diary to be distributed not only to the soldiers but also to the local citizens, so I included something in French in the newsletter every day, and soon the civilians started to read the paper. It had a breezy, gossipy, New York style, and the tidbits in it were quite different from those of the Army's Stars & Stripes and similar journals.

At first, we were mimeographing one hundred sheets a day, but the circulation quickly built and eventually we were printing six thousand per day. Since I was including something for the French citizenry, I got into the habit of signing off my column with "Votre garçon, Sidney." When the armed services radio guys got wind of our newspaper, they started quoting it in their broadcasts. "Here's something from 'Your boy, Sidney,'" they would say. This created still greater demand for the paper. Amazing! I had become a successful newspaper publisher while waiting to be released from the Army.

The captain and other officers were so pleased with my journalistic success that they procured a room for me at Dijon's Grand

Hotel, which had accommodations far superior to those at the Central Hotel, where we had been staying. I was the only nonofficer living at the Grand.

Through the newspaper, I campaigned against the gouging of American soldiers by the French at the bars and cafés. The locals were not as appreciative of the Americans as the British had been, treating our boys rudely and overcharging them at almost every turn. This did not sit well with me. After all, we had come to France to help liberate them from the Nazis. Some of our finest young men were buried in France. I began to campaign for a GI nightclub.

One day, one of the captains approached me: "Bernstein, you know this GI nightclub you keep writing about in the paper? There's a lot of talk about it and I want you to put it together."

I knew nothing about running a nightclub, but an order is an order, so I requisitioned a vacant store on the main street in Dijon. I got tables and chairs, had the place decorated and hired the loveliest French girls as waitresses. We made it a point of keeping all the windows clear so that anyone could look inside and see how well-behaved the GIs were. And we served only wine and beer, no hard liquor. The entertainment consisted mostly of records played by a deejay, and I insisted that everyone be on his best behavior. Anyone who got the least bit rowdy was asked to leave.

The nightclub became very popular, so in addition to being a newspaper mogul, I had now become a nightclub impresario. I made sure we had the latest music, arranged for the cleanup of the club and found two bright enlisted men to run the cash and keep the books. Everyone having a good time in a safe and well-ordered environment was the goal, and we accomplished it. Determined to keep my behavior professional, I made it my business to stay away from the attractive girls who worked in or patronized our club.

Almost every night, a crowd of Dijon residents would congregate outside the window. One evening, as I turned to look at the crowd that was outside peering in, I spotted the most delicately exquisite blonde standing there with a very attractive older woman, obviously her mother, who looked to be in her early forties. Both women were smiling at me, and I ventured out to say hello. My

Here I am with a fellow soldier in front of the "happening" GI Nite Club.

French had become quite good by this time, and I learned that the shy young beauty was Claudy Vilfroy, a nineteen-year-old college student at the University of Dijon.

Claudy and Madame Vilfroy accepted my offer to accompany them home, a mere eight blocks down the road. At the entrance to their building they cordially invited me up for tea, but I declined. I had to get back to the club but would enjoy having tea with them some other time. Whenever convenient, they said. I returned to the club, but thoughts of Claudy did not leave me.

Several days later, when all seemed to be running smoothly and I could get away, I walked the eight blocks to the Vilfroy apartment, where from that day forward I became a frequent guest. I was twenty-seven years old and smitten with Claudy Vilfroy.

Claudy and I spoke only French to each other, and on one occasion, as the record player was filling the room with lilting music, I asked if she would like to dance. "Oui," she said, and I was in heaven. I sneaked a kiss.

As my visits to the Vilfroy home continued, I became very friendly with Madame Vilfroy and her husband, Georges, a traveling sales-man who was often away. And, of course, I found Claudy continu-ally enchanting.

After many months of waiting, my unit was ordered back to the United States. We were to go to Reine and from there to Marseilles to board ships destined for home. On my final day in Dijon, I went to bid Claudy and her mother farewell. I was quite sad. Claudy walked me downstairs and we kissed. I gave her my address and promised to write. I hoped I could get back to France soon, I told her.

The next day we left for Reine, turning in our weapons and other gear. There, we boarded trains that we thought would take us di-rectly to Marseilles. When late that night the train stopped unex-pectedly at Dijon, I seriously considered going AWOL to go say goodbye to Claudy one more time. Reminding myself of the dire consequences of abandoning my unit, I reconsidered. A short time later the train resumed its journey to Marseilles.

Rough seas made the voyage back to the United States horren-dous; thoughts of Claudy were my only comfort. What seemed like an eternity later, we arrived at one of the Hudson River piers. There, we were loaded on buses and transported to Fort Dix, New Jersey, where we arrived late in the evening to find the ground covered with snow. After being formally discharged, we had the choice of waiting for the morning bus or leaving immediately.

I didn't care how late the hour, how bad the weather or how deep the snow—I just wanted to get out of there. So, with a few friends, I trudged through a large muddy field to the train station. Every step took us closer to home.

We caught the early morning train to New York, and after a hearty breakfast with my buddies down at Ratner's on Second Avenue, I took a cab to the Bronx. Wearing an Army coat, with a duffel bag slung over my shoulder, I entered my father's tailor shop. Tears rolled down my cheeks when I saw Pop sitting at his sewing machine. I had seen that image countless times. But how he had aged! He looked up and yanked off his glasses.

"Simcha!" he cried. We hugged for a long time. I had not seen my father in more than two years, and as we spoke to each other in

Yiddish, I was flooded with memories. I rushed home to be reunited with Mama and Bubba.

That evening, as we sat down at the dinner table in our ground-floor Bronx apartment, I thanked God for allowing me to make it through. Our small family was together again.

The next day, still in disbelief that I was actually home, I wandered around the neighborhood, getting reacclimated. I was looking forward to seeing my old friend Abe Margolies but was disappointed to learn that he and his young family had moved to Laurelton, Queens. On the other hand, I was happy to find out that Abe had achieved considerable success in business. Abe's poor eyesight had rendered him unable to serve in the armed forces, so instead he started a jewelry company, which in a short time he and a partner built into a large and successful enterprise.

CLAUDY HAD WRITTEN ME practically every day since I left France, and when I arrived home, a packet of letters awaited me. Knowing that religion was an issue between us, I did not respond for a long while. Even though I was not religious, my parents—and particularly my grandmother—would have been greatly disappointed if I became seriously involved with a girl of a different faith. Eventually, Claudy stopped writing. She was young and innocent, and I should have demonstrated greater sensitivity. I will always feel remorse over that episode in my life.

As the weeks passed, I became reintegrated into civilian life. I didn't know what I wanted to do and, as usual, there was absolutely no family pressure. I helped out my father at the tailor shop when needed, but the work was intermittent and I didn't approach it seriously. However, one day I presented my father with a business idea that turned out to be almost too successful.

"Pop," I remarked, "the Tremont trolley runs right past the shop. You know, all these returning soldiers need work done on their clothes. Why don't we put up a sign that says 'Alterations for Returning Soldiers—Special Discount Price'? Lots of people riding on the trolley will notice it."

My father liked the idea, so I went to the local signmaker and designed a large colorful placard that we hung in the shop window. Sure enough, the returning servicemen came in droves. In fact, there were so many new customers that my father had to hire another tailor and I had to spend more time at the shop. "*Simcha, vus hus di getoon? Ich hab tzu fil arbeit!*" my father said. "What have you done? I have too much work!"

ACTIVISM WAS IN MY BLOOD. I soon became itchy to get involved in a social cause once again. The people who came into the shop complained bitterly about the price of meat, which was high because the government had taken over the meat supply for use by the armed services. That meant that there was a limited amount for civilians. It would take a while for supply to catch up to demand.

I decided to start a sticker campaign. The message was "Don't Buy Meat," and again I signed it "Buddy Burnside." And, as before, tiny letters at the bottom of the sticker said that by sending a self-addressed envelope, anyone could get a supply of stickers and become an ally of mine. I got plenty of responses, and soon "Don't Buy Meat" stickers began to appear all over the city.

The next campaign was in support of affordable housing for returning servicemen. Veterans were marrying at a rapid rate, and housing was so scarce that young married couples had to move in with their parents, creating very trying circumstances. I spoke out publicly for affordable housing, even traveling to Washington, D.C., with a group of veterans to lobby congressmen and senators. There, I met a young congressman from Boston who was very sympathetic to our cause. His name was John F. Kennedy.

One day back in New York, a singer spoke at a large housing rally in Harlem. He was eloquent, extremely handsome, brilliant and charismatic. I will never forget watching Harry Belafonte command the attention of the crowd that afternoon.

During this period, I had enough money to subsist but continued to assume odd jobs, though none really interested me. My mother's health had not improved, so I also became even more involved at home, acting as the family chauffeur, helping with the shopping, and doing various other chores.

Not too long after I returned from the Army, Bubba went to the doctor complaining of chest pains. The doctor didn't like the way her heart sounded, so he admitted her to the hospital for tests and rest. I visited her every day for about ten days, and she seemed fine. Then one day we got a call that Bubba had passed away. The news was terribly shocking. My best pal was gone.

WITH THE WAR'S END and my return to civilian life, I wanted to become involved in a politically and socially liberal organization. The Veterans of Foreign Wars (VFW) and the American Legion seemed too conservative, so I joined the American Veterans Committee (AVC).

Headquartered in Washington, that group was led by bright young returning veterans, including Michael Straight, from a prominent family in Westbury; Franklin D. Roosevelt, Jr., the deceased president's son; and G. Mennen Williams, a scion of the shaving cream family.

I helped organize AVC's Henry Hopkins chapter in the South Bronx, named after FDR's longtime friend, adviser and aide. We secured a clubhouse loft on East Tremont Avenue, and I became the chapter's first president. Weekly board meetings were held at the loft, and it became a hangout where we could talk about the important issues of the day. We debated at length about affordable housing, as well as about equity and justice for black people. I wrote a weekly column, "The Burnside Chat," for the *AVC Bulletin*, a tabloid-size journal that was distributed to all of the AVC chapters. Buddy Burnside now became known nationally.

For months, an idea was percolating in my brain. I decided to organize a singles weekend for young people at the Plaza Hotel in Fallsburg, New York. I traveled up north to that Catskills hotel and met with its owners, Messrs. Orlansky and Platt. I requested fifty double-occupancy rooms, hoping that I would be able to attract one hundred singles for a Friday night to Sunday stay. Orlansky and Platt agreed to give me the fifty rooms with the proviso that should they need them for their own guests, they could take them back. I gambled and placed some ads in the *New York Post*. The reservations came pouring in, and the weekend was a hit on all fronts. To top it off, I made $12.50 per room. Orlansky and Platt were impressed, and they offered me a job for the next summer as the hotel's social director. I declined.

I was still very involved with the AVC. Since I was the Harry Hopkins chapter's first president, I knew every person by name and interacted with many members on various projects. Jay Simms, one of the chapter's founding members, worked closely with me and we became good friends. Jay knew Jack and Eve Lasher, a middle-aged couple who had rented an old Con Ed regional office on Tremont and Monterey Avenues in the Bronx and converted it into a catering and meeting hall. The Tremont Terrace, as it was called, became a popular place for weddings, bar mitzvahs, christenings or any type of social event where food was a requirement. The Terrace also held weekly Friday night dances featuring small bands.

One day, Jay told me that he had spoken to the Lashers and thought that I could be helpful to them as a publicity man for the Terrace. Jay set up a meeting. I liked the Lashers immediately, and accepted their job offer at a salary of $25.00 a week.

For a publicity man, contacts are his lifeblood, and through my AVC activities, including the many meetings I attended at chapters throughout the city, I came to know many people. In my travels, I spread the word about the events being held at the Tremont Terrace, and as a result the Terrace became increasingly popular. As a thanks for my efforts, the Lashers increased my salary from $25.00 to one hundred twenty-five dollars per week within a year.

I was on a typically showbiz schedule. I arrived at work around noon six days a week and would stay late into the evening. As time went on, I was given more responsibility, including booking the small bands and combos that were popular at the time. The Lashers looked to me increasingly for advice, and I got involved in all facets of the club business. While the Lashers were the owners and bosses, I was basically in charge of the daily operations of the Tremont Terrace. I didn't realize then that I was rapidly gravitating towards a career in the entertainment world.

6

Let the Music Begin

I N 1950, LATIN MUSIC BECAME HOT. Xavier Cugat and Noro Morales were two of the most prominent Latin recording artists, and Cugat was also often seen on television and in the movies.

With the growing prominence of Latin music, the Lashers and I decided to change the name of the Tremont Terrace to the Trocadero. The South Bronx was slowly becoming a Puerto Rican enclave, so it made sense to follow the Latin craze that was sweeping the music business. We continued to do weddings, bar mitzvahs and other social events, but the Trocadero became known primarily as a dance club where you could have a good time in a safe, secure, fun environment. People came from all over the city to dance and meet each other.

I began to buy time on radio, which reached a wide audience. The promotion worked, and the Trocadero prospered, with customers coming from New Jersey, Brooklyn, Westchester and Manhattan. The Lashers couldn't have been happier.

The club was jammed on the weekends, but I wanted to fill it during the week as well. That led to the idea of holding a Wednesday night lecture series. I had been reading about a high-school teacher who had become a very successful humorist while working in the Catskills. I contacted him, and he agreed to work at the Trocadero for the princely sum of $75.00. Sam Levenson became a hit in the Bronx and went on to become an even bigger star on TV variety shows. I also booked a young blind pianist by the name of George Shearing, who became a big draw and ultimately went on to achieve stardom as a concert and television performer.

The Trocadero had become a Bronx landmark. I was feeling really good about myself and knew that I was on a roll. It was time for something bigger. The Lashers encouraged me in anything that I wanted to do. As long as I took care of my responsibilities at the Trocadero, I was free to test other waters.

I was still active in the AVC and thought that it would be terrific to hold a big benefit dance, so I took a leap of faith and rented the huge Kingsbridge Armory for one thousand dollars. Then I hired Sammy Kaye and his band for the substantial sum of two thousand dollars. Sammy, in a class with the Dorsey and Glen Miller bands, was worth every penny. I also spent money on leaflets and posters and had them plastered all over town. At the monthly citywide meetings of the AVC, I persuaded the participants to take tickets and sell them at their respective chapters—and I gave them a commission on each ticket sold. The incentive worked.

Kingsbridge Armory did not have a facility for checking outerwear, and it was my responsibility to devise one for those attending the dance. I went up to Lefty's Pool Hall and asked some of the guys there to help me out. The dance was held in late fall, and most of the men who came to the dance wore hats, while almost all the gals came with some type of coat. More than five thousand people showed up at the armory that night, a record for a dance in the Bronx. Sammy Kaye and his band were wonderful, and a fabulous time was had by all.

When the dance ended, all the attendees rushed to the coatcheck stand being manned by my buddies from Lefty's. Here were these eight pool-hall characters trying to return hats and coats to more than five thousand people. It was utter chaos. And when all was said and done, a group of young women in tears sought me out.

"I lost my beaver coat!" "My fur is gone!" And on and on.

What could I do? Everyone knew me as the dance organizer. I had run the dance for the AVC, but I couldn't use any of the considerable profits to pay for the lost garments. So I jotted down the name and address of each young lady, noted the value of each missing garment and, over a period of the next six months, used my Trocadero salary to gradually repay each one.

After the Kingsbridge Armory fiasco, I continued to book the bands into the Trocadero. Most were Puerto Rican groups like the Curbelos, the La Playa sextet from Central America, Tito Rodriguez and the legendary Tito Puente. After trying repeatedly, I finally got Noro Morales, who had one of the best Latin sounds around.

Noro had a younger brother named Esy, a fabulous flutist and overall magnificent musician who was known for a number-one record of his own: a new arrangement of "The Flight of the Bumblebee." I was thoroughly won over by his talent. I booked Esy, and on the night he played, I went backstage to talk to him between sets. Articulate and bright, Esy spoke English quite well. He told me that he and his other brother, Humberto, a drummer, had started out with Noro but had left to form a band of their own.

"Esy, you had this incredible number-one hit, yet your asking price for tonight was much lower than I imagined it would be. Tell me, do you work a lot?"

"Truthfully, I don't. In fact, I have a very hard time keeping my band together. We don't get enough work."

I pursued it. "Do you have a manager?"

"I have a lawyer and an accountant, but no manager."

His lawyer and accountant were well known in the business, but I knew that Esy was harming himself by not having adequate representation. Without someone to exploit his great talent, he would have a difficult time keeping the band together.

"Well, Esy, don't you think you should have one? After all, that's what would keep you working and help build your career. You've got such a fine band and you've already had a hit record. You should be working more."

We exchanged phone numbers, and a few days later I called. He invited me to his home, and I met his attractive and gregarious wife, Blanche. Esy and I discussed management, and he told me that he wanted to work together. I proposed a deal: 10 percent of his earnings in exchange for finding him work and guiding his career.

We agreed that I would also become his promoter as well as his manager. This meant that I would no longer be able to handle my responsibilities at the Trocadero. I gave the Lashers six weeks' notice, and although they were upset, they wished me well. I had become like a son to them. Living only ten blocks from the Trocadero, I assured them that I would be around if needed. And whenever they called upon me after that, I was always there for them. I really cared about those folks. They gave me my entrée into the business and I learned a great deal while in their employ.

Milton Berle had worked at a nightclub in the Capitol Hotel at Fiftieth and Broadway, but after he achieved a measure of success, he left the club with a vacancy. I decided to rent the space and showcase Esy Morales there for several weekends. That was just what was needed. Esy was an instantaneous success, and as his reputation grew, the crowds did, too. Esy was delighted at his increased following. His price per performance was up and his career was booming. Thereafter, I was able to get Esy many club dates, and talk about his not being able to keep the band together was a thing of the past.

Meanwhile, word was out about what I had done with the singles weekend at the Plaza. Mrs. Lipkin and Mrs. Bush, proprietors of the Morningside Hotel, another Catskills resort, sought to hire me as their social director the following summer. They offered me good money, so I took the opportunity to spend July and August in the mountains. Since I had a responsibility to Esy, I booked him into a neighboring hotel, the Tamarack Lodge. An ideal situation: I could do my job at the Morningside and still manage Esy's career. I was making two salaries—one from Esy and the other from the Morningside. I had a car, so I could travel back and forth between locations with ease. In addition, I could afford to bring my mother to the mountains for the entire summer. Pop would join us on the weekends. Everyone was happy.

Next, I met George Scheck (father of Barry Scheck, the DNA lawyer and one of the defenders of O. J. Simpson), who was then managing Connie Francis. George owned a television show called *Star Time*, which featured kid entertainers. In addition to performing on the show, George would tour them to clubs and hotels in a prepackaged variety format. We became friends when *The Star Time Revue* came to perform at the Morningside.

I told George about Esy Morales and his band playing at the Tamarack, and he sent one of his assistants to hear them. The assistant flipped, so Scheck asked if I would be interested in having Esy star on a local CBS show called *Tropic Holiday* along with other Latin artists. Esy and I both answered a resounding yes, and before long Esy Morales could be seen on New York television every week.

Esy Morales was in the prime of life. His horizons were unlimited. But he suffered from diabetes and was very cavalier about his diet. I warned him that if he didn't monitor his sugar intake there could be irreversible damage. The advice went unheeded, and one afternoon Blanche called to tell me that thirty-five-year-old Esy had died. I fell into deep despair. How was it possible for so vibrant a man, blessed with a loving wife and a blossoming career, to be taken so abruptly from our midst?

LOU WALTERS, THE FATHER OF BARBARA, owned the Latin Quarter, without question one of the top nightclubs in America. "The Quarter," as it came to be known, featured statuesque showgirls, dance ensembles, acrobats, magicians and comedians, and its customer base consisted of the most varied group of dinner and show patrons one could imagine. The rich and famous, royalty, captains of industry, mobsters—all visited the Latin Quarter.

I knew Lou casually because Cass Franklin, his associate, would book acts for me while I was at the Trocadero. Lou wanted to expand his horizons, so he, along with Cass, started an artists man-

JUdson 6-8300

LOU WALTERS ENTERPRISES, INC.

SIDNEY BERNSTEIN
1576 BROADWAY
NEW YORK 36. N. Y.

The Latin Quarter Management Company was under the umbrella of Lou Walters Enterprises.

agement company. A wise move, I thought, because if they found talent worthy of appearing at the Latin Quarter, that performer would have a leg up on the competition. Cass ran the management company.

After Esy died, Cass approached me. "Sid, I know what a terrible blow Esy's death is for you. You did a wonderful job for him and we know that you have management skills. Lou and I were hoping that you would come work with us."

I liked Cass, so I said yes and went to work for the Latin Quarter Management Company. It was a pleasant atmosphere to be in. I was treated well, the Quarter was in its heyday, and I met lots of famous people. Those tall, curvaceous chorus girls weren't hard to take, either. I got to know some of them extremely well, including one who had caught Frank Sinatra's eye.

Even so, in the time that I spent there, we never signed a breakthrough act, one that rocketed to stardom, and that made the going tough. Without that kind of leverage, it's difficult for a management company to survive, and before long Cass was forced to conclude that it was time to disband. I was ready for something new anyway, so the dissolution of the business did not really bother me.

THE MAJOR BOOKING ORGANIZATION for Latin bands at the time was the Mercury Agency. When I was hiring bands for the Trocadero, I dealt with Mercury on a continuous basis. They had all the greats: Noro Morales, Ralph Font, the great Machito, the Cabelos, Pupi Campo and Tito Puente.

My friend Larry Meyers worked as an agent at Mercury, and I would see him from time to time. When the Latin Quarter management venture failed, Larry talked to me about coming to work at Mercury. He offered to get me an interview, so I figured, Why not?

I knew and liked Lenny and Charley Green, the brothers who owned Mercury. They were aware of my efforts on behalf of Esy. So when they asked me to join them, I accepted without hesitation. The setup sounded terrific: I had my own office and secretary, and since I was committed to a job in the Catskills the following summer, they would give me the entire summer off.

I loved being busy, and I loved Latin music, but good as the situation appeared, being chained to a desk at the Mercury Agency was not to my liking. The world of management was freer. And working with bands that I wasn't close to didn't have any particular appeal. I was really looking forward to the coming summer.

Before Esy died, I had met Cynthia Brown, whose father, Charlie, owned Brown's Hotel, home of the Brown Derby, one of the most famous nightspots in the Catskills. The action there would start at about midnight, when the staff as well as the entertainers from the surrounding hotels would gather to unwind after their long and hectic day and evening performances. Famous personalities like Eddie Cantor and Milton Berle would visit there while vacationing. The Brown Derby was simply the place to be in the Catskills—and if you worked at Brown's and had the opportunity to go there every night, you had it made. It was wine, women and song.

Cynthia was familiar with my work at the Morningside, and she wanted me to meet her father. "Gladly," I told her. When I met with Charlie Brown at the hotel, it took no time before he offered me the social director's job for the following summer.

Brown's Hotel was everything it was cracked up to be—large, well-maintained, teeming with guests. There was nonstop action, beautiful girls, a fabulous nightclub, and even more beautiful girls. Brown's had gotten a lot of press because Jerry Lewis got his start there. His parents were on staff and Jerry actually began as a teaboy. With his comedic gift, he kept people in stitches for hours, eventually working his way into the Brown Derby. After Jerry was discovered, he never forgot that it was Brown's that gave him his first break. Even as a megastar, Jerry would stop by for a month each summer to visit with his folks, take it easy and vacation with his wife, Patti. And when the spirit moved him, Jerry would perform

One of the greatest clowns in film history, Jerry Lewis was born Joseph Levitch on March 16, 1926, in Newark, New Jersey.

in the Brown Derby and have the audience howling at his antics.

My first summer at Brown's, Jerry made me an offer. "Sid, listen. I like your style. I like what you do. You have a lot of class. How would you like to come to Los Angeles and work with me?"

"Doing what, Jerry?"

"I need an assistant. I'd give you a good deal, Sid. You could live in the guesthouse on my property, which is really nice, and you'd be in L.A., which is a great place."

I was intrigued, so I agreed to spend a few days in Los Angeles. Everything Jerry said was true. L.A. was beautiful, the guesthouse was first-class, Patti was as sweet as could be, and when you spent time around Jerry, all you did was laugh.

Jerry was in great demand, and there was an indescribable spirit emanating from him. It was a terrific time. But in the end, I decided that I could not be away from my parents for an extended period. Jerry was extremely understanding.

I returned to New York to finish up the summer at Brown's. One night at the Brown Derby, I ran into Emil Cohen, a comic who lived and worked at Grossinger's but who would also occasionally appear at Brown's Playhouse, the hotel's theater.

"Sid, I'd like to bring a young friend of mine, Billy Fields, over with me the next time I appear at the Playhouse for you. He's really a marvelous singer and he's just replaced Eddie Fisher as our band singer at Grossinger's. You know, Milton [Berle] and Eddie [Cantor] have taken Eddie Fisher under their wing and he's going to be a very big star. I'd like it if Billy could open for me here at Brown's. I'm sure you'll love him, and it won't cost you anything because I'll pay him. I'd like the guests at Brown's to hear him."

"That's fine, Emil. Bring him the next time you appear."

I remember thinking then how great it was that working entertainers, men like Emil Cohen, and superstars like Milton Berle and Eddie Cantor, would go out of their way to help struggling young talents like Eddie Fisher and Billy Fields. The generosity of those established stars was special.

The next time Emil appeared at the Playhouse, he brought Billy Fields with him. Billy had a big voice, and I thought he was very talented. But even more important was the kinship that developed between us. I just liked the guy.

After the summer I returned to Mercury, and my first assignment, this time as a road manager, was to accompany Tito Puente and his band on a two-week West Coast tour. The Mexican-Americans in California were clamoring for Tito. I had never worked as a road manager, so this was good experience. I was responsible for arranging the travel, booking hotel rooms, keeping the band intact and making sure the group showed up for performances on time and ready to play. I also coordinated radio and newspaper interviews for Tito, interacted with the promoters at the various venues and oversaw financial matters.

We flew to the San Diego area, boarded a bus and worked our way north, playing in a different ballroom every night. Tito was doing it about as well as it could be done: playing to sold-out ballrooms packed with enthusiastic crowds. Tito and the band were so infectious that they kept the people up and dancing all night. Including me, my two left feet notwithstanding! The girls were exotic and were happy to dance with anyone connected with the band. For my part, I would make sure to dance near the musicians so they could see me with the lovely Latin ladies. We always had a good time with that the next day on the bus.

In Oakland, on one of the last nights of the tour, I found the absolutely most shapely girl in the entire ballroom and asked her to dance. We started to mambo, and I was having trouble keeping up with her. I could see that the guys in the band were bug-eyed, so I decided to play it up for all it was worth. I maneuvered myself and my gorgeous partner right in front of the bandstand. Just then, she did a step where she threw me out, so, being the original mambo king, I tried to reciprocate. Not a good idea. Our feet got tangled and I fell flat on my ass. That was the end of the music. Guys choking back laughter have a hard time playing their instruments!

I'm happy to say that my little dance routine did not adversely affect Tito's popularity. He stayed hot for over forty years, becoming an international star and winning every possible award in the music business. Whenever we'd meet, he'd invariably say, "Hey, Sid, still do the mambo?" and we'd both crack up. I was greatly saddened on June 1, 2000, when I learned that Tito had passed on. He was a great and talented musician and a very warm, decent human being. I was privileged to count him as a friend.

I CONTINUED WORKING at Mercury until Larry Meyers called to tell me that there was an opening for an agent at Shaw Artists, where he was employed. Shaw, located in the WNEW Building on Fifth Avenue, specialized in R&B and jazz acts and had on its roster such artists as Ray Charles, Fats Domino, Miles Davis, Muddy Waters, Stan Getz, and Ruth Brown. The agency was run extremely well by the husband-and-wife team of Billy and Lee Shaw.

Jack Whittemore, a vice-president at Shaw and a terrific agent, became my mentor. He allowed me to spend time in his office, so I got to see him in action. Jack had a way with people, and great style. I got to know many managers and promoters because we agents were the go-betweens for the artists, and I tried to let the good traits I observed in all these show-business functionaries rub off on me.

When I accepted the job at Shaw, I negotiated the summers off because I had given my word to Charlie Brown that I would continue to be his hotel's summer social director. Billy Shaw respected that I was a man of my word and agreed to give me the time off. There was also a plus side. He knew that I would book some of Shaw's acts into Brown's.

One particular act I had responsibility for at Shaw was Sallie Blair, a talented young black singer from Baltimore who I was certain was destined for stardom. Together with her manager, Biddy Wood, I worked hard to help ignite Sallie's career.

One of Sallie's favorite tunes was Harold Arlen's "Old Black Magic." Invariably, she would kick off her shoes during the song and really work the crowd. The moment she threw off those shoes, the audience went wild. They knew that Sallie would remain barefoot for the duration of the performance. That became her signature.

I booked Sallie into L.A.'s famous *Cotton Club Revue*, and her looks and charismatic presence were beginning to create quite a stir. Word-of-mouth led to many additional appearances. After L.A., I booked Sallie into a hotel in Miami Beach, where Walter Hyman, a young New York textile executive, saw her. Actually, he attended every one of her performances, and the more he saw her, the more captivated he became. Soon, Walter and Sallie became friends.

Sallie called me one day to talk about Walter. "Sid, I met this rich businessman from New York and he wants to manage me. I told him that Biddy is my manager, but he's so persistent. I told him he has to talk to you."

"Tell him to call me," I said.

The next day, Walter Hyman called me from Florida. "When I get back to New York, I'd like to come up to see you about Sallie Blair. I want you to get to know me. I'm very sincere about getting involved in her career."

"Fine, Walter. Call me when you get back."

Eventually, I met with Walter at his tastefully appointed home in Scarsdale. After some small talk, we began to discuss Sallie Blair.

"Sid, this is what I'd like to do. Sallie is going to be a star, but right now she has no money. She isn't even signed with her manager, Biddy Wood. I'll do the right thing, but you're the man to help me get this done."

I looked at him earnestly. "But, Walter, what exactly do you want to do?"

"I'll do anything I have to do to buy you and the manager out."

"Look, Walter, I'm her agent, and it's not necessary to buy me out. Our arrangement is a flat 10 percent commission. As far as Biddy is concerned, I'll talk to him and let you know what he says."

"I'd appreciate that very much, Sid. I'm determined to help Sallie become a star."

"Nothing would please me more," I answered.

The next day, I called Biddy Wood and told him about the conversation. He asked me to have Walter call him, intimating that even though he had a financial interest in Sallie, he would not stand in her way if Walter Hyman could help further her career.

The details of their agreement remain unknown to me, but Walter was able to buy Biddy out. Perhaps ironically, and perhaps owing to health problems, Sallie never did achieve the stardom Walter and I had predicted. And perhaps more ironically, because of our association with Sallie Blair, Walter and I became good friends. Years later, Walter Hyman would play a pivotal role in my life.

7

Dancing with
Gerry . . . and Judy

URING MY TIME AT SHAW, I had several bachelor friends
with whom I used to pal around. We went to sporting
events, spent summers at the same beach club and basically enjoyed New York life. A favorite dining spot of ours was the
famous Reuben's Restaurant, on Fifty-eighth Street between Fifth
and Madison. One day, Bea, the lady who ran the checkroom, approached me.

"Sid, you know that girl who is my assistant? The pretty one?
Her name is Geraldine Gale, and she's newly arrived from California. She does very nicely with me but spends almost every penny
on voice lessons, hoping to get into musical comedy. I was wondering if you could audition her and tell me what you think."

Shaw Artists specialized in jazz and R&B, so I didn't know if I
could help. But, as a favor to Bea I said I would be happy to hear
Geraldine.

About a week later, I received a phone call at the office: "Hi, this is Geraldine Gale. I'm not sure if you know who I am." The usual stuff. "I'm one of the girls who works with Bea, and you're the man who never lets me help him put his coat on!" she giggled.

"I know who you are, Geraldine. So what can I do for you?"

"Bea told me that you might come hear me sing."

"I did promise I would do that. But I don't want you to spend money on a rehearsal studio or a pianist, and I don't have a facility here at Shaw. Perhaps I could come to one of your singing lessons and take a listen."

"That would be great!" Geraldine said. "Please let me check with my coach and I'll phone you back."

The following day, Geraldine invited me to come, at my convenience, to the Osborne Building to sit in on her lesson.

As I was walking up the steps of the Osborne the next day, I passed the famous conductor and composer Leonard Bernstein. When I found the rehearsal room where I was to observe the lesson, I expected to see the young girl in flat shoes I had seen a few times at Reuben's. Instead, I saw a slender, rather shapely girl with beautiful reddish-brown hair, wearing stylish spike heels and a beige dress. *Is this the same kid I'd been seeing at the restaurant?*

Gerry was very shy. She introduced me to her coach, Eva Brown, and her accompanist and thanked me for coming. She sang two songs, one of which was "I Feel Pretty" from *West Side Story*. How coincidental, I thought, that she had picked a song by Leonard Bernstein, the fellow I just passed in the stairwell. Equally apropos, I had been thinking that Gerry was indeed very pretty. Someone was definitely trying to tell me something.

"Geraldine, you're a wonderful singer! What is it that you would hope from me?"

"I would love to audition and maybe get into a Broadway show."

"Have you gone on any auditions?"

"No, I haven't really learned the ropes yet. I don't even know how to go about getting one. I got to New York just a short while ago."

I thought for a moment. "Okay. Give me a few days, and let me see what I can come up with." I thanked Mrs. Brown and the accompanist, said my goodbyes and left.

About a week later, Geraldine followed up. I explained that I didn't think our agency could help her, but I would be happy to introduce her to some friends who specialize in Broadway talent.

I sent Gerry to Biff Liff at William Morris, one of the world's leading agencies. After Biff heard Geraldine sing, he called to thank me and explained that William Morris mostly worked with established artists and therefore couldn't sign Geraldine, but he would refer her to some theater producers and let her know if and where and when auditions were being held. As noncommittal as it sounded, Biff's efforts did eventually pay off, for it was through him that Geraldine finally landed a job in summer stock.

I LIKED GERALDINE GALE, and I would occasionally call her to find out what was happening in her life. Gradually, we started to feel comfortable with each other. . . . Meanwhile, I was still living with my parents and hanging out with my buddies.

Between summer-stock jobs, Geraldine would come home to her Eighth Street apartment. On one of those occasions, I reached her on the telephone.

"Gerry, what are you doing for dinner? Maybe the boys and I could pick you up."

"I don't have any plans, Sid. I'd love to go to dinner."

One by one, the boys canceled out, and when I arrived at Gerry's place, it was just the two of us. We went to Ratner's. There she sat, this all-American girl from Southern California, falling in love with whitefish salad, vegetarian chopped liver, blintzes, kreplach, kasha varnishkes. After dinner, which was topped off by the requisite egg cream, I walked her home.

She looked radiant as we strolled along, and after a while it felt natural that I should take her hand. As we were about to reach her apartment building, I pointed into the distance. "Gerry, look at the fella kissing the girl over there!" I said.

"Where?"

"Where? Here!" And then I kissed her.

We walked up the three flights to Gerry's apartment, and at every landing I kissed her again. It took me only three years after that date to ask her to marry me.

I CONTINUED WORKING at Shaw as an agent dealing with promoters, TV producers, and managers. One day, as I was lunching at a small restaurant on the ground floor of the building where our office was located, in walked Abe Margolies, my old pal from Lefty's Pool Hall.

Abe's jewelry manufacturing business was right around the corner from Shaw, and from time to time we would run into each other on the street, but we were both busy and never got a chance to shmooze. However, on this particular day, since we were both taking a break, I invited him to join me.

"Sid, how's it going at the agency?" he asked.

I explained that Shaw was a nice place to work, that the people were very friendly and that I had learned a great deal. Then, I added, "But, Abe, I really don't enjoy being an agent anymore. I've been thinking about making a change."

"So what do you want to do?"

"I think I'd like to be a promoter. I deal with a lot of promoters, and I'd like to try my hand at that. I think I could be successful."

"Well, Sid, why don't you give it a go?"

I laughed. "Being a promoter takes money."

"What do you mean?"

"First of all, you have to be able to engage the services of a band. Then you have to be able to pay for a venue, and finally you need money to publicize the event. It all takes cash!"

"You really don't like the job upstairs at the agency?"

"It's not that, Abe. I like the job. The people are great. I have some close friends up there. They have big and successful acts, and I'm learning about television, but—"

"How much money do you think you'll need, Sid?"

"Abe, it depends on the act and the facility I want to rent. I've done a lot of business with the Apollo Theatre since I've been at Shaw, and I once asked Bobby Schiffman, son of Frank, who owns the Apollo, what it would take to rent the place out. The Schiffmans don't really like doing that because they run their own promotions. Bobby told me that were they to even consider renting the space, it would cost seven thousand dollars a week. And they would only entertain the idea if the act being brought in conformed to the policy of the theater, which means that it has to have the potential of succeeding in Harlem."

"I understand, Sid," Abe said. "But what about the act? How much would that cost?"

"An act capable of filling the hall would cost about ten thousand dollars a week. Then you would need several thousand dollars for publicity, leaflets and posters."

"So, you're talking about twenty thousand dollars."

"That's right. The Apollo is the place for me to do it, Abe. I know the Apollo. I go there often because the agency books acts there all the time, and I think I understand the audience."

"Do it!" Abe said. "I'll put up the money. Do it, Sid!"

"What do you mean?"

"I said I'll put up the money."

"So, you want to be my partner, Abe? Right?"

"No, Sid. I just want to help you."

"No, no, Abe, I can't do that. If we make money, you're my partner. And if we lose it, how could I pay you back?"

"Forget about paying me back," he said. "Okay, we're partners. DO IT!" Abe stood up. "I've got to go. I've got an appointment. Do what you have to do and let me know when you need the money." With that, he left.

Somewhat shell-shocked, I returned to the agency. I had gone to lunch and come back with a new career and a new partner. I had mixed feelings about leaving Shaw Artists, where I had spent four years working with a marvelous crew, but I had made my decision.

The first person I saw was Lee Shaw. I swallowed hard. "Mrs. Shaw, I want to start a new career for myself, and it means I'm going to have to leave the agency."

"Sid, how can you leave? You're doing so well here, and you're seeing that lovely girl! And what if that gets serious?"

In those days, if it looked like you were going to get married and you had a well-paying job, you didn't quit to chase a hit-or-miss dream. It just wasn't done.

"This is something I must do, Mrs. Shaw."

"Did you tell Billy yet?"

"No. You're the first person I've spoken to."

"Let me talk to Billy tonight at dinner."

"My husband's really not happy about it," Mrs. Shaw said the next day, "but I told him it's something you want to do. Billy said he doesn't want an unhappy soldier here, but he wants to try to talk you out of it, so go see him later today."

At the end of the day, I went to see Billy Shaw in his office. He was cordial.

"I hear you want to leave. What is it, Sid? A matter of money?"

"No, Billy, it's not about money. It's simply that I want to do other things. I want to be a promoter."

"You know, being a promoter is risky."

"I know," I said. "But I'm a risk-taker and I want to try."

"It also takes a lot of gelt, Sid."

"I know that, too, but I can get help. I'm okay there." I told him about Abe's involvement.

"Okay, Sid. It's your decision." Billy was resigned.

The next morning, Lee and I agreed that I would stay two more weeks and finish what I had to do. They generously offered to pay me for six weeks.

"Billy told me what you're going to be doing," Lee said." So I guess you'll be around, Sid. You'll stop in to say hello?"

"I have every intention of being around, Lee." Actually, I planned to be around almost immediately, because I knew that I wanted to book Miles Davis as my first promotion at the Apollo. Miles was a Shaw artist.

And that was the culmination of my four years at Shaw.

SETTING UP THE NEW BUSINESS in our Bronx apartment was an interesting transition. For the previous six years, at two different agencies, I had worked in a busy office, and now I was by myself doing everything for myself. Of course, I spoke to Abe, who was quite generous with both his money and his encouragement. But he couldn't help with the day-to-day responsibilities. All of that fell on my shoulders.

Task number one was to persuade the Schiffmans to let me rent the Apollo for a week so that I could present the first promotion of my new career. I made an appointment to see Bobby Schiffman.

On the day of my visit, Bobby asked, "Sid, so you want to rent the Apollo? That's fine. It'll cost seven thousand dollars for the week, and you'll have to pay up front. I've already spoken to my dad, and it's okay with him, but he wants to talk to you first."

Bobby called his father, who came down from his office into the theater. "Sid, you really want to do this thing? Can you afford it? You need to pay up front, you know."

"That's okay, Mr. Schiffman. You'll have the money up front."

"Who are you bringing in?"

"I'm not sure."

"Okay, just give us enough notice, Sid. Work the details out with Bobby. And make sure your check clears," he joked.

Having secured the Apollo, my next move was to go back to Shaw and book Miles Davis. Miles hadn't played the Apollo in a long time. I felt confident that he would do well.

At Shaw, I talked to Larry Meyers, who had a close relationship with Miles. We agreed on a ten-thousand-dollar figure. Then I went to see Abe and told him what I had accomplished.

"When do you need the money?"

"Within forty-eight hours."

"It'll be there," he assured me.

I returned to the theater and told the Schiffmans that in six weeks Miles Davis would be working his magic at the Apollo. They were flabbergasted.

"Hey, you're going into competition with us now, but if you can get Miles, good luck to you!" said Mr. Schiffman senior. "We haven't had him here in ages."

I couldn't reveal that Ruth Brown, the great blues singer, was my choice as the supporting act. That first had to be cleared with Miles.

Unwritten though it was, the headliner always had approval over the supporting act.

Miles said yes to Ruth, and I put her on the bill. Everything was set. I went back to Abe the next day, and he gave me three separate checks: one for seven thousand dollars made out to the Apollo; one for ten thousand dollars to Shaw Artists, to be paid into the account of Miles Davis; and one for three thousand dollars for promotional expenses.

I placed ads in newspapers and printed posters, which Bob Maltz proceeded to hang around the city. Next, I hoped and prayed that when we opened, the crowds would be there. It would be six long weeks before I would have the answer. Remember, there was no Ticketron in those days. Ticket sales came from walk-up traffic at the box office.

When I went to the Apollo to check on the arrangements, the manager of the theater, Honi Coles, who knew me from my years as an agent, offered his support: "We're going to give you a little extra help, Sid!" That meant a great deal. I had good feelings about what was happening. It seemed like everyone was rooting for me.

Everywhere I went, I handed out leaflets and handbills. I didn't go anywhere without promotional literature ready to be thrust upon anyone in my path. In addition, I hired guys from Lefty's Pool Hall to surround Yankee Stadium during a heavyweight championship fight and hand out thousands of leaflets as the fans left.

As luck would have it, while we were handing out these leaflets, Joe Glaser, owner of one of the top theatrical agencies in the country, exited the fight with his party, many of whom were subagents working for him. A dynamo in the business, Glaser was also the lifelong manager of the great trumpeter Louis Armstrong. He never had a contract with Satchmo, but their loyalty to each other was legendary. Joe turned to his agents and pointed at me. "You see this man? He's out here with his guys working shoulder-to-shoulder. He's protecting his investment. He's going to make it. He's doing it the right way."

Then he turned to me. "Sidney, it's great to see you out here. I wish you a lot of luck." Joe Glaser's words gave me the confidence that my promotion would succeed.

It must have been an omen.

Miles Davis was a sensation at the Apollo. Two shows a day and every seat sold! My timing had been perfect. I made a bundle.

I called up Abe to share the good news. "I owe you a lot of dough," I reported.

The next day, at the Diamond Club, the jewelry industry's major New York hangout, I gave Abe the twenty thousand dollars in seed money I had borrowed. Then I took out a handwritten sheet detailing the costs and revenues for the week at the Apollo. It showed that we had made a profit of eight grand. A bonanza! I handed over another four thousand dollars, Abe's partnership share. He handed it right back. "Sid, use it for the next one," he said.

As soon as I saw the rush for tickets to see Miles, I called the Howard Theatre in Washington. The Howard was the Apollo of D.C., and I had sold them acts while an agent at Shaw. I told the manager what was happening, got a list of open dates, then called Larry Meyers at Shaw and told him that I'd like to present Miles Davis and Ruth Brown at the Howard.

"Great," Larry laughed. "You're becoming one of our best clients. The Shaws are beginning to like the fact that you left! Keep the dates comin'!" Because the Howard was a smaller theater, we agreed on a price somewhat less than the ten thousand a week we had paid Miles at the Apollo.

I went down to Washington ten days in advance of the event and plastered the town with leaflets and posters.

Miles Davis's triumphant stand at the Howard mirrored what had happened at the Apollo. Long lines waited to see him play. I was on a hot streak and having lots of fun. It was time to find my next promotion.

SHAW ARTISTS HAD A YOUNG black singer who had been playing the "chitlin' circuit," the numerous night, supper and dance clubs in the black urban areas of America. He was on the road to stardom and, in my opinion, ready for a major coming-out in New York. So on the heels of Miles Davis, I booked Brook Benton into the Apollo. Lucky for me, Brook had just released "It's Just a Matter of Time." The record was peaking, and everybody wanted to see him.

Brook Benton sold out the Apollo for the week, and this time we netted $5,500. Again Abe would take no money. "*Votre garçon* Sidney" was having the time of his life. I had reclaimed my independence, working hard but enjoying every moment.

Because Brook had recently played the Howard, I couldn't bring him to D.C. to follow Miles. But the Howard management and I were eager to do another promotion. I went to Shaw, talked to Larry, and we agreed to put Fats Domino from New Orleans into the Howard. It was one of the coldest, snowiest winters in the history of Washington. My body was shivering as I toured the supermarkets, meat markets and groceries, asking the proprietors for permission to put my posters in their store windows. That done, I rode the trolleys (at least they were warm) through the black neighborhoods and distributed leaflets and handbills to the riders. My daily supply of promo material exhausted, I would then ride over to the U. S. Senate to watch the best actors in the world perform.

During the week of Fats Domino's Howard engagement, I often spent time outside with the audience before curtain time. Fats, with his flashy rings and clothes, would leave the warmth of the dressing room and come out to talk to the fans on the ticket line. And he would never fail to ask, "Mr. Sidney, how are you doing out here?" He was the gentlest, most considerate and involved artist that I have ever met.

Fats was a big hit at the Howard. Again Abe took no money. I was building up a kitty.

By now, Gerry and I were seeing each other all the time. She had landed a role on Broadway as one of the nuns in *The Sound of Music*, and I became a "stage-door Johnny," picking her up at the theater every night after the performance. Our romance was blossoming.

While all this was going on, the folks at Shaw, who by now thought that I had the Midas touch, approached me with an idea. The Newport Jazz Festival, held each of the past seven years in Rhode Island, had become an international event. Promoted and produced by the highly capable George Wein, the festival was a major happening each summer, attracting jazz fans to Newport for three days during the Fourth of July weekend. The people at Shaw thought that the jazz artists they managed coupled with my promotional hot streak would make it possible to re-create some of the Newport excitement in Atlantic City. They even thought that we could do it in the same Fourth of July time frame. I agreed.

Quickly, I secured Atlantic City's Warren Theatre for the holiday weekend. I booked Shaw Artists' jazz lineup, including Miles Davis, Stan Getz, Dakota Staton and Maynard Ferguson. I also signed on Duke Ellington and Count Basie. For promotion, once again I took the direct route. Posters were plastered all over New York, Atlantic City, Washington, Baltimore and Philadelphia, and thousands of leaflets were handed out. Then, I hired top security and crowd-control personnel for the three-day festival. If you wanted to see or hear jazz in America on the weekend of July 4, 1960, you had to go either to Atlantic City, New Jersey, or Newport, Rhode Island. We were so successful in Atlantic City that we broke all attendance records for a live event there, even surpassing the Miss America Pageant.

On the last night of the festival, Abe, Gerry and I were in my car looking for a place to eat when we heard a radio bulletin that there had been a riot at the Newport Jazz Festival. This was the first time there had ever been trouble in the seven years that George Wein had produced the show. My heart went out to him.

By now, the Schiffmans at the Apollo were closely watching what I was doing. I must have recharged their battery, because it became almost impossible to clear dates at that venue. Based on my success, the Schiffmans decided to undertake future promotions themselves rather than rent out the space to the competition. If I wanted to continue promoting in New York City, I was going to have to find another theater.

IN THE LATE '50S, the number-one deejay in America was Alan Freed, who broadcast his radio show from WINS, in New York City. A transplanted Clevelander, Freed had a huge radio following. Some journalists credit Alan with popularizing the terms "rock-and-roll" and "rhythm and blues."

In addition to his radio work, Alan loved to present holiday rock-and-roll shows at the Paramount theaters in both Manhattan and Brooklyn. During Christmas and Easter, he would assemble the top recording acts and showcase them three times a day—and the kids would line up to get in. Of course, it was no small advantage that Freed was able to spin an artist's recordings on his radio program. That leverage made the artists and their managers feel a certain obligation to Freed. If Alan asked you to perform at his Paramount shows, you did it.

In late 1959 and early 1960, the payola scandal hit the news, and Alan Freed got caught up in it. Needless to say, taking money to play records over the Federal Communication Commission-controlled airwaves was criminal, and because of his association with the payola scandal, Freed was banned from the airwaves. A victim of the domino effect, he lost his Paramount holiday shows as well.

Owing to my recent successes, I was able to open an office in the Jensen Building, on Fifth Avenue. It was there that a shaken Alan Freed came to see me shortly after his indictment. He was seeking advice, and even though I liked him, I was powerless to help. It was evident that Alan's troubles with the law were destroying him, and in fact he died brokenhearted a few years later. Alan was a decent man who gave a tremendous boost to many R&B and pop artists.

GENE PLESHETTE, FATHER OF actress Suzanne, was director of the New York and Brooklyn Paramount theaters where Alan had presented his holiday shows. Gene had worked with Freed to make the holiday rock-and-roll events an institution in New York, and one day he called and asked if I would like to take over Alan's spot at the Paramount. He suggested staging a show at the Brooklyn theater first. This was a godsend: I needed a new venue, since I had lost the Apollo. But first, I went to Abe. "Do it!" he said.

The show I presented for Gene Pleshette at the Brooklyn Paramount turned out to be the first big mistake in my career as a promoter. In an effort to ensure sellouts, I mixed rock-and-roll with jazz acts, which was definitely a case of oil and water: the rock-and-rollers had no interest in jazz artists, and the jazz aficionados couldn't care less about rock-and-roll. The fans stayed away in droves, and we lost about eighteen thousand dollars. With just one loser in my career as a promoter, I had undone the financial gains I had made with the four preceding winners. However, I wasn't about to stop now. I told Abe that I wanted to do a show at the Palace Theatre on Broadway and, as usual, he supported me. But this time he thought we should try something a bit different.

Ray Charles, master of R&B, jazz and pop, has won a dozen Grammys and numerous other prestigious awards.

Abe convinced me to let John Drew, scion of a wealthy Irish family in Chicago, and his lovely wife, Eleanor, join our Palace promotional partnership. The Drews were eager to get into show business, and since they had financial resources, Abe thought it would be wise to include them. As soon as I met Eleanor and John, the quintessential Irishman, I agreed to Abe's suggestion.

The Palace, on a par with London's Palladium, was the best place in New York to stage a show. I had always dreamed of doing a promotion there, and in September 1961, in a coproduction with John Drew, I did just that when I presented Ray Charles and Sarah Vaughan. Larry Storch was the comedian on the bill, and we also featured Johnny Conrad, a choreographer, and his dancers. It was a great combo, but the white public wasn't quite ready for Ray Charles, and Harlem wasn't in the habit of coming down to Broadway for entertainment. Again, we failed financially.

Gene Pleshette contacted me once again: "Sid, I know you've had a couple of setbacks recently, but I still have faith in you, and so does the Paramount organization. Why don't you do the New York Paramount for our upcoming holiday season rock-and-roll show?"

I told him I would talk to my backer and let him know. I went to see dependable Abe.

"Abe, we've just had two losers, which set us back about twenty-seven grand. Now the New York Paramount wants us to stage another holiday show. I think I know what will be successful, but it'll be a financial risk. What do you think?"

"Let's do it," he said. It was always the same response when it came to Abe.

FOR THE NEW YORK PARAMOUNT, I came up with the idea of alternating the featured act. Instead of having one headliner for all ten days, I booked James Brown for four days, Sam Cooke for three and Jackie Wilson for three. As supporting acts, we had the Four Seasons, Ruby & the Romantics, Rufus Thomas, Leslie Gore, King Curtis, Terry Stafford, Diane Renay, Chris Crosby, The Sapphires and Bobby Rydell. Most of them had current or recent hit records. The WMCA Good Guys, the deejay lineup from the ever-popular New York rock-and-roll radio station, served as the show's hosts, and it was a huge success. The line for tickets stretched around the block, until the people at the end of the line met those at the front.

This time, I got more than I bargained for. Allen Klein, the manager of Sam Cooke and, later in his career, briefly the manager of the Beatles, brought me up on charges at the American Guild of Variety Artists. This was the first and only time that I ever had trouble with a union or oversight body in the industry. When I booked the three main acts to do the holiday shows, I promised each one top billing. The ads, posters and handbills showed the three top acts on an equal line, so no one had top billing or all had top billing, depending on how you chose to look at it.

Allen Klein went to my friend Jackie Bright, the head of AGVA, and complained. Jackie, who was looking out for me, suggested that I try to mollify Allen with money. I offered Sam Cooke four days' pay for three days work, and that seemed to do the trick. Neither Jackie Wilson nor James Brown, the other acts, ever complained.

While at the Paramount, I often had to talk to James Brown before his performance. Ben Bart, his manager/agent, would come to me before James was supposed to go on and say, "Sid, he's not going on. He just doesn't want to do it."

"Godfather of soul" James Brown bridged the color gap with his funky rhythmic style.

James always had a different excuse: headache, toothache, stomachache . . . always something. Ben would beg me, "You have to talk to him." So I would go to James's dressing room and tell him how great he was and how he couldn't disappoint all the fans who had come to see him. James was basically a pussycat who needed TLC. Of course, eventually he always went on, and when he did, Ben would look over at me and wink. And James would give his usual phenomenal performance.

The ten days at the New York Paramount were a huge success. The shows were all sellouts, and we even added one show, so instead of two shows a day, we did three. We netted a bundle and, thank God, were back on the plus side. But I was learning that it was hard to make money at these promotions. The margins were small, and if you charged nominal prices to accommodate the fans but didn't sell out, you were probably going to end up in the red. Basically, that meant that one had to always guess right. A succession of winners could be undone by one loser.

About a month later, I got a call from the mayor of Newport. "Mr. Bernstein, you know that we've had a disaster here with our jazz festival. The merchants are after me to continue the festival because it brings so much business to the town. The residents, on the other hand, are unhappy and want the whole thing to go away. The city council and I would like to invite you here to make a presentation, as we hope that you would consider taking over the festival from Mr. Wein."

"Mr. Mayor, I am very flattered. Are you absolutely certain that Mr. Wein cannot continue with the festival?"

"Yes, Mr. Bernstein, we are certain about that."

"Let me get back to you, Mr. Mayor. I need to confer with my associates first. I'll be in touch very soon."

I went to Abe's office.

"We are being offered the most important jazz festival in the world, Abe. It's going to be very expensive to produce a show of this magnitude. The acts will cost a lot, and the security is going to have to be extraordinary to avoid the problems that George Wein had. We're looking at fifty to seventy-five thousand."

"You know what, Sid?" Abe said. "The Russians have been calling us hooligans. When they reported the riot at Newport in their newspapers, they referred to us as the 'American hooligans.' Let's show those bastards that they're full of it. Do it!"

On the wings of Abe's ruffled feathers, I went to Newport, presented a proposal to the mayor, city council and a large assembly of townspeople, and returned home. The next day, I received a call from the mayor. "Mr. Bernstein," he said, "by unanimous vote you are hereby awarded the 1961 Newport Jazz Festival! Congratulations!"

I sent John and Eleanor Drew to Newport to act as our representatives, and we spoke on the phone continually. Our expenses were mounting—and we'd only just begun.

I used Abe's idea and told every radio show that would have me and every print journalist who wanted a story that Americans were not hooligans and that folks should let their voices be heard by buying tickets to the Newport Jazz Festival.

One day, as festival preparations were being made, John Drew called. "Sid. I'm having a problem. Eleanor and I are being called 'kikes' all around Newport. We walk down the street just to get an ice cream cone with the kids, and we hear, 'There are those kikes.' I even stopped some ladies and asked them why they were calling us kikes when I had the map of Ireland written all over my face. Their answer: 'We don't want you Bernsteins up here! We had enough of that last year!'"

The residents of Newport didn't care about the merchants or the business that the festival would generate for the town. They were worried for their safety. I told John I would understand if he felt uncomfortable and wanted to leave.

"Absolutely not!" he said.

I told him to let me think about a solution. I'd try to resolve everything in a day or two. That solution was to call Val Irving, the agent for Bob Hope, and ask if I could book Bob for the jazz festival.

"Sid, what do you want with Bob Hope at a jazz festival?"

"I need him. I'm not going to put him in the jazz festival. I'm going to put him on by himself on the afternoon of July 2."

"Okay, but it'll cost you twenty-five thousand dollars."

"You got it, Val."

I knew that if I presented Bob Hope, Mr. American Flag, the man most closely associated with the USO, the man who traveled hundreds of thousands of miles to entertain U. S. servicemen and -women all over the world, the "kike" business would stop. Anybody who brought Bob Hope to Newport would be considered a hero. Bob Hope was the Stars and Stripes.

I also called Judy Garland. I felt that we needed Judy because without tremendous star presence and the sellouts that guarantees we would lose every penny we had already sunk into Newport. She told me to call her managers, David Biegelman and Freddy Fields. I asked them if Judy could perform on the afternoon of July 3. "Twenty-five thousand dollars," they said. "Plus, you pay her conductor, Mort Lindsey, five of her key musicians, and you supply a twenty-two-piece orchestra."

"You got it. No problem."

I had just increased our expanding budget by sixty thousand

dollars—fifty thousand for Hope and Garland and ten for Lindsey and the twenty-two-piece orchestra. Word got out fast about Bob Hope and Judy Garland, and the townspeople began to treat John and Eleanor like heroes. We had diffused the anger.

The acts and dates set, we distributed posters and handbills in five cities: New York, Newport, Boston, Providence, New Haven. We also did radio advertising.

A few weeks before the festival, I got a phone call from Val Irving. "Sid, you have to let Bob out of the July 2 date. He owes Jimmy Durante a favor to be on his TV show, which is on the same day as your show, and he just has to do it. We'll make it up to you some-day, somehow, Sid, but you have to let Bob out."

Reluctantly, I agreed. I still had Judy Garland, and I knew that I could explain the Hope cancellation with a media blitz. I would lower my costs by twenty-five thousand and simultaneously get some pub-licity. We held a press conference, and I did some radio interviews to explain why Bob wasn't showing up. Everybody took it in stride.

Finally . . . we were ready for Newport. Four days of the greatest jazz acts in the world: Louis Armstrong, Count Basie, Gerry Mulligan, Maynard Ferguson, Cannonball Adderley, Dave Brubeck, Ramsey Lewis, Stan Getz, Art Blakey, Sarah Vaughan, George Shearing, Ray Charles, Oscar Peterson, Gloria Lynne, Lionel Hampton, Quincy Jones, Mel Torme and John Coltrane, among others. If you were a jazz fan and lucky enough to be in Newport during the Indepen-dence Day weekend of 1961, you would have thought you'd died and gone to heaven.

The security was fabulous. I brought in New York detectives that my cousin Leo Kitchman helped me recruit; we hired ushers from Madi-son Square Garden. The three days went off without a hitch, and John Drew and I scored a grand slam with the people of Newport.

On the last night, I featured Torme, Jones and Duke Ellington. Quincy asked me if he could have an extra thirty minutes because he was doing a live album, and I accommodated him. Quincy did his extra time, then Mel did several encores. An open-air concert that was supposed to be over at 11:30 was still in progress at 1:00 A.M., with the great Duke Ellington waiting in his trailer to go on. Then it began to drizzle. I got word soon after that the Duke wanted to talk to me. Duke Ellington was a man of great dignity and civility, and we had quite a chat.

"Mr. Bernstein. It's 1:30 A.M., it's started to rain out there, and I should have gone on stage two hours ago. I don't believe that those folks are going to want to sit in the rain at two in the morning listening to my band and me. I think I should go home."

"Mr. Ellington, those people want to see you, and they're all still here. I believe they'll stay."

I persuaded him to wait, and at 2:30 A.M., dressed in a classy jacket, the tall, elegant, regal Duke Ellington went out and wowed them. As I expected, not a soul left the concert until Duke had played his final note.

From a musical standpoint, the entire four days were magical. But our costs were inflated from the expense for Judy Garland and the extra security, so even though we broke attendance records, we once again operated at a deficit. In support of the Bob Hope and Judy Garland initiatives, I had committed unbudgeted funds for emergency advertising. Because we were functioning in a crisis, I just acted and didn't have time to confer with Abe or John. I felt that I had to bear that responsibility, so when the advertising bills came due, I decided to take care of them myself. I didn't know how, when or where, but I would find a way to get the bills paid.

In the plus column, the *Boston Herald* did an editorial about how we had saved the Newport Jazz Festival and how well it had been run. They quoted me as having said that I had come to Newport to perpetuate the great festival that George Wein had initiated. George called to thank me as soon as he heard about my statement, and we have remained friends to this very day. I may have been out some money, but the relationships I made were priceless.

DURING OUR STAY IN NEWPORT, we were headquartered at the Cliffwalk Manor Hotel. On our last day, a man came to see me with his wife and three children.

"Mr. Bernstein, I am a native of Newport, born and raised. I must tell you that I was against you and this festival from the very begin-

ning. However, after seeing how you ran these four days, the care you gave to security, how you handled yourself with our children and the great show you put on, I want to tell you, Mr. Bernstein, that if you'd choose to move up to Newport and run for mayor after Mayor Mar, we would consider it a privilege and an honor to work for your election."

How gratifying to be so appreciated! But I respectfully declined the offer.

We had accomplished much at Newport: we saved the festival, put on a wonderful four days with the best jazz acts in the world and broke all attendance records to boot. Our crowds had been well-behaved, and Abe was ecstatic that we had demonstrated to the Russians that Americans were not hooligans. I was also happy that we had put the "kike" business to rest. Despite all the positives, however, I was extremely disturbed that we ended up in the red.

Billy Fields had come to Newport to help with the festival, and we were both very down during the drive home. To make matters worse, I had booked Connie Francis and Brook Benton into the State Theatre in Hartford as our next promotion, and preliminary indications were that we were in trouble. Advance ticket sales were below expectation. A smart guy might have considered quitting the game, but no, I had to be around the music. Sid the undaunted was going to stick it out.

On the other hand, John and Eleanor called it a wrap. The financial realities had overshadowed the glitz: "It's only exciting when you win." The Drews returned to their lives in Chicago and eventually we lost contact.

Even without John and Eleanor, Abe maintained his characteristic smile, ebullient spirit and never-say-die attitude. "What's next, Sid?" he asked.

"Abe, you know Judy Garland is almost a sure thing if she shows up. Look at how great she was in Newport. The audience couldn't get enough of her."

"What do you mean if she shows up?"

"She's had all these health problems induced by her out-of-control drinking, and there's the possibility that we'll book her and she'll cancel—it's always a possibility with her. If that happens, we have to refund everybody's money. We also lose the money we put up for the venue, the advertising and the promotion. It's a crapshoot with her."

Abe considered what I'd just said for the briefest moment, then looked at me: "Let's do it!"

I nodded my head in agreement and smiled.

I HAD ESTABLISHED A GOOD working relationship with David Biegelman and Freddy Fields. They agreed to let us pay Judy date-by-date so we wouldn't have to put up all the money in advance. As long as we paid her twenty-five thousand dollars per performance, paid for conductor Mort Lindsey and five key men in her band, plus supply a twenty-two-piece orchestra, we were okay.

The first concert we did with Judy was at the Ice Palace in Haddonfield, near Philadelphia. It was the only venue in New Jersey that was both large enough and available when Judy was available. Many rural roads surrounded the Ice Palace, and on the morning of the concert a downpour made the roads virtually impassable. The police told me that cars were bumper-to-bumper in every direction. Although I was a stickler for punctuality, I held up this first Judy Garland concert for an hour and a half to accommodate all the people trying to make their way to the show.

Sitting in my temporary office in the Ice Palace, keeping tabs on audience arrival, I was summoned to Judy Garland's dressing room. What could I have forgotten? Usually, when an artist summons you to their dressing room moments before a performance, it spells trouble. I went down the checklist: we had installed the red carpet that Judy insisted always be in her dressing room; we had supplied the bottle of special liquor with the twig in the neck of the bottle; and we had installed her special lighting. Everything seemed to be in place.

I knocked on the dressing room door and was admitted by Judy's wardrobe mistress. "Miss Garland's quite angry," she whispered. Then she announced, "Miss Garland, Mr. Bernstein is here."

Judy was sitting at her dressing table, putting the finishing touches on her makeup. The bottle of liquor beside her was almost empty.

"Where are the fuckin' tissues?" she muttered, as she slowly began to rise.

"What's that, Judy?"

"The fuckin' tissues, Sid! Where are the tissues I asked for?" She was standing now, a bit unsteady and mad as blazes.

I tried to inject some levity. "Tell me what color you'd like, Judy, and I'll send for them right away."

Apparently she was not amused. "I don't give a damn what color, Sid! They should be here! I'm not going on unless my fuckin' tissues are here!"

"Don't worry. They'll be here." Without missing a beat, I had someone run out to get her the all-important hankies.

That was Judy. You could expect anything.

Finally, the cops told me that the crowd had made its way into the arena. I gave Mort Lindsey the signal to start the overture.

By now, Judy was really shaky. Freddy Fields was with her, and he helped her travel the short distance to the stage, but she couldn't negotiate the stage steps, so Freddy got under her one arm and I got under the other, and together we helped her up. We looked at each other. Would she be able to perform?

Onstage, in complete darkness, she stood. Then a pin spotlight hit her. Judy threw back her shoulders, walked to the mike and on

Mort Lindsey's cue began to sing "Somewhere Over the Rainbow." There was not a dry eye in the house. All those Garland fans knew their darling was in bad shape, and they knew why. No one at the Ice Palace that night would ever forget Judy's performance.

After the show, we all went back to the hotel. Judy changed then came downstairs to the lounge to unwind and have a bite. An ensemble played and Judy asked me if I wanted to dance. How could I refuse? So here I am—Sid the klutz—dancing with Judy Garland, who used to dance with Fred Astaire. Judy was so drunk that I had to hold her up. I was stepping all over her feet, but she was so out of it she didn't even know. How sad to see Judy like that! A great artist but a sad, lonely woman.

A few weeks later, we booked Judy into the Forum in Montreal, home of the Montreal Canadiens, the most storied hockey team in history. The Forum was a huge arena with over fifteen thousand seats. A week before the concert, Billy Fields and I drove to Montreal to let the city know we were coming in with the great Judy Garland. The luxurious Queen Elizabeth Hotel became our home base, and on our recommendation Judy and entourage stayed there, too. Near the hotel, on St. Catherine's Street, I found an incredible bakery that made the most marvelous napoleons. Every day, as a treat for myself, I would stop there and buy one or two.

On the night of the concert, determined to satisfy my napoleonic urges, I decided to leave the Queen Elizabeth a trifle early so I would have time to stop at the bakery and fortify myself with a few. The hotel is a huge block-long structure, and as I exited the elevator, I heard this big voice coming from the other side. "Hey, Sid! Sid! It's Judy! I'm on my way to the Forum. I'll give you a lift!"

I wanted to get the napoleons first, so I yelled back, "It's okay, Judy! I have a lift! I'll see you there!"

"Okay, bye!" she screamed.

Narrowly escaping, I went to the bakery, ate the napoleons and, satisfied, went to the Forum ready to work.

As usual, we were supplied with an office, a phone, some writing materials and an intercom. Billy was down on the arena floor making sure that everything was set for Judy's appearance. The intercom in my office rang. It was Judy's road manager, and he sounded very upset. "Hey, Sid, you'd better come up to Judy's dressing room. We've got a problem."

As I walked upstairs, I wondered what could be wrong now. Again, I went down my mental checklist: the red carpet was in her dressing room; Billy had personally gotten the liquor with the twig; the tissues were there.

I knocked on the dressing-room door and was admitted by the wardrobe mistress. She rolled her eyes and whispered, "I wonder how you're gonna handle this one."

"Sid's here," she announced.

Judy was sitting at her dressing table—hair coiffed, makeup artfully applied and seemingly ready to go. She was facing the mirror, fists at her cheeks, dejectedly looking downward.

"Judy, it's me, Sid! Is anything wrong?"

She looked up and spoke in a barely audible voice. "Sid . . ."

"What is it, Judy?"

She whispered again. "I can't go on, Sid. I can't speak. I can't sing. It's impossible. I can't go on. My voice is gone."

I could barely hear her, but I could certainly hear the orchestra tuning up, and I could visualize all the excited fans streaming into the Forum. I also remembered her shouting to me just an hour earlier across the hotel lobby. I went into crisis mode.

"Judy, do you have a special doctor?"

"Lester Coleman. But he's in New York, Sid."

"Judy, did you say Dr. Lester Coleman?"

"He's my doctor," she said in a slightly restored voice. As soon as I heard her voice improve, I knew that we were dealing with another kind of problem, one that had nothing to do with her throat.

I stood in front of Judy's dressing room intercom to block her view of the apparatus. I picked it up and began a conversation with myself. In my hands, the intercom became a phone, and I hoped that Judy wouldn't notice the reality.

"Hello. Is this Dr. Coleman's office? . . . It is? . . . Good. May I please speak to the doctor? I'm here in Montreal with Judy Garland, and we have an emergency."

Now, to make Judy believe that this conversation was actually taking place, I repeated everything that the other side was supposedly saying to me.

"Doctor, this is Sid Bernstein calling from Montreal. I'm presenting Judy Garland tonight, here at the Forum, in concert. The arena is sold out, doctor. There are more than fifteen thousand people waiting to see Judy, but she has a bad case of laryngitis and is having a most difficult time. Is there a possibility, doctor, that you could fly up immediately? I don't care what it costs! Charter a plane, and please come to Montreal immediately. Yes, doctor! You can? In about an hour, you say? That's wonderful, Dr. Coleman! What is the nearest airport?"

Child actress/singer Judy Garland possessed one of the most remarkable and affecting voices of all time.

I continued my imaginary conversation.

"LaGuardia? That's good. Whatever it costs, I'll pay, doctor. . . . Dr. Coleman, I cannot tell you how grateful I am, along with these thousands of people who have come here from all over Canada to hear Judy! Thank you and we'll see you soon."

I hung up the intercom and turned to Judy. She was refreshing her makeup.

"Judy, what a wonderful man! He's coming right up! He'll be here in no time flat!"

"Oh, he will? That's great, Sid. You are just the best. Will we dance later?"

"You know we will, Judy."

And then she responded in full voice: "Now, out of my dressing

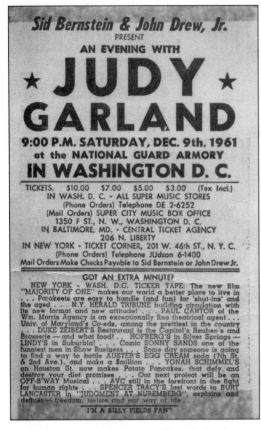

Sid Bernstein & John Drew, Jr.
PRESENT
AN EVENING WITH
★ JUDY ★
GARLAND
9:00 P.M. SATURDAY, DEC. 9th, 1961
at the NATIONAL GUARD ARMORY
IN WASHINGTON D. C.
TICKETS. $10.00 $7.00 $5.00 $3.00 (Tax Incl.)
IN WASH. D. C. - ALL SUPER MUSIC STORES
(Phone Orders) Telephone DE 2-6252
(Mail Orders) SUPER CITY MUSIC BOX OFFICE
1350 F ST., N. W., WASHINGTON D. C.
IN BALTIMORE, MD. - CENTRAL TICKET AGENCY
206 N. LIBERTY
IN NEW YORK - TICKET CORNER, 201 W. 46th ST., N. Y. C.
(Phone Orders) Telephone JUdson 6-1400
Mail Orders Make Checks Payable to Sid Bernstein or John Drew Jr.

During this period, I presented Judy in twelve cities, including the nation's capital. Her performances were always heart-wrenching.

room, Sid. I want to put on another dress."

I got out of there as quickly as I could, called Billy from the first intercom I could find and told him to tell Mort Lindsey to strike up the band. It was the sweetest music I ever heard. This was a big event. I had met so many wonderful Canadians and had helped them get tickets to Judy's sold-out concert. It had become a personal thing for me, and I just couldn't imagine disappointing all the fans because Judy was doing her shtick.

Of course, she was fabulous. She always did the job for me. I think that when Judy stepped out on a stage, she was transformed. She had been born to perform, to thrill people, to communicate with them heart-to-heart through music.

She had an indescribable magic. The Judy Garland concerts were all winners, and as a result I recouped some of our losses and much of my self-esteem.

I was beginning to see the rainbow.

8

"Tony at Carnegie Hall"

I WAS VERY TIRED. I had been going nonstop for almost three years with one promotion after another, but the winners could never seem to make up for the losers. Accumulating any kind of money was simply out of the question under those circumstances. I was sure that Abe would choose to go forward, but I had grown weary.

Stan Scotland was an agent friend who worked for the General Artists Corporation. GAC, as it was known, was one of the premier talent agencies in the world and had on its roster a Who's Who of show-business performers. When I was promoting the rock-and-roll shows at the Paramount and elsewhere, I would often buy acts from GAC.

Soon after working with Judy, Stan and I met. "Sid," he said, "I heard you took a beating at Newport and Hartford. What's next for you?"

"I just did a series of successful concerts with Judy Garland, but to tell you the truth, I've been so up and down with this promotion stuff, Stan, I think I need a change."

We spent a few more minutes talking and said our goodbyes. I thought that was the end of it. But the next day Stan called.

"Sid, I spoke to Buddy Howe, and he would like to see you. Could you come by the office today?"

I knew that Buddy Howe was the chairman of GAC. "Stan, what does Buddy want?"

"Well, he'd just like to kick some ideas around, and he asked me to invite you up."

I had known Buddy casually through the years. He had been a dancer in his younger days, and his wife, Jean Carroll, was a famous comedienne. Buddy had been a great agent with a lot of heart and had worked his way up. The following day, I went to the GAC offices. Stan took me in to see Buddy, and he got right down to business.

"Sid, Stan tells me that you're contemplating leaving promotions for a while. If that's true, we would love to have you join GAC."

My mind immediately went to all those advertising bills from Newport I still had to pay.

"I'm flattered, Buddy. What do you have in mind?"

"We'd like you to head the one-night department, which books all of our rock-and-roll acts. Rosalind Ross has been running it, but she just went over to William Morris, and I know she's going to try to take all our rock acts with her. It's a natural fit for you and us, Sid. You know the talent, and there's a lot of respect for you in the industry, and we have to make sure that Roz doesn't steal our acts. I'll pay you two hundred dollars a week to start, and naturally we'll give you your own office and secretary."

I knew Roz Ross to be formidable, bright and capable. I also knew that she would be tough competition. On reflection, however, I knew that I could compete with her and that if I took the job, I could deliver for Buddy and GAC. But I had other concerns.

"Buddy, I've just come through a very tiring and taxing time, and I don't know if I'm up to handling the responsibility of running a department right now."

"Tell you what, Sid. Why don't you come up on Monday and

work whatever hours you want. We'll give you an office away from the rest of the staff. You'll get all the company memos; you'll read the trade papers; you'll slowly work your way into it. There will be no pressure, and we'll pay you as if you were working full time."

I looked at Buddy and considered his proposal. "You're making this really tempting. . . . You've met my friend Abe Margolies. He backed me at Newport and in lots of other promotions. Well, I have a situation where I incurred some bills outside the Newport budget, but I don't want to tell Abe because he'll insist on taking care of them. I'm determined to pay those bills myself."

"Oh, come on, Sid. Abe can pay those bills easily. It's nothing for him. Why should you have the burden?"

"I know that, but—"

"Okay, here's what we'll do. Prepare a list of the creditors and give it to my secretary. We'll call each one and tell them you're joining GAC and that we are going to deduct a certain amount from your weekly paycheck and remit the money to them. That way, you'll pay them all back. They'll go for the plan because we'll stand behind it. We'll even make sure that they send the bills here to the agency. How much do you want us to deduct, Sid?"

I felt a weight being lifted from my shoulders.

"Well, I'd like to pay them back rather quickly, so if you can deduct half my salary, that'll start the ball rolling."

"Good. We'll deduct half and soon you'll get a salary increase. Before you know it, those guys will be repaid and Abe won't know a thing about it."

We shook hands. And so began my employment with GAC.

BY THIS TIME, ABE MARGOLIES had opened Les Champs, a fancy restaurant in midtown Manhattan. Opening a restaurant for Abe seemed like a good idea on paper. After all, he knew many people and his dedication to quality was well-known. The problem was that Abe's generosity made it impossible for Les Champs to ever yield a profit.

"You know your buddy Abe," one of his meat suppliers once told me. "He'll never make any money at that restaurant. He insists on Grade A stuff then charges cafeteria prices! Best meat, finest produce, home-baked goods—everything. And then, to top it off, he picks up everybody's check."

I went to Les Champs to tell Abe that I had accepted the GAC job.

"Are you sure that you want to go back to a desk job?" he asked. "You know, I'm here for you if you want to keep promoting. I think you should stay with it."

"Abe, I'm tired. You know how much pressure I've been under. Let me try this for a while and get my head clear, then we'll see. It'll be just for a while."

"Okay. As long as you're happy. If it's good for you, it's good for me. Let's eat."

The next Monday, I reported to work at GAC. Buddy had been true to his word: they put me in an office far away from everybody else. In fact, he had been so true to his word that I called it the "isolation ward." He also instructed everyone to "leave Sid alone," to let me integrate myself at my own pace. That morning, I circulated and greeted everyone, then I returned to my office to be met by the agency PR man.

"Sid, I'm here to do a press release, which Buddy wants to get into *Variety* as soon as possible. With your reputation, Buddy figures we can keep Roz from raiding our roster of rock acts, but we need to get the word out immediately."

I filled in the blanks for him, and he wrote the release. A week later, an article appeared in *Variety* and some of the other trade papers. The word was out that Sid Bernstein, who had produced shows at the Paramount, the Palace, the Apollo, the Newport Jazz Festival, and the recent highly successful Judy Garland tour, had joined GAC as head of the one-night department. For the time being, the rock acts took a wait-and-see attitude . . . and Buddy Howe's strategy paid off. No act left GAC. It was damage control at its best.

I worked my way in slowly. From the isolation ward, I read the memos, sat in on meetings and began the all-important task of getting to know the artists on GAC's roster. At that time, they had Patti Page, Dion & the Belmonts, Brenda Lee, Bobby Darin and Tony Bennett, to name a few. Buddy Howe was a frequent visitor to the isolation ward, stopping in to inquire about my well-being. That man truly had a lot of heart.

A few weeks after joining GAC, I decided at the end of a workday to catch the Second Avenue bus down to Auster's Egg Cream Stand, in Lower Manhattan. Egg creams—chocolate syrup, an equal amount of milk, and three times the amount of seltzer—had become another one of my passions. Smooth and luscious! I would think nothing of getting in my car very late at night and driving all the way from the Bronx for an Auster's egg cream.

As I was walking east from GAC to catch the bus downtown, I heard my name. I looked around and there, standing in front of the Living Room, the popular East Side nightspot, was a young man I quickly recognized.

"I'm so glad you're coming, Sid!" he said. "No one from GAC has been here to see me perform yet, and I've been here three days! It's so good of you!"

He was one of the comics I had been introduced to during my first few weeks at the agency. "When are you going on?"

"The first show is in forty-five minutes, but we can go to my dressing room and talk until the show starts."

He was so obviously delighted, I couldn't refuse. I decided to put my egg cream on hold.

In his dressing room, this bright and engaging fellow told me that his comedy routine was "very different." Before showtime, he escorted me into the club and gave me a choice of seats. I opted for the bar.

Within the first five minutes, this guy had everyone wrapped around his finger. His performance was super. After the first show, we went for a walk around the block. "I wish Buddy Howe could see my act," he said. "I know that he's not the agent responsible for me, but he is the chairman of GAC, and he could be very helpful to my career."

"Don't worry. I'll spread the word at the agency. You are different, and they should all get to see you."

We said goodnight, he thanked me again for coming to see him, and I set out once again to get my egg cream.

The next morning, I wrote a memo:

> I must say that the guy is unbelievably clever, different, and very charming . . . Although I had been on my way to get an egg-cream fix, I had the good fortune of getting a double fix, because the guy had me and everyone else howling. Everyone at GAC should make every effort to see this incredibly gifted young comic: George Carlin.

THE FOLLOWING WEEK, the phone rang in my office.

"Hi, Sid. This is Tony Bennett. How are you?"

Right, I thought. One of these jokester agents is putting me on because they know that Tony is my absolutely favorite singer of all time.

"Who is this?"

"It's Tony Bennett, Sid."

Something about the voice sounded like it was indeed Tony Bennett. Unbelievable!

"Sorry. For a minute there I thought someone was kidding around. How can I help you?"

"Sid, I read that article in *Variety* about you joining GAC, and I thought it would be a good idea for us to talk in person."

"Sure. When would you like to come up?"

"You know, I'd rather not come to the office. Why don't we meet for lunch tomorrow?"

"Great," I said.

The next day at one, we met at Schrafft's. The patrons, not to mention the staff, were thrilled to see a face familiar from television.

"Sid," he began, "I think you're going to be a great asset to GAC. Your background as a promoter with acts in the music business is quite extensive and impressive. You've worked with a lot of stars. You know, I'm thinking of leaving the agency."

"Why?"

"Well, I haven't had a hit record in a couple of years, and I haven't done *The Ed Sullivan Show* in who knows how long. Maybe they think I'm finished. Mainly, they give me saloons to work in. Take the Copa—two shows a night, seven days a week. You would think that if they have a headliner performing onstage, they would stop the food service. Instead all you hear when I'm up there are dishes and silverware clanging and dropping to the floor. It's terrible."

Tony was wound up.

"I don't have a manager at the moment, and I don't really feel like I have an agency, either," he continued. "After reading about you and what you've done, I wanted to talk to you and see if you have some thoughts about me and GAC."

The Tony Bennett sitting at the table that day at Schrafft's was a sad and dejected man. I felt bad, but I didn't know how to respond. "You know, Tony. I have to get back upstairs. Let me give our conversation some thought."

Tony's phenomenal talent has endured. A whole new generation of fans has discovered his timeless appeal.

"Okay, I'm meeting my conductor, Ralph Sharon, at Columbia to work on some new material. Would you like to go down there with me? It'll only take a few minutes."

We took the short, leisurely walk. At Columbia, Tony introduced me to Ralph, a fine, dignified Brit. "I have to get back to the office, Tony," I said.

"Shall we talk later, Sid?"

It was obvious that he was reaching out to me. "Sure, if that's what you'd like."

"I'll come up to the office at six, if that's okay with you."

"Tony, my pleasure. See you at six."

As I walked back to the office, I was troubled. Tony Bennett was a great artist. He was a man of civility who had a feel for people and treated everyone in a respectful way. He had given so much of himself to others and brought such enjoyment to countless people, including me. I wanted very much to help him.

As soon as I got to the office, I placed a call to Felix Gerstman, who with Sol Hurok was among the most prominent promoters of shows at Carnegie Hall. Gerstman was the dean of pop attractions at Carnegie. I had met him and admired what he was doing.

"Mr. Gerstman, how are you? This is Sidney Bernstein calling."

"How may I help you, Mr. Bernstein?"

"Well, I have a client here at GAC who I think would do a magnificent job at Carnegie Hall. He's worked the Copacabana and been on television and has had hit records, but as yet no one has engaged him to do a concert. I have a feeling that he'd be sensational. I'd love to see you be the first one to promote Tony Bennett at Carnegie."

"Sidney, let me think about it. Why don't you call me back in a few hours?"

At four o'clock, I called Felix Gerstman back.

"Sidney, I've done some checking and I don't think that Tony Bennett will sell out the hall. I appreciate your enthusiasm, but I won't make money with him. He hasn't had a hit record in a while. I'm sorry to have to turn you down."

"Thank you for your time, Mr. Gerstman." The man was a pro and a gentleman. He had done his homework, and even though I was disappointed, my respect for him remained undiminished.

Next, I called Bill Grummond, who over the years had produced shows at the Forest Hills Tennis Stadium.

"Bill, it's Sid Bernstein calling."

"Hi, Sid. What's up?"

"We have Tony Bennett here at GAC as a client, and I'd like to talk to you about booking him into the stadium. He's never done a concert before, and I have a feeling that he would do very well for you."

"Wait a minute, Sid. You do realize that we have a fourteen-thousand-seat capacity. Tony hasn't had a hit in a while, and I don't think he can fill the place."

"I know how big the stadium is, Bill, but he has a following. There are legions of his fans who can't afford to go to the Copa but who are dying to see him perform live."

"I don't think so, but let me think about it. I'll get back to you."

When I hung up with Bill Grummond, I knew that he would not call me back and that he had no interest in promoting Tony Bennett at Forest Hills.

It was now about six o'clock. I waited for about ten minutes and told myself that Tony was not going to show up. Probably tied up at rehearsal, I thought. But as I reached for my jacket, in he strolled.

"Sorry I'm late. We went a little over. I'm not keeping you, am I?"

I liked his gentility. I had observed at lunch how he treated the waitresses and handled the fans who came over for his autograph.

"No, you're not keeping me."

"Well, Sid, did you think about our conversation?"

"Yes, I did. I've thought about it a lot. . . . Tony, I recently came off a tour with Judy Garland. We did about a dozen concerts that were all sold out except one, all to great critical acclaim. I'd like to see you appear at Carnegie Hall. Judy did her comeback concert there, and it was unbelievable. She had Mort Lindsey conducting and her five key musicians and a large orchestra, and it was stupendous. It reignited her career.

"I'd love to promote you in concert—that's really my background—but industry rules forbid me and GAC from doing that. I've thought this out carefully. If you rented out the hall, placed the ads, printed the posters and flyers and hired the musicians, I think you could sell out the place. Tony, I'm trying to persuade and press you to do this, because I believe that it truly can work for you, and it won't cost you any money."

"Won't cost me any money? How is that possible, Sid?"

"I have a line of credit at the advertising agency and the printer." I was referring to the Newport debts that I was paying off with the help of my salary at GAC. "The only money you're going to have to put up is a deposit, and that's five hundred dollars. The musicians can be paid after the concert, and Ralph Sharon, your conductor, is already on your payroll. What I'd like to see are big posters that say 'Tony at Carnegie Hall,' the date and the price. But in really large letters, just 'Tony at Carnegie Hall.'"

"Oh, I like that. I really like that," he said. I knew then that I had him.

"Everything else will be taken care of. I'll do all the pre-concert work."

"You think I'll do good?"

"Believe me, you'll do good. We'll do a job in this town that hasn't been done in a long time. We'll print a thousand posters and put them up all over New York City."

He was really into it now. "Wait a minute, Sid. I have an artist's caricature of myself. I'd love to see the caricature on the poster instead of a picture."

"Yeah, Tony! Great idea!"

"When do you think we should do it?"

"I called Carnegie Hall before you got here, and June 2 is available." I neglected to tell him that earlier in the day both Gerstman and Grummond had passed on the opportunity to present him in concert.

"Sid, I get that I need to put up five hundred dollars to start, but we both know that if we don't sell any tickets, I'm going to have to pay all the bills, so what are we really talking about?"

"There is no way that you're not going to sell tickets, but the worst-case scenario is that you would lose ten thousand dollars, give or take a few bucks."

We continued the conversation, getting excited at the idea of actually putting on a show at Carnegie Hall.

"Do you think the show should be just me for the entire evening?"

"Yes, just you," I said. "You'll do a short first half, then we'll have an intermission. The audience will have a chance to get some refreshments and socialize, which is always a big thing at Carnegie—and after the intermission you'll go on for as long as you like, until eleven o'clock. But, remember, Tony, we can't run over, because then the costs for the house, the ushers and the rest of the staff get to be very expensive."

"Could we use a comic?"

"Not a bad idea," I said. "Who did you have in mind?"

"I'd love to get Henny Youngman. That guy really breaks me up!"

"I know Henny. He's a funny guy. I'll call him and see if he's available."

I felt great. A few short hours ago Tony was dejected. Now he was upbeat. And so was I. I was going to present the great Tony Bennett, my favorite singer, at Carnegie Hall. Even though my name couldn't be on the posters and handbills, and GAC would have to maintain some semblance of distance from the event, it didn't lessen the thrill. I was doing all this for Tony Bennett. We said goodnight, and I went home with plans for the concert stirring in my head.

THE NEXT MORNING, I arrived at work early and went directly to see Buddy Howe. I told him about the meeting I had the day before with Tony and that his continuing relationship with GAC was in jeopardy because of the lukewarm treatment he felt he was getting from the agency. I also told him about the plan I had worked out for Carnegie Hall.

"Sid," Buddy said, "I appreciate your taking the initiative on this, but do you really think Tony can fill Carnegie Hall?"

"Absolutely, Buddy, I plan to work on it after hours, weekends, whenever I have a free moment. I promise that it won't interfere with my duties here. I want this to succeed."

"Okay, but don't tell the other guys here what you're doing."

I knew from this request that Buddy Howe was concerned about the industry rules prohibiting agents and agencies from being promoters.

"Who's going to present the concert?" Buddy asked.

"Tony. Tony is going to present himself."

"That's good. That's good. And you're sure he'll be all right? I don't want him to come up here and give us aggravation when something doesn't go right. He'll be asking me, 'What did Sid get me into?'"

"Rest assured, Buddy. Everything will work out fine."

Generally, I'm not this cocky, but I had a feeling about Tony's appearing at Carnegie Hall. I called him. "Everything is set. I reserved the hall, and Henny is available to do the date. I think that you should ask Henny to do just twenty minutes. He'll warm up the audience, then you'll do your show. All I need from you now is a check for five hundred dollars."

"Fine, Sid."

The next day, I picked up the check. When Tony excused himself for a moment, I told Ralph Sharon, who was rehearsing with Tony, how excited I was about the concert at Carnegie. Ralph confided that Tony was excited but also nervous.

"It's gonna be good," I said to Ralph.

When I got back to the office, I called Julius Bloom, then head of Carnegie Hall, to reserve June 2 and tell him I had the five-hundred-dollar deposit. I asked if he wanted me to messenger it over or bring it myself the next day. He told me that the following day would be fine.

Next I called Phil Scheff, head of my ad agency, and we devised a schedule of ads for the concert. I then phoned Bob Maltz to alert him that we were going to do an extensive poster campaign and asked him to set aside the time to hang the posters. I went to the printer with Tony's caricature in hand, laid out the copy and contracted for the posters.

I called Columbia Records and spoke to Bill Gallagher, president of the label, and told him about the concert. He committed Columbia to purchasing twelve tickets for members of the press. Imagine, only twelve tickets for an artist who had made tons of money for the label. Bill was less than enthusiastic: "Sid, can you please get Tony off my back? He's constantly coming up here, urging us to do a better job with his records."

I didn't appreciate Bill's comment. I respected Tony for his work ethic and his doggedness. He had explained to me how diligently he had worked on his current release, "I Left My Heart in San Francisco," and how disappointed he was with the results and how unhappy he was with the label's lack of commitment to the record. Tony was a pro and his frequent visits to the record company were little more than an attempt to get Columbia to push his song. I felt that, if nothing else, the concert was going to help Tony at Columbia.

We were ready to go, and I was as excited as I've ever been about any project. I told Buddy Howe that everything was in place and we were prepared to start promoting the concert.

"Sid," Buddy said, "I told Herb Seigel, owner of GAC, about what you're doing. He wants to talk to you."

A little while later, Siegel came to the isolation ward. "I want you to know, Sid, I've been telling everyone here that I don't want us to lose Tony Bennett. Do you think this will enable us to keep him?"

"It'll be no problem, Herb."

"Thanks, Sid. I'm counting on you."

Soon, Bob Maltz began plastering New York City with posters publicizing the event. Bob could distribute posters better than anyone else. In addition, I took several hundred posters to hang myself. Gerry would drive my convertible to every Italian neighborhood in Brooklyn, the Bronx and Long Island. She would keep lookout, ready to honk the horn if she spied a cop. There was a law against hanging posters without a permit, and we didn't have the time to wait for the city bureaucracy to issue one. We were like Bonnie and Clyde. I would find a wooden lamppost or another spot suitable for a poster, jump out of the convertible, whack in four staples and leave. Hit and run. Remember that I had lots of experience from my previous sticker campaigns.

Gerry and I did this every free minute we had. The posters looked great. The caricature of Tony was really distinctive, and the copy was spare. Every once in a while, in the Italian neighborhoods, I would hear people exclaim, "Wow, Tony in Carnegie Hall!" He was, after all, one of their own.

Four weeks before the concert, our first ads appeared. Since I was being very careful with the limited budget, I scheduled three small ads for that first weekend: one each on Friday in the *New York Post* and the *Daily News* and one in the Sunday Arts & Leisure section of the prestigious *New York Times*.

The following Monday, I visited the Carnegie Hall box office to check on our progress. Nat Posnick was one of the top box-office professionals in the industry and I was interested in hearing what he had to say. I was also eager for any advice he might offer. When I got to the box office, I really didn't know what to expect, but I was hopeful. Mr. Posnick buzzed me in and invited me to sit.

"How are we doing on the Tony Bennett concert, Mr. Posnick?"

"There's been no big rush yet. We have three people working these windows, and I know some tickets have been sold."

We agreed that I would check with him again in a few days, but I didn't know what to think.

Two days later, I called him back. "Nat Posnick, it's Sid Bernstein. I'm checking on the concert."

"Just a minute. Let me see."

He got back on the phone. "About a hundred seats."

"Is that good?"

"Yes, it is. You've sold eighty-six tickets since you were here on Monday, and that's very good. It's really good. Tell me, Sid, when are your next ads running?"

"Not this week, Mr. Posnick. I thought we'd wait a week because of how costly the ads are and run them again the week following."

"Well, that'll be fine," he said. "I think it's going to be all right. Call me again after the next ads."

I did exactly that. He told me that he thought we were going to sell out. Two hundred seats had been sold thus far.

"Two hundred tickets? Nat, there are 2,830 seats in Carnegie Hall. We've sold a grand total of two hundred tickets. There are two and a half weeks to go till the concert, and you think we're going to have a sellout? How can that be?"

"Sid," he reassured me, "the sales are gaining momentum. Your next ads are scheduled for this weekend. Don't worry. It'll happen."

After the next ads, I checked again and we had sold a total of three hundred tickets. It was now two weeks before the concert. When I called Nat again the following Monday, he told me that the hall had been half sold. Nat then said quite convincingly, "Sid, it's a sellout."

"Can I tell Tony?"

"Absolutely."

Tony was overjoyed at the news. "Really, Sid? Sold out? Sold out!?" He couldn't believe it.

During that last week before the concert, I visited the offices of Columbia Records. I was giving away tickets to everyone from the mailroom personnel up to the people in the president's office. If an employee was married, I gave two tickets. Everyone was appreciative, and I told Tony it was an investment I believed would pay off.

I SECURED A REHEARSAL ROOM for the Friday of the concert. Every time I went outside during those hours, I would see people lined up at the box office trying to buy tickets to Tony's concert that evening. They were all turned away, and I could see the frustration on their faces.

Later, when I arrived at Carnegie, it was still early and there was a large

Born in Liverpool to American parents, comedian Henny Youngman was famous for his one-liners, most notably, "Take my wife—please!"

crowd milling about in front of the closed doors. Many had seats, but others came to see if they could buy them off the scalpers.

Tony's show that night was the hottest ticket in town. When the doors finally opened, there was a rush to get in. Everyone in that majestic hall—ticket-takers, ushers, musicians, audience—was energized, counting the minutes to showtime. It was the kind of excitement one feels only at a sold-out concert.

I went to see Tony in his dressing room. Henny Youngman was already there loosening Tony up with his wonderful humor. We reminded Henny that he should do only twenty or twenty-five minutes. "Sure thing," he said.

I sought out Bill Gallagher, who had again asked me to get Tony off his back when I delivered the twelve tickets that the label had bought for the press.

"How are we doing, Bill?" I asked.

Viewing the sold-out audience and thinking of potential record sales, he gave me a big smile and a thumbs-up. Everybody loves a winner!

When Henny's opening bit was finished, we had a short intermission. The anticipation in the hall was at a fever pitch. These were diehard Tony Bennett fans.

After the break, Henny came out to introduce the main attraction. Impeccably dressed in a beautifully-cut suit and a gorgeous tie, Tony walked onstage to deafening applause. As he looked down at the people in the orchestra, they began to rise from their seats as the applause grew in volume. The crowd screamed and whistled. "Tony, Tony! Hey, Tony!" they called in that inimitable Italian way. I knew now that all the time Gerry and I had spent in the Italian neighborhoods had paid off.

Tony began to look up through the various levels of Carnegie Hall. The entire crowd was now on its feet. He began to blow kisses to the audience and to hold his head in disbelief. He was overwhelmed. I knew that the audience was in for the show of their lives.

The fabulous welcome charged Tony up, and he gave the fans his all. I also knew that from that moment on Tony Bennett's career was going to take a new and exciting path.

When I finally worked my way to Tony's dressing room after the performance, family and friends surrounded him. It was a truly festive atmosphere. We hugged, and he whispered in my ear, "Thank you, Sid. Thank you, thank you." I felt a friendship that was deeply genuine and very special. Gerry and I then left Tony and his family, so we could celebrate on our own. I was floating on air.

ON MONDAY MORNING, I was greeted like a conquering hero. Tony Bennett had sold out Carnegie Hall, and the reviews of his concert were unanimously glowing. GAC had secured one of its biggest and most important artists. Buddy Howe came to the isolation ward to congratulate me. He gave me a raise and suggested that I move from the ward to an office in a more mainstream location. Late morning, Tony telephoned.

"Sid, I called to thank you again. I really don't know what to say. I haven't talked to him in more than two years, but Ed Sullivan called and he wants me on his show. Can you believe that? Sid, I don't know how to thank you!"

"Sure, I believe it! Why not? You're great and Sullivan read the reviews! Good for you, Tony!"

"Sid, I'd like you to come up to the house in Englewood Cliffs on Sunday for brunch. Can you make it?"

"That's nice. I'd love to come, but I usually reserve the weekends for my folks."

"No problem, bring them."

On Sunday, I loaded my parents into the car, and we took the short ride from the Bronx over the George Washington Bridge to Tony Bennett's house in Englewood Cliffs, New Jersey. We spent about an hour with his wife, Sandy, and his two boys, Danny and Dagal, just chatting and reliving the concert. My mother, familiar with Tony from his TV appearances, sat right alongside him. She leaned over, gently took hold of his throat and said in her Yiddish accent, "Tony, you know vy you sing so gut? Because you have such a beautiful gurgal!"

"Sid, what's a gurgal?" he asked.

"An Adam's apple," I said. We all roared with laughter.

The Monday following Tony's triumph at Carnegie Hall, Columbia Records executives met and decided that "I Left My Heart in San Francisco" was to become what in the business was called a "push" record. Everyone up and down the line was instructed that it was to be worked, worked and worked some more. With all the extra effort, "I Left My Heart in San Francisco" sped up the charts. It has since become Tony Bennett's signature song. Those three hundred tickets that we gave away at Columbia paid off a million times over.

The following workweek, I got a call from the head talent booker at the famous Red Rock Amphitheater outside Denver. "Mr. Bernstein," she said. "I've been directed to speak to you about booking Tony Bennett for Red Rock. Can you please tell me what he gets for a concert?"

"Ten thousand dollars," I answered. I picked that amount because it felt right.

"That's fine." She chose a date, and the deal was done. I immediately called Buddy Howe and related to him the phone conversation with Red Rock.

"Wow! Ten thousand dollars? That's fabulous, Sid! Have you told Tony yet?"

"Not yet, Buddy, but I will after I hang up with you."

"Good, Sid. And by the way, I'm sending a memo to all the GAC offices around the world that if anyone wants to book Tony Bennett, the price from now on is ten thousand dollars per performance, and they have to clear it with you first."

In one fell swoop, I had gotten Tony out of the seven-day/two-shows-a-night/five-thousand-dollar-a-week salary to ten thousand dollars for one night's work. I had also gotten him out of the "saloons" with four hundred or five hundred seats and into concert halls with thousands of seats filled with fans hanging onto his every note.

I called Tony. He was ecstatic. No more clattering dishes. No more unruly dinner patrons who were getting a show with their supper. Tony had arrived! He couldn't have been more thankful, and I couldn't have been happier for him.

A few weeks later, Tony stopped up at the office. We chatted for a while. "Hey, Sid, I'd like you to think about coming on the road and working with me. I'll pay you more than what you're getting here. Give it some thought."

I promised him that I would think it over. . . . He was starting to make really big money. If I took the job, I could hear him sing every time he worked. Tony's offer was very tempting. . . . But the following day, I called him to explain that I would have liked to accept the proposal but needed to stay in New York near my folks and help them out. I assured him that I would continue to do all things necessary for him from the office. True to form, Tony accepted my decision with absolute graciousness.

YEARS LATER, AFTER I WAS no longer his agent, Tony was booked into the prestigious Empire Room of the Waldorf-Astoria, where Lena Horne, Victor Borge, Maurice Chevalier and other international superstars appeared. Tony invited Gerry and me to come as his guests. The room was packed. Dinner was served. Before he came onstage, all dishes, flatware and glasses were removed from the tables. Times had certainly changed for Tony. Even the waiters and busboys moved to the back of the room so that there would be no distractions during his performance. Tony was magical as usual. In the middle of his performance, he made the following statement:

"Ladies and gentlemen. I want to talk about a gentleman sitting in the audience here with his wife. I want to tell

Here's Tony doing what he does best—crooning his way into our hearts.

you that this gentleman has been such a dear friend, and I respect him so much. I'm so glad that he's here in the room, and I want to acknowledge him and thank him again for the wonderful friend he's been to me."

I thought that he was talking about a songwriter who had written one of his hits. Tony often did this while performing. I surveyed the room.

"Sid, he's talking about you," Gerry whispered.

"You're kidding!"

"Sid, could you please step up here?" Tony said. "Ladies and gentlemen, my friend, Sid Bernstein."

9

You're Going to Lose that Girl

MY BOSSES AT GAC LOVED MY CONCERT STRATEGY. Buddy and Herb were so pleased I had "saved" Tony Bennett for them that they gave me the immediate go-ahead when I told them I wanted to do the same kind of promotion with two other GAC artists, then up-and-coming Nina Simone and the wonderful Italian singer Jerry Vale.

I persuaded Nina's record label to promote her at Carnegie, and she played to a good-size audience. Jerry presented himself at Carnegie, so as with Tony, we had no agent/promoter rules to worry about. It worked like a charm, and Jerry's concert sold out. The concerts kept alive the fire in my belly and made the day-to-day agenting at GAC less onerous.

A MEMORABLE EVENING WITH
**one of the Great Artist Performers
of our time**
Nina Simone
IN CONCERT AT
Carnegie Hall
FRIDAY, APRIL 12th, 1963
at 8:00 P. M.
(I'M A BILLY FIELDS FAN)

ONE OF THE THINGS I ENJOYED most about being an agent was accompanying clients on occasional trips. Meeting new people, discovering new cities and, of course, new dining establishments were all perks. I had a particularly memorable adventure when I accompanied Billy Fields to Europe to promote a new record of his. We arrived in Paris, the final destination of the seven-city tour, on a Friday, took care of business on Saturday and were prepared to take an early morning flight home on Sunday.

I wanted very much to bring my family éclairs from Le Coqelin, the famous pastry shop on the Rue Passy. So early Sunday morning, Billy and I took our suitcases, got in a cab and went to Le Coqelin. We arrived to find the doors of the shop shuttered and the shades drawn. The sign on the door was unmistakable: Fermé.

"Okay, Sid. It's closed. Let's hurry to the airport so we don't miss our flight."

"Wait a minute, Billy. I'm sure there must be someone here. They're probably baking in the back."

I rapped on the door for several minutes. No answer. Not a soul around to ask about the opening time. I continued knocking.

By now, Billy was pretty agitated.

"Sid, we're going to miss our flight. Let's go already!"

"I'm not leaving until I get my éclairs!"

After another fifteen minutes of intermittent knocking and peering in the window, someone lifted the shade and opened the door. In French, I explained my mission to the visibly annoyed proprietor. The man quickly boxed up some éclairs, and Billy and I made a mad dash for the airport.

We missed our plane, and Billy and I ate most of the éclairs—which, by the way, were velvety smooth, rich but not too sweet . . . très délicieux—while waiting for the next flight to New York. Did I dare suggest that we return to Le Coqelin to get more? Not unless I wanted to take my life in my hands. Ah, well . . . the folks back home would just have to understand.

GERRY AND I HAD BEEN dating for almost four years. She had been through my roller-coaster career as a promoter, and I had watched her blossom into a beautiful woman with a promising Broadway future. We frequented the best dining spots, caught all of the new shows and movies, and enjoyed each other's company immensely.

One of the things we did not do was introduce each other to our respective families. My Jewish parents, I was sure, would be less than overjoyed to see us together. And Gerry felt that her parents, particularly her career Army father, did not have much use for Jews.

We were sitting in my car one night in front of Gerry's apartment building on Upper Broadway, having a pretty serious conversation, when Gerry blurted out: "Sid, let's get married."

"Gerry, do you know how old I am? I'm forty-one, and you're twenty-two. I'm much too old for you."

"I don't care. What does it matter?"

"Gerry, we're of different faiths, and you know your parents will be livid. My parents are from the old country, with the old beliefs and traditions. Forget the age difference for a minute; we have other obstacles to overcome. Think about it, Gerry. We have a lot of problems."

"I don't care!" she said through tears.

"Okay, love, let's think about this. It's late. I'll take you upstairs and then I'll go home and we'll talk about it tomorrow."

I pondered the dilemma all night, weighing the pros and cons and concluding that it was unfair of me to waste any more of Gerry's time. I could not spring a non-Jewish wife on my parents, and I also didn't relish the idea of incurring the wrath of Gerry's parents.

The next day, I took Gerry to the Brasserie, our favorite post-theater hangout. I told her that I simply did not know what to do. I loved her and cared about her, but I could not marry her now. She started to cry, then I started to cry. We talked and talked but found no answer.

The next day, Gerry called me at GAC.

"Sid, I don't want to give you any more pressure. I know you're concerned about your mother. Let's just be good friends."

"Gerry, we're more than good friends."

"Well, then let's just be whatever we are, Sid. But, we'll leave the subject of marriage alone."

"Okay," I said. "That's a good idea."

"Sunday is supposed to be a beautiful day. Let's spend the day in the park."

"But I promised my folks I'd take them to dinner at Manero's, in

Gerry and I spent many an evening dining out and enjoying one another's company. We cherished our moments alone together.

Greenwich, Connecticut. . . . Maybe the four of us should go to-gether."

"Are you sure you want to do that, Sid?"

"I'm sure, Gerry. I'll just tell them I'm bringing a good friend."

"Okay, if you think it won't be a problem."

On the fateful day, I picked up Gerry at her apartment in Manhat-tan, we got my parents in the Bronx and then all drove to Manero's. We had a lovely, if subdued, dinner. Gerry tried hard, but my folks knew from the way Gerry and I interacted that this beautiful young woman was not just Simcha's good friend. They knew that serious business was going on here.

After dinner, I dropped off my parents and took Gerry home. When I returned to the Bronx, the lights were still on. Mom and Pop were clearly not yet asleep. I cracked open the door.

"Simcha," my mother said, "*zeyer a shaine maidel. Sie is frum California?*"

"Yes, she is a beautiful girl, and she is from California."

"An actress?"

"*Nicht an actress, a zinger,*" I said.

"*Sie zingt zeyer shain?*"

"Yeah, she sings very beautifully."

"*Bist far leibt in ir?* You're in love with her?" The interrogation continued.

I told them that I liked her a lot, that she is a very fine girl, but very young. Then I reassured them. "Not to worry," I said. "*Erger sig nicht. Es is nicht zeyer serious.*"

I chickened out . . . A music guy who couldn't face the music.

My parents went to sleep, and the next day I went to see Abe.

"You're out of your mind," he said. "This is a beautiful, charming girl and you've been seeing her for four years. Where are you going to find another girl like this? You're going to lose this girl. You want to have a family. You're always talking about having children. How long are you going to wait?"

I didn't have an answer.

"Maybe you don't want her," Abe said. "You're coming up with all these excuses: age, your parents, her parents, religion—who knows what else. Maybe you don't want to marry her!"

Abe wasn't the only one disgusted with me. All of my friends advised me to stop procrastinating and "do the right thing and marry Gerry before you lose her!"

Now that the subject of marriage had been broached, it found its way into every conversation Gerry and I would have.

"I'm going to California on vacation," she announced one day. "Would you like to come meet my grandparents?" Not her parents, mind you, but her grandparents, whom she adored.

"No," I said. "Later. Not now."

I knew that if I went to California with her, I would have had to meet her parents as well, and I was not ready for that. So Gerry opted to stay in New York, too. "We'll spend more time together," she said.

During her vacation, Gerry came to the office more often and got to know my business associates. We had a nice time, but behind the curtain of seeming acceptance, the tension was building. A few weeks later, unexpectedly, Gerry said, "Look, Sid, I have another vacation coming up, and if we're not going to get married, I'm going home, and I'm not coming back. I'm going to stay in California. I don't want to come back to New York."

An ultimatum. I knew that she meant every word.

"Gerry, are you going to walk away from *The Sound of Music* and your career, just like that?"

"Yes, I don't want to come back."

I let her go. I can't really say why. I didn't fight it. I just let her go.

The first week after Gerry left was unqualified misery. I wouldn't write. If her parents saw a letter from Sid Bernstein, they would certainly make a nasty remark about my Jewishness. Nor did I want to phone. "Who's calling please?" "Sid Bernstein . . ." The name would certainly reveal my ethnicity.

Finally, after a week, I couldn't take the depression anymore. I was in love with that woman, and I didn't care who picked up the phone or what they thought about my background.

Her sister answered.

"Hi, Kathleen, it's Sid Bernstein calling. Is Geraldine at home? I'd like to say hello."

"Yes, Sid. She's at home. Hold on, please." Kathleen sounded very pleasant.

Gerry came to the phone. "How are you, Sid?"

"Miserable, Gerry."

"So am I."

"Are you coming back, Gerry?"

"Do you *want* me to come back?"

"Yes, I want you to come back. I miss you."

"I miss you, too. I'll be home."

"When, Gerry? When will you come back?"

"I have to come back to the show again next week."

Obviously, she hadn't given notice to the producers.

"What flight are you coming back on? I'll pick you up . . ."

GERRY RETURNED TO NEW YORK and *The Sound of Music*. After weeks of avoiding the subject, we again began to discuss marriage and finally made plans to wed. My parents were elderly, and by now my mother was in need of almost constant care. Gerry was sensitive to that and suggested that we find a two-family house. My parents could live on the ground floor, and we would live on the floor above.

My father had given up the tailor shop on East Tremont Avenue. We tried to sell it, but when no buyer emerged, he just closed the doors and walked away. Pop was too active to retire completely, so he took a job at the Sutton Cleaners and Tailoring Shop, on First Avenue between Fifty-eighth and Fifty-ninth Streets. Three days a week, without fail, he would take the subway to the shop. He needed to be busy. Fortunately for us both, Sutton Cleaners was a short walk from GAC, and I could surprise him with an occasional visit.

On Monday, April 15, 1963, my father and I had a lunch date. I was looking at my watch, thinking that I had to get ready to meet him, when the phone rang. "Sid," said the voice from Sutton Cleaners, "your dad had a heart attack, and they've rushed him to New York Hospital."

The hospital was not far from GAC. At the inquiry desk, I was instructed to go straight to the emergency room. "Your father has had a severe heart attack," the attending doctor told me, "and we're trying to save his life. He is conscious, and you may see him for a moment."

When I got into the room, I saw my father surrounded by a team of physicians. He looked ashen. I held his hand and kissed him several times. "Pop, you'll be fine. You'll be okay. I'll be right next door."

The doctors asked me to leave the room. About a half-hour later, with Gerry and Abe by my side, one of the doctors came out. "Mr. Bernstein, I am sorry to tell you that we couldn't save your father. We did everything we could, but the heart attack was just too severe. I'm sorry."

Just like that. One minute my father was a reasonably healthy and functioning human being, and the next minute he was gone. I was devastated. Gerry and Abe drove me home, and Gerry stayed by my side. Mama had been spending most of her time in bed, going through still another health crisis. I dreaded having to tell her.

When Gerry left for the theater, I went in to see my mother.

"Papa had a heart attack. We won't be seeing him tonight," I said gently.

"When will we see him?"

"Not tonight or tomorrow or ever again, Mama. He's gone."

She began to sob uncontrollably. I held her and held her. Neither of us slept that night.

We had the funeral the next day, as is the Jewish custom, and my dad was buried in the Elmont, New York, cemetery. It all went by in a blur. Mama and I sat *shiva*, the seven-day mourning period, and were visited by family and friends. Immediately after, I arranged for my mother to have full-time help and companionship. Mama would receive the care she needed, while I returned to work at GAC.

One of the great and beautiful lights in my life had been extinguished. I was useless when I returned to my job those first weeks after my father's death. I went through the motions but accomplished little. But everyone at GAC understood. The "leave Sid alone" policy was again in force.

Each day, when work was over, I would rush home to be with my mother. When she was asleep, I would hurry back down to the city to be at the Lunt-Fontanne Theatre to pick up Gerry when the curtain fell on *The Sound of Music*. My life was harried and hectic.

ON JULY 16, 1963, two months after Papa died, Gerry and I eloped. We drove to Cape Cod and the next morning went looking for a justice of the peace. We couldn't find one, so we took the very next ferry to Nantucket. There, we were referred to a man named, of all things, Coffin, who came from an old New England family. Justice Coffin married us, with his secretary serving as the other witness. Sid, the confirmed bachelor, had finally run out of excuses. He was now a married man.

We had a lovely honeymoon week on Cape Cod. When we got back to New York, we moved into my old buddy Walter Hyman's luxurious Fifth Avenue apartment. He and his family were off on a six-week vacation in Cannes, so, as his wedding gift, this incredible place—complete with a wraparound terrace and view of Central Park and the city skyline—was ours.

My mother came with us to Walter's apartment. It was a pleasant time for her. She so enjoyed sitting on that terrace, taking in the beautiful view of New York. During our entire stay, religion was never brought up.

Gerry and I found an apartment of our own in Greenwich Village, and by the time Walter returned from Cannes, we were ensconced on West Twelfth Street.

Mom was safely back home in the Bronx. I went back to work at GAC. Gerry got pregnant. Her show-business career was over, and mine was about to go for the ride of the century.

PART THREE

Ride of the Century

10

Ahead of the Beat

A FTER THE HONEYMOON, I went back to GAC and straight to Buddy Howe: "We need to talk. I appreciate everything you've done for me and I've really enjoyed working here, but I feel the time is right for me to get back to promoting. I've decided to leave the agency."

"Sid, hold your horses! I know you love promoting, but it's such an iffy business. You just got married, and your wife is pregnant. Don't you think you should give this careful consideration? Your future is secure here. Let's table this idea for a while, and we'll revisit it after you've had time to think."

Buddy didn't want to have to deal with replacing me. He was such a nice guy, and I felt an allegiance toward him since he had allowed me to work myself into GAC slowly after I had been bruised and battered by Newport. I let Buddy put me off.

One of the good things about working as an agent was that I had more free time than I did as a promoter or manager. To keep my mind active and my spirits high, I decided to take some courses at the New School for Social Research, in Greenwich Village. The brilliant Dr. Max Lerner, who was also a prominent columnist, first with P.M. and then with the *New York Post*, was one of the school's best lecturers. He would always fill up the seven-hundred-seat auditorium.

Max Lerner explained that if we wanted to learn about democracy in America, it was incumbent upon us to read about other great world democracies. He distributed a reading list comprised of works on the evolution of that institution in England. Since I had little time, I decided that in lieu of the recommended reading I would buy some British newspapers and immerse myself in things English.

I went to Hotaling's, the international newsstand now on West Forty-second Street but then located in the basement of the old *New York Times* building. I started reading the *London Times* and several other publications. Reading those papers brought to mind my time as a soldier in Great Britain and all of the wonderful British people I had encountered there. For the first time in my life, I was enjoying school.

Each Wednesday, it was my custom to buy a British newspaper at Hotaling's. On one such day in late 1963, I picked up a copy of an airmail edition of the *Daily Mirror*, a breezy tabloid which, I believe, was the largest circulating paper in England. I took it back to the office and browsed through the news section. When I reached the entertainment page, I paid more attention. There were noteworthy items about theaters, concerts, movies, and the like, and I happened to notice a small, one-column five-line item. It had a Liverpool dateline and talked about a group called the Beatles, which consisted of four local boys who were attracting big crowds and causing some hysteria. The word "hysteria" particularly caught my eye.

The next week, again I browsed through the *Daily Mirror*. I wasn't looking specifically for a mention of the Beatles; the item of the previous week had been almost inconsequential. But there it was—another item about the four boys. The two-column article reported that the group was now attracting huge crowds *outside* of Liverpool. Again I noticed that word "hysteria," and again my interest was piqued. The only time I could remember a word like that being used in entertainment circles was in reference to Frank Sinatra and Elvis Presley.

A week later, I picked up several newspapers in addition to the *Daily Mirror*, and in each I saw articles about the excitement that the Beatles were generating. Now the newspapers reported that the foursome's shows were selling out and people were being turned away. Under any circumstances, sellouts were uncommon; it was clear that the cash register was ringing for these four boys. They had become an attraction, and not just in Liverpool.

The following Wednesday I picked up my papers with anticipation, but this time I bought some of the more conservative dailies. Because I was also interested in what the music trades might be writing, I purchased *Melody Maker* and *The New Musical Express*. All had features about the Beatles. Maurice Kinn, publisher of the latter, wrote under a pseudonym that the Beatles were going to "explode all over England and the British Isles."

There was a kiosk at Fifty-seventh Street and Eighth Avenue that sold *Melody Maker* and *The New Musical Express*, and I began to pick up copies there and read them religiously. At breakneck speed, the trades reported, the Beatles were gaining momentum in England. I realized that any day now the excitement might find its way to American shores.

I was still running the one-night department at GAC and, being a devoted employee, was committed to doing the best job I could. My thought was that the audiences for the shows I had put on at the Palace and Paramount were probably similar to the Brits who were getting turned on to the Beatles. Maybe there would be an American audience for this new British group. Beatles frenzy was feeding on itself, and stories documenting it were proliferating geometrically. Even I, who could never pass geometry, knew that this meant more press and increased fame. Surely, the phenomenon would eventually spread beyond English borders.

I soon added other British newspapers—*The People*, *The Observer*, *Reynolds News*, *Manchester Guardian*—to my reading list. I wondered how the elite dailies were reacting to this burgeoning musical development. Interestingly enough, almost all reports noted the group's long hair and the frenzy the group created in the clubs. No one wrote about the quality of the music or the musicianship. One day,

I noticed a headline on the third or fourth page of *Manchester Guardian*: "Beatlemania Is About to Sweep Great Britain." It was then that I became determined to find Brian Epstein.

Many articles had named Epstein as the entrepreneur guiding the Beatles' careers. His family owned a large retail furniture establishment in Liverpool, and he had established a record shop in the store. One day, a customer requested a record by the Beatles, and Brian Epstein became curious about this new local group. He had found them working in a tiny Liverpool nightclub and was so impressed that he succeeded Alan Williams, a local theatrical agent and manager, as their guiding force.

Vic Lewis was in charge of the GAC London office. I sent him a memo:

> Vic, I have been reading about a group, the Beatles, out of Liverpool, that's creating a furor in England. I'd like to contact their manager, Brian Epstein. Do you know anything about the group and can you get me Brian Epstein's phone number?

In a few days, Vic responded with a memo of his own:

> Of course I know about the Beatles, but Sid, no one in America cares or will ever care about them. It's a local phenomenon. There's currently no airplay in the U.S. Epstein books the band himself, so they don't need agents. There is nothing here for GAC to pursue. Forget about it.

As the newspaper articles about the Beatles grew in frequency and enthusiasm, I sent Vic a series of memos, becoming more insistent with each. After a while, perhaps considering me less than rational, he stopped responding to my communications entirely. In Vic's defense, bands like the Beatles were, until that time, not appearing in the U.S., nor were they getting any radio airplay. But in spite of everything, I still wanted to pursue the idea of bringing the Beatles to America. I went to the top: Buddy Howe.

"Buddy, I've been writing memos to Vic in London about a band in England that's got the kids going wild. They've had no airplay in the U.S. and not that much in England, so Vic thinks they're just a fad. Their manager, Brian Epstein, books them himself, so Vic thinks there's nothing there for GAC, but I think that something is going to break and that we should try to sign them."

Buddy stared at me blankly. "What do you want me to do about it, Sid?"

"I'd like you to talk to Vic about getting involved in this. I think we should try to sign the group. Something is definitely going on."

"Okay, Sid. I'll call Vic."

The next day, Buddy stopped by my office to tell me what I already knew—that Vic felt it would be a waste of time to chase the Beatles. It was clear that Vic wanted me off his back, and Buddy was preoccupied with the day-to-day operations of GAC. He had to look out for the bottom line, and a group with no airplay in the U.S. and a manager who booked the group himself represented zero dollar-potential to the agency. Buddy's message to me was loud and clear: Stop bothering Vic. Forget about the Beatles.

Time was passing, and I was growing really antsy. Overall, my time at GAC had been good. I had that terrific experience with Tony Bennett and had orchestrated Carnegie Hall debuts for both Jerry Vale and Nina Simone. I had repaid most of my advertising debts from the Newport Jazz Festival. However, my first love was promotion. Now, I thought, now would be my chance to escape and still walk the moral high ground. I had tried every way I knew to interest GAC in the Beatles. It was time to take the initiative. I wanted to promote the Beatles in the United States.

I called information in Liverpool but could not get a listing for Brian Epstein. I called information in London, thinking that now that the band was exploding all over the British Isles, Epstein would have an office there: "No Brian Epstein in London, sir." I wracked my brain trying to figure out a way to contact Epstein without attracting too much attention to myself at GAC.

A few days later, I was sitting in Stouffer's thinking about how I could get Epstein's phone number when in walked Bud Halliwell, a successful independent record promotion man. Although record companies keep promo men on their staffs, they often hire indies to augment their permanent personnel. The goal of the indies is to develop contacts at radio stations in order to get airplay, the life-blood of the record industry.

I invited Bud to sit with me. We exchanged chitchat, Bud remarking about my success with the Tony Bennett concert and the giveaway of three hundred tickets to the Columbia Records staff, which had become well-known in the industry.

"A stroke of genius," Bud said.

"Thanks, Bud. You know, I've been reading about this group in England called the Beatles—"

"I know them, Sid. I'm promoting their records."

My jaw almost hit the floor. "You are? How's it going?"

"Not great. No one in America wants to play them. No one wants to hear about the Beatles. No one cares."

"That's too bad, but that'll change. Eventually, you'll be able to get their records on the air. . . . Tell me, would you happen to know their manager, Brian Epstein?"

"Sure, Sid. That's who I'm working for. He's the guy who hired me."

"Do you happen to have his phone number?"

"Childwall 6518. It's in Liverpool."

I repeated the number and scribbled it on a napkin. It was as easy as that. When God wants it and it's destined, it happens. In Yiddish, we say it's *bashert*. I rushed back to my office and asked my secretary to place a call to Childwall 6518 in Great Britain. In a minute, she buzzed back.

"Sid, I have your call. It's a woman on the line."

A very pleasant voice said hello.

"Hello," I said. "It's Sid Bernstein calling from New York. I would like to speak to Brian Epstein please."

"Sure, I'll get him," Queenie Epstein said. "Mr. Bernstein, may I ask a question of you before I call my son?"

"Certainly. What would you like to know?"

"Does *The New York Times* still print its Book Review section? I have not seen it in the longest time."

"Yes, Mrs. Epstein, every week, like clockwork."

"My gosh! I used to read it all the time but can't find it now."

"Mrs. Epstein, may I have your address? I get *The Times* every Sunday, and I'll mail the book section to you."

"Oh, that's too much to ask."

"Not at all. It would be my pleasure."

She gave me her address, told me that she hadn't visited the States in ages and proceeded to ask me a series of questions about New York. And, yes, I did send her the Book Review section every week.

"Oh, Mr. Bernstein, this

HENRY EPSTEIN

The charming Brian Epstein. With one word, a simple "yes," he changed my life.

call must be costing you a small fortune. Let me call my son. . . . Brian, there's a gentleman from New York wanting to speak to you. I've kept him on the phone far too long."

In a moment, a male voice said, "Hello, this is Brian Epstein."

I was immediately struck by his dignified tone and manner. I was finally on the phone with Brian Epstein. I froze. Somehow, I knew that this was the most important phone call of my professional life. I was literally tongue-tied.

" . . . Mr. Epsteen. This is Mr. Bernsteen," I finally said.

"Excuse me, Mr. Bernsteen. My name is pronounced Epstyne."

"Oh, I see. My name is pronounced BernSTEEN and yours is EpSTYNE. Mr. Epstyne, this is confusing. Perhaps we could call each other Sid and Brian?"

"Fine," he said. "How may I help you?"

"Brian, I have been reading about your group, the Beatles, for some time now, and I would like to present them here in America. I'm sorry to call you at home, but it's the only phone number I could get for you."

"I understand," he said. "Tell me, Sid, why would you want to present my boys? They've had no radio airplay in America at all. I'm having great difficulty breaking through or getting any response from the American market, and I will not permit my boys to play to a house that is not 100 percent full."

"But you will, Brian. You'll get your airplay. I'm sure you will."

I wasn't just trying to sell him. From what I had read in the newspapers, I could tell that the Beatles' success would not be limited to the British market. I had a gut feeling that they would be a phenomenon in America, too.

"Tell me, Brian, has anyone else called you from the States?"

"No, you are the first. Tell me, Sid, where would you present them?"

I was not prepared for the question. I had planned only to chat with Brian and win him over—just a hello, not a detailed discussion.

" . . . Carnegie Hall."

"What? You want to present my boys at Carnegie Hall?"

"Yes, it's one of the most cherished concert halls in America."

"I know it well. Not three or four days ago, I saw a movie on British telly. It was called, of all things, *Carnegie Hall*."

"That's the place."

"Wait till I tell the boys at Isow's!" Brian said.

I didn't know that Isow's was a popular London hangout for managers, agents and publishers, but in case Brian thought I was plugged into the British pop music scene, I didn't want to reveal my ignorance. "Oh, yeah! Good!" I responded.

Brian continued. "Have you any idea how much my boys are earning in England right now?"

Oh, no, here it comes, I thought. "Uh . . . no, I don't know, Brian."

"We are earning top dollar. The equivalent of two thousand American dollars per show. This is what we earn in the music halls of Great Britain."

I breathed easier. I had paid Judy Garland twenty-five thousand dollars per night. I had been prepared to pay Bob Hope the same amount for one afternoon. I had gotten ten thousand per show for

Tony Bennett. Two thousand dollars for the Beatles was definitely something I could handle.

"What are the capacities of those music halls, Brian?"

"Oh, easily upwards of fifteen hundred seats, and at some venues even better," he said.

"Carnegie Hall has 2,830 seats, but I believe the Beatles will fill it. Not to worry."

"Sid, so many requests are coming in for the boys that it is nearly impossible to fill them all. We are getting superstar money."

Four months had passed since I started reading about the Beatles, and my instincts had now been confirmed. They had indeed become a phenomenon.

Brian's questioning continued. "When would you present them?"

"Three months from now," I said arbitrarily. "Brian, I will offer you $6,500 for two shows in one day at Carnegie Hall."

He was delighted. "Wait till I tell the boys at Isow's that an American is offering me $6,500 for two shows in one day! . . . But three months is too soon."

"Then, let's make it four months."

"No, Sid. I do not want my boys to play to an empty house."

"Okay, Brian. When would you want to come over?"

He thought for a moment. "Not till early next year."

Next year?! I had been dreaming about this for several months. It was paramount that I get the Beatles, and especially that I be first. I had to be first. It would be a long wait, but if I agreed, I would have them. And my intuition told me that this man would keep his word.

"All right," I said. I turned to February 1964 in my calendar. It was after the Christmas holidays and New Year's festivities. The first holiday in the new year was Lincoln's Birthday. That was also a Wednesday, and I thought that Carnegie Hall would probably be available on a weekday. "How about February 12, 1964, Brian? It's a legal holiday here in the States. The kids will be out of school and we can do the two shows."

"Okay. The idea of playing Carnegie Hall is intriguing, and the money is sufficient. I will agree to everything, with one proviso. If my boys still haven't gotten airplay in America by this coming

October—October of nineteen hundred and sixty three—I have the right to cancel."

"That's fine," I said. By now, I was prepared to agree to almost anything.

"If we have to cancel, Sid, how much will that cost you?"

"If you have to cancel, so be it. I'll take the loss. But I'm confident that the airplay will materialize. Don't worry about it. I can handle it."

I was struck by the man's decency. Brian Epstein was a businessman, to be sure, but he also had great sensitivity, which would remain evident throughout the years. He was a mensch.

"Fine, Sid. We're going to be busy for a while now. Why don't we talk again in about six or eight weeks."

"Okay, Brian, I will call you again the first week in May. Meanwhile, can I go ahead with my plans?"

"Yes, go right ahead. However, I just want to reiterate that if there's no airplay in your country by October, I have the right to cancel. That's the only condition."

"Agreed," I said. "Goodbye, Brian. It was a pleasure speaking with you."

"No, Sid, the pleasure was mine. Until next time . . . Cheers!"

I was ecstatic. I did a jig around the office. I would be the first to bring the Beatles to America!

Immediately, I called Julius Bloom at Carnegie Hall, who informed me that Iona Satescu had become the head booker. I was transferred to her office and made an appointment to meet with her.

At 12:30 p.m. the next day, I went to Mrs. Satescu's office on the tenth floor of Carnegie. Gilda Weissberg, her secretary, ushered me in. I took a seat opposite Mrs. Satescu.

"I have an act from England, Mrs. Satescu, that I would like to present next year, and I was wondering if you have February 12, 1964, available."

She leafed through her calendar. "Yes, Mr. Bernstein. It's available."

"Would it be possible to do two shows that day?"

"What times did you have in mind?"

"Well, one would be at 7:00 p.m., the other at 9:30. Would that be workable?"

"Gilda," Mrs. Satescu said. "Are there any rehearsals or special events at that time?"

Gilda checked her book. "The hall is free that day."

"Great!" I said. "Mrs. Satescu, what would the costs be?"

"For the afternoon and evening, with staff and liability insurance, the two shows would run about five thousand dollars."

"That's fine."

"You do not have to give me the five thousand dollars now, Mr. Bernstein. All that is required is a five-hundred-dollar deposit. By the way, who are these people that you want to bring?"

"Four young men who are a phenomenon in Great Britain. Just four."

"And what are their names?"

"They're called the Beatles. B-E-A-T-L-E-S."

"Uh. . . .Ohhh. . . . How very interesting. . . . Have a good day, Mr. Bernstein."

Gilda led me into her office so that she could type up the contract. After filling in the required information, she asked me for a check. I needed to stall for time.

"Gilda, I'm so sorry. May I come back tomorrow? I completely forgot that I would need to give you money today."

"That's okay, Mr. Bernstein. The contract will be here tomorrow, and if I'm not here, see Mrs. Satescu. Make the payment out to Carnegie Hall."

I thanked both ladies and hurried back to GAC to call Abe Margolies.

"Abe, I need five hundred dollars."

"I can't do it right now, Sid, but let's have lunch tomorrow."

"Okay. I have something really important going on."

"Come to the office for lunch, Sid, and I'll take care of it."

No questions asked. The five hundred dollars for Carnegie Hall was as good as mine. All I had to do was pick it up. The next day, I took an early break and went to Abe's office. We had a sandwich, and he took out his checkbook.

"Who's this for, Sid?" His pen was poised.

"Carnegie Hall, Abe. I have a show that I must do."

"Who are you presenting?"

"It's an act from England. You've never heard of them, so what's the difference?"

"Sid, tell me who it is so I can at least tell my kids. Tell me."

"The name of the group is the Beatles. B-E-A-T-L-E-S. Beatles, with an 'a', Abe, not with a double 'e.' Beatles that make music, not insects that sting. The Beatles are from Liverpool, England."

"The Beatles, Sid? The Beatles?!!" The look on his face said it all. "What kind of a name is that?"

I turned my palms heavenward. "Abe, that's their name."

"Sid, do you think for one moment that I'm going to tell my kids or anybody that I backed you or loaned you five hundred dollars for a music group with a name like that? In the last days of my life, I will never let anybody know that I backed you to put a group called the Beatles in Carnegie Hall. Never."

"Okay, Abe, but I'm telling you, I've got a feeling about this. Don't worry about it."

He wrote the check. "Sid, I don't want to be your partner on this one. By all means, do it. You know I always wish you luck no matter what. I hope you're right, but I don't want to be involved. . . . And Sid, you have to promise me one thing: you will never let anyone know that I had anything to do with this thing."

I took the check and left. Abe really thinks I'd gone off the deep end, I thought. I hoped he wasn't right.

Of course, Abe told some of his closest friends and associates about my new venture. For a few months after that, mutual friends would say, "Hey, Sid! What's with that group you sold Abe? You know, that insect group? What's happening? We don't hear a word!" Everybody was having a good laugh at my expense.

I took the check for five hundred dollars directly to Carnegie Hall and gave it to Mrs. Satescu.

"Mr. Bernstein, we're not aware of this group. Who are they? I haven't seen them in any of the music periodicals."

"Believe me when I say they're a phenomenon in Britain." I quickly signed the contract, turned over Abe's five hundred dollars and got out of there as fast as I could. Then, I headed over to see my friend Nat Posnick at the box office. Aida, his assistant, buzzed me in.

"How've you been, Sid?" Nat asked. "We haven't seen you for a while. That Tony Bennett concert was great. Fabulous job you did! What's up this time?"

"I just came from Mrs. Satescu's office, Nat. I signed a contract for a group from England that I'm bringing in next February, on Lincoln's Birthday. No one has heard of them yet."

"Good, good, Sid. You want to give me the details so we can print the tickets?"

I started to give him the copy for the tickets and realized that I had a serious problem. Since I was an agent, I was precluded by industry rules from acting as a promoter. You could be either an agent or promoter, not both. My name could not appear on the tickets, the posters or in any of the ads. There would be no "Sid Bernstein Presents." And I couldn't use Abe's name. I had a big problem.

"Nat, I just thought of something. Can I call you back later or tomorrow with the copy?"

"Sure, Sid. Whatever you want."

As I walked back to GAC, I tried to come up with a plan that would enable me to forge ahead. I decided to call my old friend Walter Hyman.

"Walter, I just booked an act you've never heard of. They're doing very well in England and I'm bringing them to Carnegie Hall next year. I'm going to be the first one to bring them to America. Their manager told me I was the first American to call him."

"Well, what's the deal?"

"I have a problem, Walter. I'm going to promote this concert, but I'm still here at GAC as an agent, and you know I can't be an agent and a promoter at the same time. Abe Margolies, who has always been my backer, can't get involved in this for unspecified reasons. He can't front for me and I can't use his name. Would you do it? Can I use your name?"

"Sure, Sid! My buddy Hank Barron has been telling me for the long-

THEATRE THREE PRODUCTIONS

PRESENT

THE FIRST NEW YORK APPEARANCE OF THE

BEATLES

CARNEGIE HALL WED. FEB. 12

2 SHOWS 7PM & 8·30PM

PRICES $4·00 $4·50 $5·00   TICKETS GO
ON SALE AT CARNGIE HALL FROM JAN 27

Due to the pre-concert frenzy, this poster was printed with glaring errors. Not only was the name of the hall misspelled on the bottom line, but the ticket prices were wrong as well.

est time that he'd like to get involved in show business, and he's been saying to me, 'Let's do something with Sid!' You can put his name and my name on the tickets and posters."

"Walter, that's great. I'll do it any way you guys like."

"Okay. Let me call Hank and discuss it with him, and by tomorrow we'll have it figured out. Call me tomorrow, Sid."

The next day, I called Walter. "Hank's in," he said, "but he wants to use the name Theatre Three Productions. Don't ask me why. He likes it."

"Great, Walter! It's a good name. We'll use that." Once again, my friends had come through for me.

I went back to Nat Posnick at Carnegie. "The name I want to use, Nat, is Theatre Three Productions. Two shows on Wednesday, February 12. One at 7:00 and one at 9:30."

"Fine, Sid. And what do you want to charge?"

"What do you think, Nat? What is the going price these days?"

"If you really feel the act is that good, Sid, and you think they're going to make it, then charge top dollar."

"What's top dollar, Nat?"

"Hot acts are $3.50 for the balcony, $4.50 for the golden circle, and $5.50 for the orchestra."

"Okay. If that's what you think is best."

"The tickets will be ready in ten to twelve days. I'll call you when they arrive."

I thanked Nat for his advice, said goodbye to Aida and left. I can never say enough about how wonderful and helpful those Carnegie Hall people were. Ten days later, Nat called and I went over to pull some tickets for the press. I pulled twelve of the best seats and told Nat to put the rest away until I had a need for them.

Since the Beatles concerts were still eleven months off, there was no immediate pressure to raise additional money for ads, posters and handbills. I continued picking up the British newspapers and music trade papers and reading with delight that Beatlemania in England was raging.

In early May, as agreed, I called Brian to confirm our verbal contract. He was effusive about the progress of his boys, but he continued to lament the lack of airplay in America.

"Don't worry, Brian. It'll happen. You'll get your airplay. It'll come."

"I hope so, Sid. I hope so."

No one hoped so more than I. The waiting game was now on.

MEANWHILE, I WAS STILL busy handling other acts.

Anything I wanted to do with Tony Bennett had the support of my bosses at GAC. I had an idea and called Bill Grummond, who had previously turned down the opportunity to have Tony appear at Forest Hills.

"Bill," I said, "Tony filled up Carnegie Hall."

"I'm well aware of that, Sid."

"Well, let's put him in Forest Hills."

"No, Sid. I still don't feel it. This venue is too big. Tony won't fill it."

"Okay, how about if Tony buys the venue and pays for everything himself? Then would you give him a date?"

"That's fine," Bill said. "It'll cost you nine thousand dollars for everything. It's your house. I'll have nothing to do with it. It'll be your show."

"Good. But can we at least say it's a Forest Hills production? As an agent at GAC I can't have my name associated with the show."

"I understand, Sid. You can use the Forest Hills name. It's okay with me."

I called Tony and told him about my idea and my conversation with Grummond. I explained that it would cost about nine thousand for the house, and with advertising, the band and other expenses, he would be on the line for about eighteen thousand.

"Once we get past the eighteen, Tony, the rest will be yours. I don't want any of the money because I'm working at GAC."

"Sure, Sid. I'd like to try it. It's a go."

Tony had renewed confidence since his success at Carnegie. He had appeared on *Ed Sullivan*, was in demand both nationally and internationally, and he had a new self-image. I was so pleased for him and his success, and I knew that Tony trusted me and my advice.

"Do you think we'll be all right, Sid?"

"Yes, Tony. I'd bet on it."

Gerry and I went to work. We were again the poster-posting pair. She would drive the car through the Italian neighborhoods, and I would hang the posters on every available surface. Four staples with the gun and go. Hit and run, then off to the next target.

I had handbills printed and did an ad campaign. We sold 10,500 seats out of a 14,000 capacity. Not a full house, but close. The concert was held on a beautiful summer's evening, and Tony gave another spectacular performance. After recouping the eighteen thousand dollars, he walked away with about eight thousand. More important, Tony's reputation as a live performer had been solidified.

After the concert, Tony again asked me to join him on tour.

"I can't leave my mother, Tony. Sorry."

When I went to see Bill Grummond, he took the money and shook my hand. "Sid, I guess I don't understand this Tony Bennett thing like you do."

"Guess not, Bill. Guess not."

ED SULLIVAN'S SUNDAY NIGHT variety show was the highest-rated television program in the country. Everybody in the entertainment business considered it the most important vehicle for achieving stardom. If you appeared on Ed's show, you'd made it.

One fateful day, Ed and his wife, Sylvia, were returning to New York from a European holiday when they were delayed at Heathrow Airport. The Beatles were returning from an engagement on the Continent that same day. While waiting for their flight, the Sullivans saw hundreds of excited teenagers milling about the airport, carrying placards that read: "Welcome Home Beatles!" "We Love You Beatles!"

Sullivan walked over to a uniformed airport attendant. "What are Beatles?" he said. "A circus act? An animal act?"

"The Beatles, sir, are England's foremost singing quartet."

Back in New York, Sullivan called Brian Epstein to discuss airing the Beatles on his show. Brian told him that a New York promoter by the name of Sid Bernstein had booked the Beatles into Carnegie Hall for February 1964.

"I know Sid. I'll talk to him," Ed said.

Sullivan called me. "Sid, let me ask you a question."

Ed always got right down to business. "Go right ahead, Ed."

"I was in Heathrow Airport last week and saw this rather large crowd waiting for a singing group called the Beatles. I called Brian Epstein, their manager in Liverpool, and he told me that you're bringing them to Carnegie Hall on February 12 to make their first U.S. appearance. Is that true?"

"Nothing but."

"What do you think of them?"

"Ed, they're a phenomenon. An absolute phenomenon."

"That's all I wanted to know, Sid. Thanks."

Ed Sullivan booked the Beatles on his show for Sunday evening, February 9, and for the following week, Sunday, February 16. He would make television history.

When I found out that Sullivan had made a deal with Brian Epstein, I was elated. Having the Beatles appear on national television three days before Carnegie Hall would almost guarantee a sellout. I wouldn't have to borrow money. I wouldn't have to sweat it out. This was the break I was waiting for. Home free, I thought.

COURTESY OF TONY ISOLDI – ROCKARTS.COM

Ed Sullivan with George Harrison. Ed presented a really big "shoe" when the Fab Four appeared on his stage. The fit was perfect.

I KNEW THEN THAT I COULD double or triple the ticket price for the Beatles, but I opted not to. My plan had been to do the shows on Lincoln's Birthday so that the kids who were off from school that day could see the concert. I was not about to price the tickets beyond their means. No, I thought, I'm going to do just fine financially on these two Beatles concerts. We'll leave the ticket prices just where they are.

By October, I was more excited—and more nervous. The four guys were piping hot in England, so hot that they had to disguise themselves in public. Brian had campaigned vigorously for EMI, the British parent company of Capitol Records, to release and promote Beatles records in America. The appeals were in vain. EMI would not consent to Capitol releasing Beatles records in the U.S. This gave me *agita*. Would Brian exercise his right to cancel because there was no American airplay?

In December, an American airline stewardess who had experienced Beatlemania firsthand brought home from England a copy of "I Want to Hold Your Hand." She gave the record to Carroll James, a deejay for a Washington, D.C., radio station. James put the single on the air and the audience reaction was instantaneous and unprecedented. The station received a flood of phone calls, burning out the switchboard.

From Washington, D.C., the wildfire spread to New York City, where Jack Spector of the WMCA "Good Guys" spun the record. The reaction in New York, the number-one radio market in America, was a carbon copy of that in D.C., and almost overnight all of New York's pop radio stations were playing Beatles music. Beatlemania had finally crossed the seas!

Capitol Records was completely unprepared for the enormity of the American reaction to Beatles music. Several months earlier, they had staunchly refused Brian Epstein's requests that they release the group's records in the U.S. Now, every Capitol Records plant was pressing Beatles records day and night trying to keep up with the demand. Within two weeks, "I Want to Hold Your Hand" was the number-one record in the States. As I drove around in my Plymouth, continually switching radio stations, I was elated to find nothing on the airwaves but Beatles music. Brian Epstein would not cancel now. I was counting the days until February 12.

THE BEATLES' BREAKTHROUGH had opened up the music scene for everybody in Britain. In the fall of 1963, the British music trades and popular daily newspapers began reporting on a group called the Rolling Stones. The buzz was that the Stones was another longhaired group like the Beatles, but with a rougher, harder edge. They also had more of a working-class following than the Beatles did. According to the press, the popularity of the Rolling Stones' was rapidly building. They were playing to sold-out venues and creating their own unique brand of hysteria.

I decided that I wanted to introduce the Rolling Stones to America, too, and got the phone number of their manager, Andrew Loog Oldham, whose name I had seen in the trade papers.

I placed the call and was greeted by a secretary.

"This is Sid Bernstein calling from New York City. I'd like to speak to Andrew Oldham."

A moment later, a charming, soft-spoken voice came on. "Sid, this is Andrew. I was hoping that you were going to call me."

He caught me off-guard, to say the least. "Really, why is that?"

"Well, I've heard through the grapevine that you are the man who's bringing the Beatles to the States to play Carnegie Hall."

"Who told you that?"

"I don't recall exactly, but I know it was someone at Isow's."

"Yes, Andrew, it's true. But let's keep it a secret between us. I have special reasons for not wanting everyone to know about that just yet." Remember that everyone knew that the Beatles were coming to Carnegie Hall, but no one knew that Theatre Three Productions was really Sid Bernstein.

"No problem, Sid. It's just between us."

"Now, Andrew," I continued. "I would also like to bring the Rolling Stones to play Carnegie Hall."

"How marvelous! When would you like to do that?"

"How does this March sound to you?"

The Rolling Stones took their name from a Muddy Waters song, "Rollin' Stone." Formed in 1962, the original group included, left to right, Bill Wyman, Keith Richards, Mick Jagger, Charlie Watts, and Brian Jones.

"We are committed for the spring of 1964. But, the chaps would be available after that."

"How about sometime in June?"

"That would be just fine with us, Sid. Since we're so far away from the date, why don't we firm it up in December? We won't pick an exact date until then, but we'll leave the first two weeks in June free."

"Great, Andrew. I'll look forward to talking to you in December, then."

I hung up feeling very good about our conversation. The Rolling Stones did not have the popularity of the Beatles, but I knew that something really huge was happening on the British music scene, and I was in the loop.

But I was still working at GAC. I would be calling Carnegie Hall to book the Rolling Stones, and again I would have to put someone else's name on the tickets. I didn't want to ask Walter Hyman and Hank Barron to do a repeat Theatre Three deal, because I knew that the Stones were definitely not their kind of music. So, I called Billy Fields.

"Billy, I just booked a group called the Rolling Stones to play Carnegie Hall sometime in June of next year. They're not the Beatles, but they're making lots of noise in England, and they're gaining momentum. I'm still here at GAC and I'm not sure when I'm going to leave, so I'd like to book the concert under your name. Is that okay?"

"Yes, Sid. Go right ahead."

Next, I called Abe. "My friend, I need five hundred dollars for a deposit for another group from England."

By now, Abe had heard and read all about the Beatles. He knew I was onto something. "Come to the office anytime, Sid. The check will be here waiting for you."

"Thanks. I'll pick it up tomorrow."

"By the way . . . what's this group's name?"

"The Rolling Stones."

"Whew! What a relief!" he said.

The next day, I picked up the check and went to see Mrs. Satescu. We agreed on a date in June 1964. The British Invasion was beginning to take shape.

ON FRIDAY, NOVEMBER 22, 1963, I was working in my office at GAC when the news came that President John F. Kennedy had been shot. We all huddled around the television set in Buddy's office, listening and hoping against hope that the president would survive. At one o'clock in the afternoon, we, along with millions of other Americans, heard Walter Cronkite announce in an unsteady voice that the president was dead.

The country now had to deal with the unthinkable. A beautiful family had been torn asunder. Our youthful, enthusiastic, witty, stylish leader—a man whose efforts on behalf of civil rights had long struck a chord with me—was gone. I remembered that time years earlier meeting the young John F. Kennedy when I was in Washington to campaign for affordable housing. I was still Buddy Burnside then. . . . Losing a hero was painful, but somehow the nation summoned up the strength to move on.

About this time, I moved my mother and her caretaker from the

Bronx into an apartment in the same Manhattan building where Gerry and I had set up house. Having my mother in close proximity afforded me great relief. Gerry would often look in to see how my mother was faring, and I could now keep an eye on Mom without having to travel back and forth between boroughs. An obvious solution to a logistical nightmare. I wondered why I hadn't thought of it sooner.

Meanwhile, the American press had finally caught up to the Beatles story. Wherever one went, in whatever newspaper or magazine one looked, there were stories about the Beatles. *Time, Life, Newsweek*—all ran features on the boys. Of course, my involvement was still a secret. I was tingling with anticipation.

Brian Epstein called me in December.

"Brian, how good to hear from you! How in heaven are you?"

"Well, you can imagine, Sid! All hell has broken loose! I'm being besieged from all corners. The press wants to interview the boys constantly, and the demand for appearances is nothing short of incredible! . . . Of course, we can't be everywhere. It's a challenge!"

"I can well imagine. . . . Tell me, Brian, how can I help you?"

"Well, I'm concerned about the boys coming to America and particularly stepping off the plane practically into Carnegie Hall. I was wondering if some kind of warm-up date out of New York might not be in order. I want them to get the feel for an American audience."

"Not a bad idea, Brian."

"Could you set up something not too far from New York for us? Someplace that we can get back and forth to in the same day?"

"It's a great idea and you should do it, but it's not a good time for me to leave New York. My mother is not getting along very well. If I take this on, I'll have to spend time away to make sure that the arrangements are handled properly. Brian, my apologies, but I can't commit myself to that now. Please know how sorry I am."

"Not at all, Sid. I understand fully. I'm sorry as well. But, I'm happy that you concur about it's needing to be done, and we will set it up. By the by, we'll be arriving on Friday, February 7, and staying at the Plaza Hotel. Capitol Records is hosting a reception for the boys in the hotel at around three o'clock. Why don't you drop by our suite prior to that and meet the boys, and then join us at the reception?"

"Thank you, Brian. I look forward to that."

"Thank you for everything, Sid. Cheers!"

Brian was a gentleman as always, but I could tell from his tone that his responsibilities and concerns were all-consuming. He had entered the fast lane.

The holiday season came and went. It was a bittersweet time, as the country was still mourning the fallen president. But the joyous, effervescent, hopeful music coming from those four boys from Liverpool helped to salve the terrible wound Americans were struggling to heal.

The build-up for the Beatles was in high gear. Every pop radio station played them incessantly. "Love Me Do," "I Want to Hold Your Hand" and "She Loves You" flooded the airwaves.

WHILE BEATLEMANIA WAS ESCALATING, recording artists working in more traditional musical styles were also faring well. One of the hottest acts at GAC was Trini Lopez. His record of "If I Had a Hammer" had gone to number one on the charts, and he was in big demand for personal appearances. In January 1964, Trini was booked into the Olympia Theatre in Paris. That was a prestigious venue, and Norman Weiss, a GAC vice president, was dispatched to the City of Lights to cover and provide service for Trini. It was common practice for agencies to have representatives in attendance when their acts performed, and the more lucrative the act, the greater the attention.

The Beatles were being presented on the same bill as Trini Lopez, and it didn't take long for Norman Weiss to recognize that the four Liverpudlians were indeed the real deal. As fate would have it, Norman crossed paths with Brian Epstein, and he told Brian all about GAC, how it was the second-largest theatrical agency in the world, how it had considerable power and prestige in the entertainment world, and so on and so forth and so on.

Norman gently asked Brian if he might consider allowing GAC

to handle the Beatles in America. "All GAC would ask is 10 percent of all bookings," Norman said.

"Yes, we would consider GAC as agents, but I will not pay 10 percent," Brian answered.

Norman told Brian that he would report back to GAC that the Beatles would not pay the standard fee and get back to him with the agency response.

When Norman Weiss returned to New York and reported to Buddy Howe about Brian Epstein's reluctance to pay 10 percent, Buddy decided that GAC would make an exception to get the Beatles for the GAC roster. The agency would accept a commission of 5 percent.

The deal was made and the Beatles were signed. Without delay, a memo was circulated throughout the agency's worldwide offices. "GAC has scored a coup," it read. I headed straight for Buddy's office.

"Buddy, why wasn't I sent to Paris? I found the group! Neither you nor Vic had any interest. I'm the guy who alerted everybody to the Beatles."

"Sid, now wait a second. I sent Norman over there to cover Trini. He met Brian Epstein by coincidence and one thing led to another. Norman is a vice president. He saw the opportunity and seized it."

I was fuming. It became clear what having stripes and a title meant. I called Walter Hyman and relayed the sequence of events.

"Sid, here's what's really happening. . . . First of all, no one knows who Theatre Three Productions is, including your boss. Everyone is running around trying to get a piece of the Beatles' action. . . . Tell me, how much are you going to make from the two performances at Carnegie?"

"Easily ten thousand dollars after expenses."

"That's a little less than you make for a full year's work at GAC," Walter said. "You don't need GAC anymore. This is your concert. You're Theatre Three. Neither Hank nor I want a penny of the ten G's. You found the group, you did the work. All we did was come up with a name. It's your deal. . . . If I were you, I would go see my pal Buddy Howe and tell him you're leaving GAC unless you get a vice presidency and a hundred-dollar raise. They'll make you a veep. Mark my words."

I took Walter's advice and laid it on the line to Buddy.

"Listen, Sid, it took me four years to become a vice president at GAC. . . . You've been here less than two years. I can't make you a VP just yet, but you've got the raise. I know you can use it."

I called Walter. "Quit, just quit," he said. "No one in the business knows anything about your relationship to the Beatles because you've managed to keep it a secret. Listen to me. . . . You quit, announce it to the world and take your bows. You're the first one to bring the Beatles here. For heaven's sake, take the credit." Walter was angry.

I went back to Buddy. I was really charged up.

"Buddy, I'm leaving. I owe you a lot for bringing me in, but I'm going to walk away, and I'm going to present the Beatles at Carnegie Hall."

The cat was out of the bag.

Buddy sat up straight in his seat. "You're Theatre Three? . . . Uh, are you sure you're doing the right thing here, Sid?"

"Never more sure of anything in my life, Buddy. I started on this thing months and months ago when I was sending memos to Vic Lewis in London. I tried to get you to intervene. I did the right thing, and you guys dropped the ball. I think I'm entitled to have my name attached to all the activity surrounding the Beatles. That's why I have to go. Forget that I've even been asking about a vice presidency. This is my chance to get back to being myself—to being Sid—to being what I've always wanted."

"Okay. If you've made your decision and that's what you want, I wish you good luck."

"We'll still be friends, Buddy. You and Jean and me and Gerry. But I have to live my dream."

I gave him three weeks' notice, then set up an office in my West Twelfth Street apartment.

Events were moving at warp speed.

Mrs. Satescu from Carnegie Hall phoned and informed me that a February 15 show had been canceled and would I be interested in taking the date. I took it. I had been in Los Angeles months before, covering an act for GAC at the Whiskey A Go Go. Someone told me that I absolutely must catch a young black female entertainer from

Under the nom de plume *Theatre Three Productions, I was able to keep my day job and promote at the same time!*

Wales who was appearing at Charlie Morrison's Macombo. On a free evening, I rushed over to the Macombo to see Shirley Bassey, an incredible young talent.

When I accepted Mrs. Satescu's February 15 offer, I had Shirley Bassey in mind. I called Charlie Morrison to inquire about her availability, and he told me that her husband, a Yugoslavian count, was acting as her manager. I immediately placed a call to him, who couldn't accept fast enough.

This would be another first. I would take Shirley out of the night-club circuit and put her in a concert venue for the first time. Walter Hyman put up the money, but this time he would be my partner in every sense of the word.

Mrs. Satescu called again. "Mr. Bernstein, we have an opening for February 21. Could you use that date as well?"

I rang up Tony Bennett and offered him the twenty-first. Tony said yes, the eve of George Washington's birthday would be a fine date. All that he would require was a good band. . . . So I got him Count Basie.

When I called Mrs. Satescu to accept the February 21 date, she said, "My, but you're a busy man, Mr. Bernstein."

Busy indeed. Everybody wanted to extend me credit—and I was prepared to keep rolling the dice. Promoting was what I was born to do.

I started to think about how I would publicize the three upcoming events. And then it dawned on me. I would run an ad that said: "Bernstein Presents—The Beatles, Bassey, Bennett & Basie."

I liked the ring of that.

11

Yeah! Yeah! Yeah!

O N JANUARY 27, 1964, AT 9:00 A.M., the Beatles tickets were put on sale. When I went to see Nat Posnick at noon to gauge sales, I noticed a trail of cigarette butts, gum wrappers and other assorted garbage from Sixth Avenue and Fifty-sixth Street all the way to Carnegie Hall at Seventh Avenue and Fifty-seventh Street. Aida, Nat's assistant, buzzed me into the box office. They both looked stunned.

"Nat, don't they ever clean up around here anymore?"

Nat let out a howl. "Sid, what just happened here has never happened in the seventy-four-year history of Carnegie Hall. It's simply unbelievable! Some of the kids camped out all night waiting to buy tickets. When we opened, the line stretched all the way around the block. You should have seen it, Sid! We sold out in forty minutes flat . . . and they're still coming! We could have sold those tickets at three or four times the price."

"It's okay, Nat. I wanted the kids to be able to afford the tickets."

"Sid," Nat said in wonderment. "This is big!"

"Yes, sir," I laughed. "And it's getting bigger!"

THE UNRELENTING DEMAND for Beatles tickets had a down side: I didn't have enough for press and friends. Abe Margolies (Mr. "Promise me, Sid, you will never *ever* tell anyone that I had anything to do with something called the Beatles!") all of a sudden wanted three hundred tickets.

"Abe," I would tell him, "we're sold out! I'm getting requests from press people all over the world! The phone doesn't stop ringing! Where do you expect me to get three hundred more tickets?!"

"Don't worry, Sid," he would say calmly. "You'll figure it out." And the next day, he'd call to request still more.

That was the problem: supply vs. demand.

Then, about ten days before the concert, Doc, the Carnegie stagehand I knew best, came to me. "Listen, Sidney, I'm not asking for myself. Some of the guys have kids and they want them to see this concert. It would really be nice if you could accommodate them."

"So what do I do, Doc? I can't even accommodate my oldest and best friend! Doc, I don't sleep nights. People are calling me from all over the world at all hours day and night. I don't know what to do. I can't give out tickets that don't exist."

"I'll tell you what, Sidney. You're allowed a limited number of seats onstage. Tell the stagehands it's okay to bring their kids. Limit them to two tickets per family and ask them to fit as many folding chairs onstage as possible. We know the guys at the fire department, and we'll talk to them. Ask Nat to punch out some special tickets for our people and for your best friend. We'll put some seats in the wings. We'll put others behind the band. After all, it'll only be four boys up on there. I think we can get you three hundred extra seats without creating a stir. You've got enough security here."

Voilà! I had just found six hundred extra seats—three hundred for the early evening and another three hundred for the late show. I was spared a very frightening fate indeed.

I couldn't wait to tell Abe the good news. "I knew you would work it out, Sid!"

The Beatles land on the American music scene and change it forever.

WHEN THE BEATLES ARRIVED at Kennedy Airport on Friday, February 7, 1964, they had six records in the Top 100. (Eight weeks later, they would have the number one, two, three, four and five records on the charts.) The WMCA "Good Guys" and Murray the K, a top New York deejay, had broadcast lots of Beatles information on their radio shows, including the arrival time of their Pan Am flight. As a result, hundreds of press members and thousands of kids showed up at the airport.

I skipped their arrival and instead decided to meet the Beatles at the Plaza, as per Brian Epstein's suggestion. I arrived to discover barricades surrounding the entire hotel, with foot police and mounted police everywhere. Out front, there were fifteen hundred to two thousand kids waving signs, plus some adults and members of the press. The Beatles were not yet there, so I stood among the kids for a while. It was a party atmosphere. People were singing Beatles songs, looking up at the windows of the hotel, screaming and having a ball. I thought, *Here I am in the middle of this amazing crowd, responsible for all this, and nobody even knows who I am!*

Standing there in the midst of the excitement, I realized that what I had been reading about in the papers for months was real. I had been right. These kids waiting out in the cold were an army—a peaceful one to be sure, but an army nonetheless. Their lives would be influenced significantly by the four mop-tops from England.

Tea time. Four proper British gentlemen enjoy the calm before they take New York by storm.

Not only would social and cultural change come to pass, but political change as well. There was a lot of power outside the Plaza that night.

Suddenly, an entourage of limousines drove up to the front of the hotel. Brian had told me that for security reasons the boys would not travel in the same car—and I don't know to this day how it was arranged—but it seemed as if all four Beatles appeared at once. They all waved perfunctorily, then ran up the stairs and through the Plaza's revolving doors. Only Paul McCartney turned, waved and blew a kiss to the crowd gathered across the street.

I spent another fifteen or twenty minutes taking in the scene, then I worked my way to the front, past the barricades, up the steps and into the lobby of the Plaza. Whereupon I was abruptly stopped by a security man. "Excuse me, sir. Are you a guest of the hotel?"

"No, I am—"

"Then would you please state your business here, sir."

"Yes, I am here to see Mr. Brian Epstein."

"Your name, sir?"

"Sid Bernstein."

The security guard glanced through a notebook. "Okay, yes, sir. You may proceed. The elevator operator will take you right up. And, thank you, sir, for your patience."

Nodding to the security guard, I boarded the elevator. "Mr. Epstein's floor, please." The instant the elevator doors opened on the twelfth floor, another guard directed me down the hall to a gentleman stationed in front of the suite. I gave him my name and he opened the door.

As I entered the suite, I immediately recognized several Capitol Records executives. Brian Epstein was on the phone, and a photographer with many cameras suspended from his neck was working the room.

Brian finished up his phone call and turned to me. I walked the few steps toward him and extended my hand.

"Brian, I'm Sid Bernstein."

"Sid! It's good to finally meet you! I'm so glad you came. The reception will begin in a bit."

Brian, a very pleasant-looking young man in his early thirties, wore shirtsleeves, and his tie was loosened around his neck. He seemed both exhausted and exhilarated.

"Sid, I'd like to introduce you to the boys," he said, taking me over to a closed door that opened into another suite. He knocked, and the door was opened by yet another security man. As we entered, all four Beatles were standing at the window, gazing at the large crowd assembled below.

Ringo was the first to come forward.

"Ringo, this is Mr. Sid Bernstein, our promoter," Brian said.

Ringo reached out his hand.

I reciprocated. "Welcome to New York."

The other three then came forward, and Brian introduced me to each.

My first impressions of these four lads will remain with me always. They were well-groomed and neatly dressed, and although I

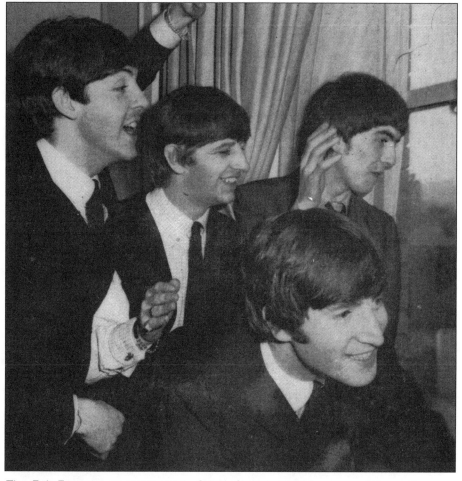

The Fab Four are as enamored of their fans as their fans are of them. It seems like only "yesterday" . . .

was initially thrown by their long hair, after talking with them for a few moments, that became a nonissue. Ringo struck me as being a funny guy. Paul was handsome. George and John looked like excited kids just having a good time with all the special treatment.

"The reception at the airport was overwhelming, but the crowds here at the hotel are utterly amazing," Brian said.

"This is one crazy place," John said.

George kept gazing out the window: "Can you believe this? Can you believe it?"

"What do you think of New York?" I asked.

"A happening place!" Ringo said.

"Fantastic," Paul piped in.

"You haven't seen anything yet," I told them.

"Unbelievable! Just unbelievable!" John kept repeating.

"Listen, guys," I said. "If you get a chance and can manage to get out of here, you should go to Paolucci's. It's the best Italian restaurant in New York. I'm sure you'd all love it."

Brian smiled. Between the crowds and the press, it would be difficult to go anywhere.

The boys went back to stare out the windows at the throngs below, while I brought Brian up-to-date on security. I had contacted the precinct responsible for Carnegie Hall, had spoken to the police chief, and had been assured that the police were prepared for any eventuality. Brian's people had also been in touch with the New York police, and he was satisfied with their reassurances.

I changed the subject. "Brian, the demand for tickets is nonstop. The phone rings twenty-four hours a day. I'm getting requests for press credentials from all over the world. There is even a contingent coming from Japan."

"That's great!" Brian said.

"How about Washington? Are you all set for the warm-up concert there?"

"Yes, Sid. We were going to fly, but because of the snow we're going to take an early train on Tuesday, do the show that night and come back early on Wednesday for your two shows at Carnegie Hall."

I remember hoping a major snowstorm wouldn't strand the guys in Washington. If I had been able to arrange the out-of-town warm-up as Brian had requested, I never would have let the Beatles perform there. A little too far from New York for comfort.

Brian had everything planned out: "Tomorrow we start rehearsals for the Sullivan show, then Sunday is the actual broadcast. I left Monday open for a rest day, and on Tuesday, as I said, we go to Washington." A tight schedule indeed.

Brian and I walked over to a window. "You know, Sid," he said, "the fever in the States even exceeds that in England."

YEAH! YEAH! YEAH! 145

"America loves the Beatles, Brian, and the love affair is just beginning."

I looked at my watch and saw that the reception was less than a half-hour away. "I'm really pleased to have met all of you and want you to know how proud I am to present you at Carnegie Hall."

"We're delighted to be here. Thank you for presenting us," John said in his inimitable way.

We shook hands all around and I returned with Brian to the outer suite, chatted with him a few more minutes and exchanged pleasantries with the Capitol Records gang. When Brian escorted me to the door, he was quite pleasant. "I'll see you downstairs in a bit. Thanks for coming by, Sid."

THE RECEPTION WAS TEEMING with hundreds of press people and record executives, some of whom I knew but many of whom were unfamiliar. I circulated, greeting old friends and making new ones. But once Brian ushered the Beatles into the reception area, everything became all too hectic. It was time to make my exit.

On the way home, I felt elated. I was finally doing what I liked to do best. I had married the girl I loved and soon she was going to have our first baby. My mother lived nearby and I could look out for her well-being. I had just met Brian Epstein, a man with whom I knew I could and would do further business. And, I had met the four boys and they turned out to be quality kids. This Beatles thing was going to get bigger and better, and I was an integral part of it.

THE MOMENT I GOT HOME, I called Bob Precht, Ed Sullivan's son-in-law and executive producer, to request a ticket for the Beatles appearance. Bob and I had an acquaintanceship because I often covered GAC acts that appeared on Ed's show. Gerry preferred to watch from the comfort of home, so my chore was made a bit easier.

"The demand for tickets is unbelievable," Bob said, "but for *you?* Of course I have a ticket!"

"Tell me about unbelievable, Bob!" I laughed.

I had been to the CBS studio where *The Ed Sullivan Show* was broadcast, but the excitement that Sunday in February was different.

Heightening the mood was the presence of many celebrities in the audience of seven hundred fifty. (Ed loved to introduce famous folk to his national television viewers.) The Beatles did their thing and wowed everyone. As I sat there in the electric environment, I realized that there were people all over America seeing and hearing the magic that I had only imagined more than a year before. At that moment, I was truly grateful for the medium of television. The estimate was that over seventy-three million people had seen the broadcast that night. Mind-boggling. If the energy was so high in a television studio, what would it be like at Carnegie Hall? I couldn't wait to find out.

WHEN I ARRIVED AT OUR West Twelfth Street apartment after the show, dozens of people were congregated outside, milling about on the sidewalk and perched along the cement balustrade that framed the walkway to the building's entrance.

"Got any tickets to Carnegie Hall, Mr. Bernstein? Any price, any seat. We gotta be there when it happens."

"Sorry, folks. Sorry to disappoint. There's not a ticket to be had."

Early the next morning, I was besieged with requests. We had taken the phones off the hook to get some sleep, but as soon as we replaced a receiver on its cradle, the ringing started all over again.

Struck by the magnitude and fervor of the fans, early Monday morning I called John Goldner, head booker at the old Madison Square Garden on Fifty-second Street, with an idea.

"John, it's Sid Bernstein. I was wondering if the Garden is free a week from this Wednesday or Thursday, February 18 or 19?"

"Eighteenth no, nineteenth yes. Why, Sid?"

"I don't have approval yet, but I'd like to book the Beatles in the Garden. I think we could sell out."

"Sid, from what I saw last night on Sullivan and from what I've been reading in the newspapers, you probably could."

"If I can get clearance from the group to do another show, how long would it take for you to print tickets?"

"Twenty-four hours—if we push it."

"Okay, John. I'm going to call the Beatles' manager and discuss it with him. If there's any possibility of pulling this off, I'll bring him down to the Garden. I'll let you know."

"Fine, Sid. We'll help you in any way we can."

I called Brian at the Plaza.

"Good morning, Sid. How are you?"

"Great, Brian. That show last night was spectacular."

"Quite splendid, Sid. And the audience! Sullivan's people and the papers are saying seventy-three million! That's absolutely astonishing!"

"What's even more astonishing, Brian, is that all seventy-three million seem to want tickets to Carnegie Hall!"

He laughed.

"Brian," I continued, "I'd like to propose an idea. . . . Actually, I'd rather show you in person. Could you possibly spare an hour? It'll be well worth your while. I promise."

We agreed that I would pick up Brian at the Plaza at 12:30. I then called John Goldner at the Garden and told him we were coming and when to expect us.

Accompanied by my cousin Leo Kitchman, who wanted to meet Brian, I arrived at the Plaza at 12:15 sharp. This was not a day to be late.

Promptly at 12:30, Brian exited the elevator, and I showed him to the cab. I introduced Leo and started to present my idea.

"We're going to Madison Square Garden." Brian knew the arena from the political rallies and championship fights he had read about over the years. "The Garden has an open date a week from this Thursday, and I would like to present the boys there. That means you would have to come back from your Florida holiday a few days early. The Garden has seventeen thousand seats, but I can guarantee a sellout—and you and the boys can keep all the money. I'm not interested in making a penny. I just want to accommodate the thousands upon thousands who are desperate to see the boys in person."

"You're sure we can sell it out, Sid? You know that I will not let the Beatles appear in a venue with empty seats. Seventeen thousand seats is far more than we've ever filled!"

"Positive. Right now, I think we could sell out a venue five times the size. Not a problem."

We had reached the Garden. We waited in the reception area for a moment, then John Goldner emerged to greet us. He brought us right to the middle of the Garden floor. Brian stood there and turned around slowly.

"Hmmm, hmmm," he kept saying as he looked into the uppermost reaches of the cavernous space. I could see him visualizing the Beatles playing in front of its biggest crowd yet.

"What do you think?"

He took another look, doing a complete 360.

"The public and the fans will eat this up, Brian. I think you should do it. I figure you can take home one hundred thousand dollars clear."

"Let's keep them wanting, Sid. We'll do it another time."

And that was that.

I thanked Goldner. His disappointment showed.

"We'll do other stuff," I told him.

During the ride back to the Plaza, Brian told me that the boys loved New York City and somehow had managed to sneak out to a nightclub with Murray the K, the city's top deejay and by now the self-proclaimed fifth Beatle.

"See you on Wednesday," Brian said when the cab pulled up to his hotel.

True, I was let down. But I felt great that Brian would consider the Garden at a future date. I was already envisioning it.

GERRY WAS SIX MONTHS PREGNANT with our first child, and on the morning of February 12 she told me that she was concerned about the crowds at the concert and thought it would be best if she didn't attend. She was adamant about keeping herself and the baby safe.

In the days and weeks leading up to the Beatles' appearance at Carnegie Hall, I was working hard, supervising every aspect of the concert, from security to publicity. Operating in a state of frenzy was the rule rather than the exception, and it must have been in one of those harried moments that I approved the program for the evening as well as the two posters that were to hang right outside Carnegie Hall. It wasn't until hours before showtime that I discovered two glaring errors: Carnegie Hall was spelled *Carngie* Hall and the Beatles were listed as Ringo Starr, George Harrison, John Lennon and *John* McCartney! There was nothing to do but cope with my embarrassment and hope that Brian Epstein would not be utterly mortified.

I decided to get to the hall early to check on the house and talk to Aida and Nat in the box office about the other concerts that would follow the Beatles, particularly Shirley Bassey, whose ticket sales were painfully slow. When I arrived at about four o'clock, the Beatles' road crew was already setting up.

Nat was preoccupied: "Sid, we've got to be careful about how we bring the group into the building. The kids are all over the place. They're lined up near the stage door, trying to figure out a way to get in here and break through. We gotta be careful."

"The police chief told me that they're prepared. They told me not to worry, Nat. I feel confident that they have it covered."

"Well, they sure have plenty of cops around here," Aida said.

"That's good. That's the way it's supposed to be," I said.

The last thing I needed was an out-of-control crowd.

Outside the box office, people were scrambling for tickets and scalpers were waiting to pounce. Tickets selling for $5.50 were for going for a hundred and fifty bucks—almost thirty times their face value.

At 6:00 P.M., one of the stagehands came over to me. "Mr. Bernstein, your act is in the building and in their dressing room." Good news! They made it back from D.C. without delay.

Not a moment after I entered the Carnegie lobby, Al Aronowitz, the dean of rock-and-roll reporters, walked over and put his arm around my shoulder. "Sid, history is being made here today, and I'm going to say so in the *New York Post* tomorrow." Al recognized the enormity of the occasion. He was right on the money.

As I entered the hall and hurried down the aisle in the direction of the stage, I turned and noticed an usher standing near the entrance doors. He was pointing straight at me and speaking to an

CARNEGIE HA

Wednesday Evening, February 12, 1964, at 7:00 and 9:30 o'cl

THEATRE THREE PRODUCTIONS

presents

The Briarwood Singers

New York disc jockeys' salute to The Beatles

THE BEATLES

John Lennon
Ringo Starr
John McCartney
George Harrison

The Beatles record for Capitol Records.   The Briarwood Singers record for United Artists Records.

CARNEGIE HALL PROGRAM

11

(Above and below) The Beatles with Ed Sullivan.

(Left) Paul was incorrectly named John (circled) in this program. Luckily, a Beatle by any other name is still a Beatle!

imposing state trooper sporting a pinched three-cornered hat and high black boots. The trooper started heading straight toward me. Trouble already? The evening hadn't even begun.

"Mr. Bernstein, I am here with the governor's wife, Mrs. Nelson Rockefeller. She's in the lobby, sir, and is short a ticket for one of her daughters. Is there a possibility that you might have an extra?"

I remembered that I had Gerry's ticket in my pocket. "Uh . . . as a matter of fact, yes, I do, sir. I happen to have a ticket for the seat next to mine."

"Might the governor's daughter use that ticket, sir?"

"Uh . . . Why yes. Certainly."

I handed the gentleman the ticket and he walked to the back of the hall, out the doors and into the lobby. In a moment, he returned with Mrs. Rockefeller and several young girls. The governor's wife stepped forward, expressed her gratitude and introduced her daughter Wendy. She would sit right by my side. As we entered our row, I noticed that in front of us sat a young girl of about thirteen with a cast on her leg.

I leaned over. "What's your name, sweetheart?"

"Kelly," she whispered.

The bell rang, and the audience started to settle down. To open the evening, I had booked the Briarwood Singers, a folk act. I knew that they required little in the way of equipment, so it would be easy to reset the stage for the Beatles. The Briarwood Singers gave a very creditable twenty-minute performance, then there was a short intermission.

I tapped Kelly on the shoulder. "Would you like to meet the Beatles right now?"

Kelly looked up. "Yes! Oh, yes! I would love to."

And so, Wendy, Kelly and I made our way backstage to see the Fab Four who were about to carve a page in history. Mal Evans, the Beatles' security man and a helluva guy, knocked on the door, and we were admitted.

I went right to Brian. "How are you, my friend?"

"Tired, Sid."

"I can imagine. I really can. . . . Brian, this is Wendy Rockefeller,

Happy Rockefeller pictured here with two of her four children, Wendy and James, at the Beatles concert in Carnegie Hall.

the governor's daughter, and this is Kelly."

"How do you do, young ladies?"

"Brian, would it be possible for Kelly and Wendy to meet the boys and perhaps get their autographs?"

"I think we can manage that straight away."

We followed Brian farther into the room, where the Beatles were sitting in their shirtsleeves, tuning their instruments, drinking sodas and enjoying the fruit I had provided.

John came over and immediately started joking with the kids. He signed Kelly's cast and Wendy's program.

"Hey, Ringo," John said. "Come here. I'd like you to meet Wendy and Kelly."

Ringo ambled on over, made a funny face at them and set them giggling. As he gave each an autograph, I could almost hear the pounding of those two young girls' hearts. Paul and George were next in line to say hello and give their respective John Hancocks. I was so pleased to have been able to give those two girls an experience they would never forget.

"Thanks, guys, I appreciate this. See you later! Have a great show!" I walked back to the auditorium—the girls floated.

As the bell signaling the end of intermission rang, I could feel the walls of Carnegie Hall pulsing with excitement. This is it, I thought. The moment of truth.

As full as the experience with the Beatles had been so far, there was only one thing left: to realize the dream I had pursued from

First-class seats. The Beatles are joined by adoring fans for the first-and-only time in Carnegie history that an audience was permitted to sit onstage.

the minute I read about those boys, to see all my efforts come to fruition as I watched them perform in a concert venue. An act's live performance determines its ultimate value to a promoter. I had been in the music business now for more than twenty years. I knew that clever producers and audio engineers using state-of-the-art equipment could make a marginal act sound decent and a decent act sound good. The only way to know if a singing act really has it is to hear them live. They either have it or they don't. It's that simple.

The hall was packed. The people in the folding chairs were so close to the Beatles that the hall had the feel of a small club. You could cut the anticipation with a knife.

Then, all of a sudden the words of the emcee: "Ladies and gentlemen . . . The Beatles!" The four boys, dressed in their mod suits, ran onto the stage to earsplitting screams of welcome from the audience. It was unlike anything I had ever experienced. The boys took their places, checked their instruments briefly and began.

For the next thirty-four minutes, the Beatles created sheer magic. They were superb in every respect: the finely honed musicianship,

the seamless blending of their voices, their synchronicity. The audience was mesmerized.

As soon as they finished their last song, the fellows were spirited to waiting cars and driven back to the Plaza. No encores or curtain calls. They just played their songs, bowed once and left. Everybody was left wanting more.

Except for Abe. After the first concert, he came over to me. "Sid, are you kidding? This is music? Everybody is crazy!"

He simply didn't get it. He had been brought up on Benny Goodman, Glenn Miller and Frank Sinatra. He simply didn't understand the power of the Beatles.

I smiled and motioned to the crowd. "Those four boys have changed the music business forever, Abe. Better learn how to twist and shout!"

FOR THE NEXT HOUR, the Carnegie Hall staff cleared the house and prepared for the second show. From the moment the Beatles had left the building, the three hundred fifty members of the assembled press bombarded me with questions:

"How did you learn about the group, Sid?"

"When did you contact them?"

"What's your impression of the Beatles, Mr. Bernstein?"

"Sir, please tell us— what was the deal you made with them?"

I did my best to answer, but the audience for the next show was beginning to enter the hall. Though the Carnegie staff and the police had done a fantastic job clearing the house, cleaning it up and managing the crowds, we were running very late. We brought the Beatles back into the building at 10:30 P.M. and ushered them through a cordon of police and heavy security. I had real concerns about the lateness of the hour. Tomorrow was a school day, and I didn't want to be responsible for kids sleeping in. At the pace we were going, there was no way that the late-show audience would leave Carnegie Hall before midnight.

When I visited the boys and Brian in the dressing room before the second show, I found them relaxed, drinking sodas, kidding around, but understandably tired. I complimented them on their incredible performance and commented on how their American fans had raved. "You guys own New York," I said. "You know, Al Aronowitz told me you're making history here today."

The boys knew that Al was an influential New York rock critic, and they couldn't believe their ears. Modesty seemed to be a shared characteristic.

I thanked John, Ringo, Paul and George, told them to have a great second show and wished them well on their trip to Florida the next day.

Brian walked me out of the dressing room and took my hand. "Sid, thanks for everything."

"No, Brian, thank you," I said. I knew that our friendship was cemented and that we would do other historic things together.

I went back into the hall. The Briarwood Singers had warmed up the late crowd, which was already at fever pitch. The bell rang and everyone was seated. At 11:15 P.M., one hour and forty-five minutes later than scheduled, the Beatles came out and proceeded to send the late-night audience into a frenzy.

I was immensely impressed with the Beatles' professionalism. True, they were young men brimming with energy and enthusiasm, but they had to cope with a backbreaking, whirlwind schedule and the accompanying pressures. Their first day in New York had been spent meeting with record executives and answering questions from the press. The next two days were spent at CBS rehearsing and preparing for their appearance before the largest American television audience in history. It wasn't until Monday, after appearing on the *Sullivan* show, that the boys finally had a chance to rest. On Tuesday morning, they were off on a train to do the warm-up concert in Washington, then they dashed back to New York and were now doing the two shows for me. It had been an exhausting time, yet their second show was as good as their first. The Beatles played the same music and connected with the audience as they had with the first. Exactly thirty-four minutes after they started, they took their quick bows, rushed out the stage door and were whisked away to the Plaza, accompanied as always by Brian Epstein.

When I got home, it was well past midnight, and I was astonished to find dozens of kids waiting for me. What now? I thought. The concert's over! They can't be waiting to get tickets!

"Do you have any ticket stubs, Mr. Bernstein?" the kids implored.

"No. Sorry, I don't."

"Did you shake hands with the Beatles, Mr. Bernstein?"

"Yes, I did."

"Have you washed your hands yet?"

"Nope."

"Can we please shake your hand?"

I shook the hand of each and every kid waiting for me and hoped that, in some small way, it made up for their not being able to attend the concert.

I went upstairs and related the evening's events to Gerry. "This was a once-in-a-lifetime thing," I told her. And I went to sleep with the sounds of the Beatles resonating in my head.

THE NEXT MORNING, the newspapers unanimously extolled the Beatles. History had indeed been made, and I was hailed as the man who had brought the Beatles to America. I marveled at the power of those four boys from Liverpool. They had made me into an overnight celebrity as well.

There was little time to relax and enjoy. I had two more Carnegie concerts coming up in the next eight days. The Shirley Bassey performance was just three days off, and it was not going to sell out. Shirley's limited New York following and lack of a hit record were the main factors behind the low ticket sales. I made peace with the fact that we would lose money, but it wouldn't be a disaster. On the other hand, Nat Posnick told me, the Tony Bennett/Count Basie concert was doing extremely well. A sellout was assured.

Shirley's concert in a half-filled Carnegie Hall was an artistic triumph. Her thrilling voice, beauty and incredible stage presence evoked memories of a young, dynamic Judy Garland. The audience showered her with flowers.

Six days later, Tony Bennett and Count Basie performed to a full house at Carnegie. Following his fifteen- to twenty-minute warm-up, The Count stepped up to the microphone: "Ladies and gentlemen, please welcome my friend, Tony Bennett." Tony came out to tumultuous applause. "I Left My Heart in San Francisco" had been a top-ten record, his albums were selling well, and he was playing all over the world to packed houses. His career was in full bloom and his renewed confidence was evident throughout the evening.

Tony took a moment between numbers to tell the audience how honored he was to work with Count Basie and his great band. The Count acknowledged Tony in return. It was the rare teaming of two great artists.

After the show, I rushed to Count Basie's dressing room and expressed my appreciation.

"Sid, anytime, anywhere, I'd do this again in a heartbeat."

"Thanks, Count. I'll keep that in mind." I paid him and left.

By the time I reached Tony's dressing room, the crowd of well-wishers had all but gone. Tony threw his arms around me. "Thanks, Sid. Thanks. You did it again!"

"No, Tony, you did it. It was a great evening. Special. Very special."

For some reason, when I had booked this concert, Tony and I had neglected to talk about money. I leaned over to him and whispered, "What do I owe you? I want to pay you."

It was customary to pay the artist right after the engagement. I expected that Tony would charge me between five thousand and sixty-five hundred dollars, even though his customary fee was ten thousand dollars a night, because he knew that I would be paying Count Basie as well.

"All I asked was that you get me a great band, Sid. We're even."

"What did you say, Tony?"

"That all I asked for was a great band—and you got me one."

"But we did very well. We sold out. I have to pay you something!"

"Sid, I wanted the band and you gave it to me. . . . Thanks!"

Tony then turned away to be with his guests.

I was amazed. It was unheard of for a performer not to get paid for a concert appearance, unless, of course, it was for charity. As a promoter, that had never happened to me before. At that precise moment, I recalled an old Italian adage: "If someone offers you something, take it with two hands." So, I took it . . . with gratitude.

Grazie, Tony. *Grazie*.

ON MAY 3, 1964, ADAM WAS BORN. I was almost forty-six years old and thrilled to finally be a father. I now had an outlet for many of the loving feelings that were pent up inside. How could I thank Gerry enough?

I didn't want to miss a moment with Adam, so a baby carriage accompanied me as I wandered about the neighborhood, through Washington Square Park and the surrounding area. This was the home of New York University, and it was filled with people of all ages, heritages and experiences.

Before long, I literally developed a following in the park. College kids began to trail me like I was the Pied Piper. They were eager for any and all tidbits on the Beatles, the Stones . . . and, equally important, wanted to know who would be the next hot group that I would import from England.

Speaking of imports, the Stones were on fire. The phones began to ring incessantly. Their June 1964 concert at Carnegie Hall sold out immediately. As we got closer to the concert date, those still trying to land tickets were again waiting in vain for me outside my building. Boys outnumbered girls. Stones fans overall had a tougher look than the Beatles fans.

When the Stones arrived at the airport, a contingent of youngsters and a small gathering of press were there to meet them, but their reception was nothing like the one the Beatles found when they arrived in New York. Finally, they made their way over to the Park Sheraton, across from Carnegie Hall, where they were staying.

I didn't meet with them until the day of the concerts. This time I booked one show for 2:00 P.M. and the other for 7:00 P.M. I got to the hall early, and the group was already doing a sound-check. I introduced myself to Andrew Loog Oldham, Mick Jagger, Charlie Watts, Brian Jones and Keith Richard. They were all extremely nice fellows, not nearly as wild as the British press had portrayed them.

Charlie and Brian were particularly friendly, pressing me with questions about where the action was in New York.

The Stones did a great show. Their fans were a blue jeans-and-motorcycle-jacket crowd, and when the band played, the kids jumped up and down on the seats. After the first show, I went backstage to tell the Stones that I was impressed with their energy and showmanship. They appreciated that and seemed eager to please. I invited them next door to Carnegie Tavern, a German-style beer and sandwich pub. Only Brian Jones seemed interested.

Brian and I exited through the backstage door, which was only a few feet from the tavern. We took the most out-of-the-way booth we could find, and Brian positioned himself so that his back was to the front door and window. After just a few minutes, I could see several young faces pressed up against the windowpanes. That number quickly multiplied, as if someone had made a public announcement that one of the Rolling Stones was in the pub. The crowd of onlookers swelled, and some of them came into the restaurant.

When Brian and I had first entered, there had been only a handful of patrons, but now, in no time flat, the tavern was mobbed and the crowd pressing against the windows was frightening. The manager, a big burly guy, told his staff to lock the door and allow no one else inside. Then he approached us and very cordially—but matter-of-factly—suggested that we leave immediately.

As the doors to Carnegie Tavern were unlocked to let us escape, I realized that the only way we could get back into Carnegie Hall was to go around to the front. We would have to negotiate our way through the crowd that had left the first concert and some of the new crowd that was assembling for the next show. I motioned for Brian to follow me, and we made a mad dash across Seventh Avenue to the Park Sheraton. If we could get into the lobby of the hotel, I figured we would be safe.

Eluding a mob of kids that was chasing us and grabbing at Brian's long hair, we managed to make it safely through the doors of the hotel. Security did the rest of the work. I took a rest, then made my way back to Carnegie Hall. Brian, escorted by police and security, followed shortly thereafter.

The evening crowds were even more unruly than those attending the afternoon show. After the performance, at around 9:00 P.M., members of the press were interviewing me when Mrs. Satescu came over.

"Mr. Bernstein, can I speak to you in private, please?"

"Yes, Mrs. Satescu, what can I do for you?"

"Mr. Bernstein, the pictures on the walls were shaking. The kids were jumping on our plush seats and armrests. They were rude and disobedient to the ushers, and you are lucky, Mr. Bernstein, that no one was hurt here today. Please do not bring any of your presentations here again!"

The woman was livid. I tried in vain to placate her, but she just kept repeating, "Mr. Bernstein, please do not come back to Carnegie Hall. Please do not come back to Carnegie Hall. . . ." She made her point. I was not wanted there anymore—period. I had managed to get thrown out of two places that day.

"Mrs. Satescu," I said, "I promise that this will never happen again. I just did not expect this kind of enthusiasm from the crowd. It will not happen again, I assure you."

"I know, Bernstein, because you will not be here."

I loved Carnegie Hall and the people who worked there. Mrs. Satescu's anger disturbed me. Fortunately, I had begun negotiating with other venues. The word was out to the managers and agents in Great Britain that American audiences filled concert halls to hear British groups. The British Invasion was in full swing, and I was the lead "general." If you wanted your act to play the United States, Sid Bernstein was the man to contact.

I WAS EAGER TO BRING the Dave Clark Five to the States but, being *persona non grata* at Carnegie, I needed a new venue. I was also in preliminary negotiations with the Animals, the Kinks, Herman's Hermits, the Moody Blues, Manfred Mann, and Gerry and the Pacemakers. Eventually, I signed them all and had the privilege of being the first to present to America eleven of the top thirteen British rock acts. It was imperative for me to find other theaters, other spaces to present these acts.

The Paramount Theatre, one of my old stamping grounds, had ceased to function as an everyday venue. Instead, it was being rented for special events and concerts. I went back to my old friend Gene Pleshette.

"Sid! You're really doing it with these bands from England! I'm happy for you!"

"Thanks, Gene, but I need help."

"What's up?"

"They don't want me in Carnegie Hall anymore."

"Why is that?"

"I'm not really sure, Gene. Maybe they don't like rock-and-roll. You know,

My son Adam takes centerstage with some big-name musicians!

Carnegie's a venerable old hall, and rock-and-roll is, well, not what you'd call venerable."

"I understand, Sid. We're here and we're available."

We made the deal, and I had the Paramount for the Dave Clark Five, and even though it was a bigger venue than Carnegie, we sold out. In fact, we had to turn a few thousand away.

The Five was a clean-cut group—more on the style of the Beatles—and Gene Pleshette was not a guy to be crossed. In Yiddish, we'd call him a no-*chochmas* guy. No fooling around. What you see is what you get. When Gene told his ushers and staff to control the kids, that's exactly what they did. There was no jumping on the seats at the New York Paramount!

Next to invade the States from Britain was Eric Burdon and the Animals. Their record "The House of the Rising Sun" was a gigantic hit, and it seemed as if every time I switched stations in my car, if I didn't hear a Beatles record, I heard Eric Burdon and the Animals. I got carried away with the enthusiasm for the Animals and made a bad business decision. Instead of booking them into the Paramount for one or two days, I rented the venue for a week, thinking that the hit record would generate sellouts or near-sellouts every day.

The Animals sold out for the first two dates, but by then they had peaked. They were neither the Beatles nor the Stones, and attendance diminished daily. The Paramount had given me a good deal, but not good enough to make up for five days of a 50 percent house.

After the financial disaster at the Paramount, I decided to move to the Academy of Music on Fourteenth Street, which had two hundred fewer seats. It was there that we presented The Kinks, Herman's Hermits, the Moody Blues and Gerry and the Pacemakers. The British invasion was still in full swing, and Americans were welcoming the invaders with open arms.

On the home front, we had a momentous occasion: Denise, our first daughter, was born. My awareness of the importance of family grew ever stronger.

12

A Whole New Ballgame

IN LATE OCTOBER 1964, I called Jim Thompson at Shea Stadium, home of baseball's New York Mets.

"Jim, it's Sid Bernstein calling. I'm the guy who brought the Beatles to New—"

"Sid, I know who you are. What can I do for you?"

"Well, I'm going to bring the Beatles back as soon as I can, and I was considering presenting them at Shea."

"Sid, we have never had a concert here, and we have fifty-five thousand seats. Are you aware of that? Fifty-five thousand seats!"

"Yes, I know, but I think the Beatles can fill them."

"Okay, here's what's involved." Jim began enumerating. "First of all, you'll need a stage, because we do not have one that can accommodate your needs. Second, you'll need insurance. Ours won't cover you. Also, you have to pick a date when the Mets are on the road, and it must allow for several days after the concert in case there's any damage to the grass that requires major repair. Our first concern is that the field be left in good playing shape. That's a league rule."

"That's fine. That all sounds reasonable. Could you look at your schedule and tell me what date would work for you?"

"Well, let's see. The Mets will be away the second week in August for an extended road trip. We could do it in the middle of August."

"Nothing sooner?"

"Well, there's another extended road trip in mid-June. Not as long as the one in August, but we could do it. You might want to take a date in that time frame."

"No. . . . I don't think that would work. The kids are all still in school and they've got finals and graduation. I think August is better." I glanced at my calendar. "How about Sunday, August 15, eight o'clock in the evening?"

"Yes, Sid, that would be fine, as long as you supply the stage, the insurance and the extra security. I forgot that. This thing is going to need extra security."

"I'm always concerned about security, and we'll have more than enough. Don't worry."

"Good."

"Now, Jim, what's this going to cost?

"We've never done this before, but how does a guarantee of fifty thousand plus a percentage sound?"

"No, not possible. I can't give you a percentage because I've got to give that to the group. Also, the stage is going to cost me a bundle, so is the insurance, and then we have to get into the security issues. On top of that, I need a reserve for grass repairs. If I give you fifty thousand, I won't make anything for myself. I can't do it. If that's your price, I need to look elsewhere, maybe Yankee Stadium."

"Point taken, Sid. What's your budget?"

"I was thinking more in the neighborhood of twenty-five thousand dollars. At that number, I think I could do it."

"Okay, twenty-five thousand guaranteed gets you the venue, ushers, lights, dressing rooms and scoreboard. You take care of the insurance, stage and extra security, and we've got a deal."

"Great, Jim. Put a hold on August 15. I'll get back to you."

"Sounds like we have a deal here, Sid. Good luck."

Next, I called Brian Epstein in London. He had established a large office to handle what had become a major enterprise.

"Brian?—"

"A treat to hear your voice, Sid. How are you?"

"I'm fine, Brian. How are you?"

"Hectic, everything's hectic. I'm fielding calls from all over the world—requests for the boys' endorsements and the like. By the way, Sid, thanks so much for sending those Book Review sections. My mum really enjoys them!"

"I'm glad, Brian. Send her my regards and assure her that I will continue to send them. And how are the boys?"

"Working hard. Recording in the studio, playing locally and doing a lot of TV. The studio work is just superb. George Martin, our record producer, tells me that the musical growth of the boys never fails to astonish. I'm delighted. I've also begun to sign some new acts, Sid, so we'll have to talk about bringing them to America. Actually I was thinking of calling you. You beat me to it."

"Brian, when would you consider bringing the boys back to the States?"

"Not until next summer. That is the earliest."

My timing seemed perfect.

"We made history ten months ago. Let's do it again. We have a ballpark in New York called Shea Stadium. It's in Queens, on the grounds of the most recent World's Fair. It has fifty-five thousand seats, and I'd like to present the Beatles there. It would be another history-making event."

"Fifty-five thousand, Sid? Do you really think that we can fill so many seats?"

"Absolutely, Brian. If I didn't, I would never present this to you."

"Tell me, Sid, what would you sell the tickets for?"

"I was thinking of $4.50, $5.00 and $5.65."

"And you really think we can fill a fifty-five-thousand-seat stadium at those prices? "

"Yes I do. I'm so sure that I will pay you $10.00 for every unsold seat."

He chuckled. "Even though the top ticket price is $5.65, you would be willing to give us $10.00 for every unsold ticket? Why, for heaven's sake?"

"Because there will be no unsold tickets. We'll have a sellout and the boys will gross three hundred thousand dollars and be able to clear one hundred and fifty thousand for one night's work. It's never been done. . . . What I am saying is that I'll guarantee the Beatles one hundred thousand dollars against 50 percent of the gross to play Shea Stadium in New York on August 15, 1965."

"Fabulous! Quite astonishing, really! Let me talk to the boys, and I'll get back to you tomorrow."

"I'll look forward to that, Brian, and remember me to Queenie."

"I shall gladly do that. Cheers!"

The next day, as promised, Brian called.

"The boys are keen on coming back to New York. We require only two things. First, the hundred-thousand-dollar guarantee is fine, but we would like 60 percent of the gross instead of 50 percent. And, second, we will need a fifty-thousand-dollar deposit up front."

"No problem, Brian. You've got it."

I expected this from a fellow like Brian. A good manager would want half the guarantee up front and always push for a little more. Brian was a *great* manager and had the hottest act in the world, so I was prepared to give him whatever he asked.

"When would I be required to give you the fifty thousand dollars?"

"As soon as possible."

"My money is tied up at the moment. What would be the latest I could give it to you?"

"Investments and the like, Sid?"

"Yes. But I will be liquid in the not-too-distant future."

"You know, I will be at the Waldorf-Astoria on the tenth of January. Why don't we meet then, and you can give me the deposit."

"That's perfect. I'll have no trouble giving you the money in January."

"Brilliant, Sid. We'll firm it up then."

"Brian, can I advertise the Shea concert?"

"No. We'll need the deposit in hand before you advertise."

"How about PR, publicity, interviews?"

"No. Please no publicity, no ads, no interviews until we firm up in January."

"Okay, Brian, but can I talk about it?"

"Of course! How can I stop you from talking about it? That wouldn't be fair, now would it?"

I could see the grin on his face. That was my saving grace. I wasn't sure exactly how, but I knew that the freedom to talk about the concert would some-how get me the cash I needed.

"Great, my friend, that's all I need to know. You have my

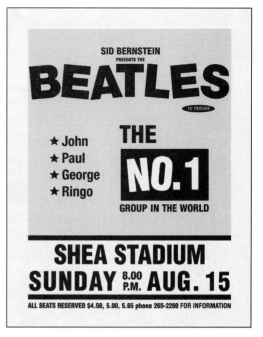

This poster was designed but never printed because the concert sold out by word-of-mouth. Now that's what I call direct marketing!

pledge. I'll see you at the Waldorf in January. Tell the boys I'm really excited and look forward to seeing them soon."

"I shall, mate. They'll be equally excited, you can be sure. Playing before fifty-five thousand New York fans is a heady prospect. Let's call it a deal, Sid. I'll see you in New York."

"Bye, Brian. Be well."

I called Jim Thompson at Shea and relayed the good news. "Jim, we're good for August 15. But, it's absolutely a secret. We can't do any PR or publicity yet, but that'll be for only about two months, so bear with me. Just hold the date for me—and mum's the word."

"You got it, Sid. Call me when you want to move forward."

THE FIRST TWO ELEMENTS—the Beatles and the date at Shea—were set. Next, I had to see to the insurance, the stage and, most impor-tant, the fifty-thousand-dollar deposit. First person to call was Chip

Munk, the top lighting and sound consultant who created stages, lights and sets for most of the major rock acts.

I told Chip that I envisioned a stage somewhere around second base so that everyone in the ballpark would be able to see. The stadium lights would be sufficient. When he asked who was going to appear, I was purposely vague. "The acts haven't been firmed up yet," I said, which happened to be the truth. Finally, I asked him for a guesstimate of the total cost so I could plug it into my budget. "Ten thousand bucks to design and erect the stage," he said. He told me to call when ready.

I telephoned some insurance friends and got the sense that finding coverage for this event was not going to be easy—and they were right. It took five weeks before my friend Jerry Rosen made contact with Lloyd's of London, who finally agreed to work out a deal at a cost of ten grand. I was happy to get it.

Now to the toughest part. . . . How in the world would I get that fifty thousand dollars? I always knew that if push came to shove, I could go to either Abe Margolies or Walter Hyman. But for some reason, I vetoed that. This was my baby. I had to do it on my own.

A day or two after speaking with Brian, I was pushing baby Adam's carriage in Washington Square Park when a group of kids converged on me. "Mr. Bernstein, what's next? Who are you going to present next?"

I waved them close and spoke in a whisper: "The Beatles at Shea Stadium . . . August 15."

Word spread like wildfire, and in no time there was pandemonium in the park. I was surrounded.

"Mr. Bernstein, can I give you the money now?"

"How many tickets can I buy?"

"I'm broke right now, Mr. Bernstein. Can I send you the money? How much per ticket?"

"Hold it, kids! Listen for a split second. I don't have tickets printed yet. When I come back later, I'll give you all the information."

I took Adam home and rushed over to the Old Chelsea Post Office on Eighteenth Street between Seventh and Eighth Avenues. I filled out some papers, paid a four-dollar fee and was given the key to Post Office Box 21. Then I returned to the park. The moment I entered, a mob surrounded me. Tickets to Shea was their only concern. The grapevine was obviously in full operation.

"Okay. Here's what you have to do. Send a check or money order to Box 21 at the Old Chelsea Post Office. Whatever you do, don't send cash. Make out the payment to Sid Bernstein. The prices are $4.50, $5.00 and $5.65. Make sure you write how many tickets you want."

Pens and small pieces of paper were zealously being passed around. The next day, again I was besieged in the park, but by a different group of kids than the day before. The grapevine was working overtime.

During the next few weeks, as Gerry, Adam and I walked around the neighborhood, a modest but steady flow of young people would approach and request the ticket information. I would happily oblige.

Three weeks to the day that I had gotten the okay from Brian Epstein, I went to the post office to check out my P.O. box. If I have fifty pieces of mail, I'll do a jig right there in the post office, I thought. If I have a hundred pieces, I'll celebrate by getting drunk— a big deal for me since I never touch alcohol. The amount of mail received would be a pretty good indication of what word-of-mouth could do to generate a demand for tickets.

As I walked up the post-office steps, I realized that I had forgotten the key to the box. Nonetheless, I walked over to Box 21, looked through the frosted glass and saw that it was jammed. To the right of the box was an inquiry office.

"Excuse me, sir. I seem to have forgotten the key to my box. I know you're closing soon, so I don't think I have enough time to run home and get it. Would you be able to give me my mail if I show you my driver's license."

"Box number, please?"

"Twenty-one. My name is Bernstein, Sid Bern—"

"You're Sid Bernstein? Hey, wait just one second. . . ." He turned and shouted across the room to a giant of a man stuffing boxes. "Eddie, guess who's here? Mr. Box 21, that's who!"

"Box 21, Mack? Wow! Gotta meet this guy." Eddie started to saunter across the floor in my direction.

"Here, Mack," I pulled out my license and showed it to him.

By now Eddie was hovering over me.

"Hey, buddy, what's your racket?"

"Racket?"

"Well, you got a heck of a lot of mail! What do you do?"

"I'm in the mail-order business."

"Yeah, but what're you selling? Must be some hot item, buddy!"

Mack looked at Eddie. "Hey, I'm going to need some help. Ed, come in here and give me a hand."

Eddie and Mack dragged out three huge duffel bags from the inquiry room.

"It's a mistake, fellas," I said.

Eddie opened one bag and Mack another. Each took out a handful of envelopes.

"No mistake," Eddie said, "All addressed to Sid Bernstein, P.O. Box 21. It's all yours."

"Yup," Mack said. "All yours."

How can I tell you how flabbergasted I was? In my wildest dreams, I had never expected a reaction even remotely like this.

"Uh . . . Look, guys, I have a bad back. Do I have time to go home and get my car? I'm only six blocks away."

"Sure," said Mack, "but be quick. We're closing soon."

I dashed back to the garage, got my car and shot right back to the post office. At the loading dock, Eddie and Mack helped me shove the three bags into the trunk. Then I hurried back home, lugged the mail into the elevator and upstairs into the apartment.

Gerry was aghast. "Why in the world are you bringing those bags in here?"

"This is our mail. From that post-office box."

"Oh, come—"

"Look for yourself. It's all addressed to Sid Bernstein. Checks . . . money orders. I even hear coins in some of the envelopes."

What did I expect? A lot of these kids didn't know from a check or money order. Despite my pleas, I felt sure we would find a lot of cash in those envelopes.

I collapsed on the couch to catch my breath.

"Gerry, what in the world have I done?! How in God's name are we going to process all this stuff?"

". . . You know what, Sid? Let's call Kathleen and see if she and some of her friends can help."

"Great idea."

Kathleen, a student nurse and sometime babysitter, lived across the street in the St. Vincent's nursing school residence. I should tell you that the student nurses all vied for the opportunity to babysit for the Bernsteins. They hoped and prayed that one night while under our employ a phone call might come from Mick Jagger, Paul McCartney or any rock star of note. Suffice it to say that we were never left without a babysitter.

I telephoned St. Vincent's.

"Hi, Kathleen. It's Mr. Bernstein calling. I have a job to do and could use the help of eight or ten people. I wonder if—"

"What kind of work, Mr. Bernstein?"

"Basically it involves opening a lot of mail. Nothing terribly difficult. We'll all do it together. Should be fun. I can offer babysitting wages."

"Let me talk to the girls, Mr. Bernstein. I'm sure we can work something out."

"Thanks, Kathleen."

The following Monday evening, Kathleen and seven of her friends arrived at the apartment. We set up a system whereby everyone sat around a table in the living room. Two of the girls would slit open the envelopes. The checks would go to one person, the money orders to another, the five- and ten-dollar bills to a third, the singles to a fourth, and the coins to the last girl. Each order would be recorded on an index card. If the envelope had a clear return address, the number of tickets ordered would be recorded on the envelope itself. Sounded like a workable system.

Every night, five days a week, for three months, we followed this procedure until we made our way through all the envelopes. That's how many there were. The bulk of the orders were for the better seats, and we filled those first. When we ran out of the best seats, we assigned the next-best-available. When we reached the sold-out point, we were still staring at more than three thousand unfilled orders. There would be a lot of disappointed people. We wrote "Return to Sender" on the envelopes and mailed them back.

When all was said and done, our take was $304,000! And I had kept my word to Brian. This was accomplished without running an ad, printing a poster, sitting for an interview or doing any public relations. All I did was tell a couple of hundred kids where they could send money if they wanted to see the Beatles at Shea on a summer night in August. The mail had come from around the globe: Japan, England, Europe, even behind the Iron Curtain. That's how far the grapevine extended. The power of those four boys was beyond description.

ON JANUARY 10, I WENT to see Brian in his Waldorf suite. It seemed to me that he was there alone.

"Sid, nice to see you."

"Likewise, Brian! How are you?"

"Truly? When I first started with the Beatles, I never anticipated that it would turn into this. Rather overwhelming, to say the least." He was clearly under tremendous pressure.

"How's your mom?"

"Quite well, but she complains of never seeing me and worries that I am working myself to the bone. By the by, you can stop sending her those Book Review sections. I am able to get them for her now that I spend so much time in London. How very nice of you it was, Sid, and we both appreciate it. Mother has very fond feelings for you."

"Queenie is a lovely lady, Brian. Tell me, how are the boys?"

"In the studio presently, which is why I took the time to come Stateside and attend meetings. They are very excited about coming back to New York this summer."

With that, I handed him a check that I had drawn that morning.

"Sid, there seems to be an error. You were to give me fifty thousand dollars, not one hundred thousand."

"Yes, Brian. I've done well, and I thought it best to take care of the guarantee now. It's not a mistake."

"Sid, your investments must have done really well for you!"

"Yes, I'm quite liquid now."

"The boys will certainly be happy to hear of this. How does the Shea concert look?"

"Not to worry, Brian. I don't believe you'll be getting that ten dollars for every unsold seat!"

"You're not going back on your word, Sid?" he laughed.

"No, I'm just feeling very good about it."

"Splendid! As soon as things get less hectic, I want to talk to you about some other acts I've signed recently."

"Great, Brian! Anytime you're ready, we can get into that."

I knew how busy he was, so I didn't dawdle. "Send my regards to Queenie and the boys. Tell them I'm looking forward to August."

"I definitely shall, Sid. And much thanks for the hundred thousand dollars!"

As I left, I thought about the price this man was paying for the comet ride he was on. A hefty one, to be sure.

While we were still filling orders for Shea, Andrew Loog Oldham called from London. "I want to bring the Stones back on an American tour in the spring, Sid. Can you promote a New York concert for us then?"

The Beatles concert was not until August. I knew that the Academy of Music was available and that the Rolling Stones would be a guaranteed sellout.

"Andrew, I think I can do it, but we can't do it in Carnegie Hall because you guys got me thrown out of there!" We both laughed. "I've been using the Academy of Music. It's larger than Carnegie by four hundred seats—and it's a wonderful theater."

"Okay. If you say it's a good place, we're in. When do you suggest?"

"The first of May, Andrew. Ten thousand dollars for two shows; how's that?"

"Brilliant! You got a deal, Sid. See you on May 1. I'll talk to you or Billy Fields before that."

I hung up. *Not bad, Sid. Not bad,* I thought. *The Stones in May and the Beatles in August!*

DURING THE NEXT FEW MONTHS, I busily prepared for the upcoming events. We did some ads and billboards for the Stones and, as projected, they sold out both shows.

On the day of the Stones concerts, I arrived at the theater early and visited with the band. It was amazing to me that the calm gentlemen in the dressing room turned into, shall we say, "jumping jack flash" onstage. Before leaving the guys prior to showtime, I said, "Listen, take it easy out there. We don't want to get thrown out of here, too!"

Take it easy? Not for a minute. They did their Stones thing, which meant Mick Jagger strutting, bouncing, dancing around with boundless energy—and the fans went wild. The Academy of Music was an old vaudeville house with an orchestra pit separating the audience from the stage, and the kids got so excited they began to rush the stage, trying to leap over the chasm of the pit. There were so many bodies pushing in the same direction that they overwhelmed the security men, and Billy and I found ourselves flat on our fannies. Bodies were flying all over the place, and some kids landed right in the pit, one on top of another. Tiny, our six-foot six-inch lead security man, jumped right in there and started throwing the kids back out. It had to be an act of God that no one got hurt. Fortunately for the Stones, they had their own security men, who blocked off stage right and left.

It was something to behold—that day in May 1965 when the Rolling Stones rocked the Academy of Music!

WE WERE BUILDING UP TO the Beatles. . . . The workload was fantastic, the hype and demand for tickets beyond belief.

Right in the middle of this extremely hectic time, I got a call from Walter Hyman.

"Sid, I'm out here in the Hamptons vacationing with my family. Some guys took an old French barge and turned it into a discothèque. It's wild. You have to walk across a gangplank to get onto the barge and into the disco. . . . But, here's the important part. They have a band playing there called The Rascals, and they're fabulous and drawing big crowds. I want you to come and see them."

The Stones. Top, left to right: Bill Wyman (1964); Mick Jagger (1964).
Middle: Keith Richards (1964); Brian Jones (1964).
Bottom: Mick Jagger & Keith Richards (1971); Charlie Watts (1964).

"Walter, are you serious? I'm getting ready to do the biggest concert in the history of rock-and-roll. My wife is pregnant. My mother is sick. I don't know where to go first, and you want me to drop everything and drive two hours out to the Hamptons?"

"Sid, I'm telling you . . . these guys are great! And all the rich and beautiful out here are lining up to see them. I saw Senator Javits here last night. Bette Davis is a frequent attendee, and Ahmet Ertegun from Atlantic Records comes here all the time and wants to sign them."

"Sounds great, Walter, but not now. Maybe after the Beatles. Sorry. Call me after Shea."

The next day, Walter called again.

"Sid, you've got to come out here. I'll send my car and you'll be here in no time. I told these guys that you're a friend of mine and that you're coming to see them. Please, don't make a liar out of me!"

"No, Walter. Not possible right now. Sorry."

The next day, a Monday, as I exited my office, two very strong arms wrapped themselves around me in a viselike grip. "You're coming with me," a voice announced. As I was maneuvered toward a car, I saw that it was Walter Hyman's Checker limousine. Walter, having a grand old time in the back seat, was laughing hysterically. His chauffeur, Mike, shoved me gently into the car.

"You're coming with me to the Hamptons. Don't worry, I cleared it with Gerry, and I promise that I'll get you home at a reasonable hour."

We drove right alongside The Barge, as the disco was called, and Mike stopped the limo in front of the gangplank. Inside, the four members of The Rascals—Felix Cavaliere, Eddie Brigati, Dino Danelli and Gene Cornish—were waiting, dressed in knickers, shirts with Lord Fauntleroy collars and pilgrim shoes. How ridiculous, I thought, Walter must be off his rocker. But then they started to play, and I knew immediately why they had become the "in" attraction of the Hamptons summer scene. Though they did songs by other artists, they played and sang them in their own unique style with high energy and great showmanship. They had the intangible "it." I knew that if they could get some original material with hit potential, they could emerge as a major band. When they finished, I talked with them for a while, then Walter, as promised, drove me back to New York.

The moment we were en route, he began to sell me: "I want to be your partner on this deal. I'm crazy about this group. The reaction of the people who come to see them, not just the kids, but the adults, is fantastic!"

Although they officially split up in 1972, the Rascals continue to stand the test of time. They have an animal magnetism that extends way beyond their name!

He pulled out his checkbook.

"I'm going to write out a check for ten thousand right now, and if you need more, let me know. I want you to take them into the studio immediately and cut a record."

"Wait a minute, Walter. . . . Yes, we can be partners. After all, you found the group. But we can get a record company to pay for their recordings, so put away your checkbook. What we really need is a lawyer. Get one, and on August 16, the day after the Beatles appear at Shea, we'll meet The Rascals at your apartment with the lawyers, and we'll sign them right then and there. In the meantime, we'll invite them to the Beatles concert."

"Consider it done, Sid. August 16 it is. And I have the lawyer. His name is Steve Weiss."

ABOUT A MONTH AFTER my meeting with Brian, I got a call from Barry Gotterer of Mayor John Lindsay's office.

"Sid, are you aware the mayor has stuck his chin out for you on this Beatles concert?"

"How? How is that?"

"Well, Shea Stadium is owned by the City of New York. We had to approve its use for the concert. The mayor and all of us here on his staff are concerned about security. Fifty-five thousand wild-eyed, screaming youngsters represent challenges in crowd control, and the mayor wants to make sure it comes off without any hitches."

"I appreciate that, Barry, and I'm grateful to the mayor for letting the concert go forward. I've built a reputation as someone who is ultra-concerned about security, and the mayor should have no cause for concern."

"Sid, it would make us more comfortable if during the numerous meetings you have with police, traffic and security people over the next few months, we could send a person or two from the Mayor's Office."

"It's unnecessary, but if you want to tag along, it's fine with me."

I had many meetings about security over the next several months, and the Mayor's Office always sent a representative. Dick Aurelio, who later became a vice president at Time Warner Cable operations, was the deputy mayor who attended most meetings. Dick is a brilliant guy and gave valuable input.

Our first concern was how we were going to get the Beatles in and out of Shea Stadium quickly and safely. I had numerous conversations with Brian and his staff about that, and slowly a plan emerged. Initially, we thought we would take the Beatles in limousines under police escort from the Warwick Hotel, where they would be staying, to a Wall Street heliport and fly them directly into Shea. When we presented that plan to the police, the Mayor's Office nixed it immediately. They thought that taking the helicopter into Shea would be too dangerous, particularly if there was a rush of kids to get to the Beatles. We finally agreed to land the helicopter in the World's Fair grounds, across from the stadium. The Beatles and Brian would exit the helicopter and get into a waiting armored car, which would proceed through the Shea Stadium outfield gates. Once under the stands, the Beatles would run to the umpires' dressing room and prepare for their appearance. In the exit plan, the vehicle would wait outside the stadium until the Beatles had completed their last song. As they were taking their bows, the outfield gates would be opened and the car would pull up right to the stage. The boys would hop in and speed out of the stadium to the waiting helicopter for the short flight back to Manhattan. The security people, the Mayor's Office and I felt that once we got them through those outfield gates, we would be home free.

After several months, the plan to get the Beatles in and out of Shea had everyone's approval, including the most important one of all: Brian Epstein's.

"Sid, are you absolutely sure the boys will be safe under this plan?" Brian needed one last assurance.

"Absolutely, Brian. Security plans for this concert are as extensive and well-thought-out as if we were protecting the president of the United States."

"Okay, I trust you. We will be arriving at the Warwick on the thirteenth. Why don't you come by and say hello?"

"That's fine. See you then."

My overriding concern over the months leading up to the concert continued to be security. Chip Munk kept telling me that the ten-thousand-dollar estimate he had given for the stage was off; it was going to cost at least twice as much. And the initial insurance estimate that I received was also off by more than half. However, these issues paled next to the issue of security.

Until this time, no one had ever attempted a rock concert of this size and magnitude. Further complicating matters, the Beatles were the number-one group in the world, with a fan base of hormone-driven teenagers. The potential for disaster was enormous, and I was determined that this concert would take place without incident. I had made that promise to Brian, to the mayor and to myself—and I meant to keep it.

We first decided on triple barricades between the seats and the field. In addition to the stadium ushers and security men patrolling the aisles and the corridors, I asked my cousin, Leo Kitchman, to provide moonlighting cops who would act as a buffer between the barricades and the stadium security, just like we had done at Newport. Finally, I hired forty karate black belts to give an exhibition before the concert. In reality, they were there to serve as the final barrier to anyone trying to rush the stage. So, to recapitulate, anyone trying to reach the stage would have to overcome the ushers and extra security personnel, leap over the stadium field gates, the three barricades, past the uniformed security people, past Leo's moonlighting cops and then make it past the black belts. And then the foolish individual would have to run two hundred feet to the stage, where Neil Aspinall and Mal Evans, the Beatles' road manager and assistant, would be waiting, prepared to give their lives for the boys.

I figured that anyone who could negotiate all that probably deserved the right to shake the Beatles' hands. Ultimately, in case the concert ever got out of control, a full contingent of New York City cops and mounted police were poised outside the stadium, prepared to enter on a moment's notice.

How could I not be confident in the security?

MURRAY THE K WAS EMCEE for the evening. He had developed a close relationship with the Beatles and Brian Epstein. Murray was an extremely engaging guy who had a winning way with kids, and he and I were good friends. His wife and Gerry were also good friends, and we often socialized together. Murray was a natural to host the concert and was honored when I asked him.

I booked King Curtis and his band, Brenda Holloway, Cannibal and the Headhunters, Sounds Incorporated and some dancers to warm up the crowd. King Curtis and I had known each other since the Shaw Artists days, and Murray suggested the dancers.

About ten days before the concert, Ed Sullivan called.

"Ed, how are you? Are you ready to get up in front of those fifty-five thousand screaming kids?" I had previously asked him to introduce the Beatles and he had accepted. When my secretary told me he was on the line, I hoped he wasn't calling to cancel.

"Looking forward to it, Sidney! What I'm calling you about is that I'd like to film the concert. Would that be okay?"

"Sure, Ed, go right ahead. Have your people talk to Billy Fields, and we'll issue the necessary passes."

The demand for tickets was again insane. No matter how many

seats I had for the concert, I always needed more. I issued 1,100 press passes, an unheard-of amount to any event. People started calling my home and accosting me at the front entrance. I dealt with the madness as best I could, but without the Carnegie Hall stagehands to save me by adding seats, I had to say no more often than I liked. I tried to get Shea to let us put seats on the field, but Jim Thompson nixed the idea, saying that if they allowed that, they could never get the grass into playing condition in time for the return of the Mets from their road trip.

MARC WEINSTEIN – ALLBEATLES.NET

At Shea, the "gorgeous" Beatle picks the strings of his guitar while tugging at the heartstrings of countless female fans.

LATE IN THE DAY ON FRIDAY, August the thirteenth, two days before Shea, I went to the Warwick to welcome Brian and the boys back to New York. The scene was reminiscent of the one in front of the Plaza in February 1964. The hotel was surrounded by police and barricades, and kids were screaming and waving placards. When I reached Brian's suite, he was very warm and pleasant. By now, he knew that there was a sellout.

"Well, you were bloody right. We're not going to get that ten dollars a ticket!" he smiled.

"You never had a chance."

"Sid, after New York we're going on a whirlwind tour around the U.S. and Canada—something like seven cities in fifteen days. I hope they're as good at security as you are."

"You'll be fine, Brian. Don't worry."

Security was his main concern. Not the music, not the performance, just the safety of his boys.

"Come in. I'm sure you'll want to say hello to the boys. They're just next door."

He took me into the adjoining suite, and the Beatles were there, hanging out, having a good time.

Paul, John, Ringo, George . . . They all greeted me effusively.

"It's nice to be with you, again," Paul said.

"I love New York!" John chimed in. "It's still a crazy place!"

Ringo remarked about how girls were trying to get at them in the hotel and that he heard that some had even booked rooms weeks in advance in the hope of getting to see the Beatles.

"Gentlemen," I said, "New York loves the Beatles and there is great anticipation for this concert. It's never been done before—a sold-out stadium the size of Shea. It's going to be spectacular!" They beamed.

"We'll be making history again," I continued. "I'll see you on Sunday. I'm *really* looking forward to it." They expressed their own enthusiasm, I said my goodbyes and left.

On Saturday, Chip Munk began to erect the stage. By then, the cost had escalated to twenty-five thousand dollars. I was in no mood to complain about the fifteen-thousand-dollar overrun; I just wanted to see it done.

On Sunday, the day of the concert, I got to Shea Stadium very early. Chip was putting the finishing touches on the stage, and I must say it was first-rate. The groundskeepers and the security people were setting up the barricades. Billy and I circulated around the huge ballpark, checking and rechecking arrangements.

The Mayor's Office assigned an extremely well-dressed, super-bright intern to spend the day with me. He was very well-mannered and had a keen eye. That young man was Jeffrey Katzenberg, who today is partners with David Geffen and Steven Spielberg at DreamWorks.

In mid-afternoon, we assembled all the security people for final instructions. I explained that no matter how they might be provoked, no matter what the young fans might do, the concertgoers were to be handled with kid gloves.

"If anyone tries to rush the stage, just lift them off their feet, let them dangle and put them back over the gates as gently as possible. If they don't go, carry them out of the ballpark. Under no circumstance are you to hit them or use any force whatsoever."

We opened the gates to Shea at about six o'clock, and there were crowds already waiting to get in. I knew we were in for something extraordinary. The Rascals got to the concert early. I had issued them passes and put them in the third-base dugout, so they could be as close to the action as possible. As irony would have it, some of the kids on the first-base side saw them and thought they were the Beatles. It was very early yet, around 6:30 or so, and kids began to filter down from across the stadium for their autographs. When they realized that this was another group, they

Meditative George looks out at the adoring crowd as he plays to a packed house.

were undaunted and clamored for their signatures anyway. I took that as a good omen about taking on the Rascals. If they could command attention as unknowns, their future seemed promising.

Since it still was early and the fans were well-behaved, I allowed them to come into the third-base dugout in small groups and get The Rascals' autographs. In addition, Billy Smith, a friend of the group, had made up buttons saying, "I'm a Rascals Fan," and he gave them out to the congregating kids. Before long, two thousand people were roaming the stands wearing Rascals buttons.

While I was in the dugout with what later became "my four boys," Bill Tooley from the Shea Stadium staff came to me.

"Sid, the stadium is yours for the night, and that includes the message board. What's your next event? We'll advertise it on the board."

"Thanks, Bill," I said. "With this and the recent Rolling Stones concert, I haven't really had time to plan another event, so I have nothing to promote at this time."

"But, Sid, you paid for it. You might as well use it."

"Okay, if that's the case, here is what I'd like to say: PLEASE, FOR YOUR SAFETY AND YOUR NEIGHBOR'S SAFETY, STAY IN YOUR SEATS THROUGH-OUT THE CONCERT. FAILURE TO DO SO COULD RESULT IN THE CANCELLA-TION OF THIS EVENT."

"Sid, you can get another message up there."

I thought for a second and then said, "Okay. Tell them to flash: THE RASCALS ARE COMING! . . . THE RASCALS ARE COMING!"

"You got it," he said, and left to make the arrangements. That flashing message turned out to be fortuitous.

Everything went off as planned. The Beatles were taken by police escort to the heliport in Manhattan and flown to the fairgrounds in Queens. Before landing, the helicopter did a turn around the stadium to let the boys see the stands, which were almost filled by 7:30. No one but a few of us knew that the Beatles were in the ballpark.

The screaming was unbelievable. The place was in a frenzy.

I went to see the Beatles in the umpires' dressing room. They were absolutely in awe. They could not believe what was happening. Here they were—in Shea Stadium in New York, fifty-five thousand seats—and the place was packed. No rock-and-roll act had ever played to an audience anywhere close to that size. The screams reached us in the dressing room.

The boys were tuning their instruments, getting dressed and preparing for the momentous performance. I had never seen them nervous before, but this event was unique.

Five minutes before showtime, we proceeded from the dressing room along a walkway to the visitors' dugout. When we reached the entrance, I said to the boys, "Okay, guys. I'm going to get up onstage and introduce Ed Sullivan. He will come up and introduce you. When he does, and I hope you can hear him, just run up these dugout steps onto the field and up to the stage. It's only a short run. There are a few steps at the left rear of the stage. You'll be surrounded by security, so don't worry about safety. We have everything under control, but be prepared. There are lots of people out

In their dressing room, George and the other guys tune up their guitars before the first Shea concert.

there. If you think it's loud now, wait till you step out of the dugout! It will be absolutely deafening!"

They nodded. I wished them good luck and left them to their Shea Stadium debut. I walked across the infield. When I reached the stage, Murray the K introduced me as "The Man Who Had Brought the Beatles to America." I stepped forward to introduce Ed Sullivan.

What can I say? It was somewhat humbling to stand up in front of those fifty-five thousand people moments before the Beatles were to come onstage. The little boy from Zisselman's Farm was about to introduce Ed Sullivan, perhaps the greatest name ever in American television, and Ed was going to introduce the number-one act in the world. Unbelievable!

I introduced Ed as a great American, which he was. Ed walked out and, with little fanfare, thanked me for the introduction and spoke these few but indelible words: "Honored by their country, decorated by their queen, and loved here in America, ladies and gentlemen—the Beatles!"

The boys ran out of the dugout, waving and turning and surveying the crowd as they made their way to the stage. Thousands of
flashbulbs went off. I wondered if the Beatles were in as much wonderment about the scene around them as I was. They got up onstage,
checked their tuning, looked at each other and began to play "Twist
and Shout." Brian and I stood stage right, next to each other.

"This is quite amazing," he shouted in my ear. "I hope we can
get them out of here."

One would think that Brian would take a moment to bask in the
glory of the evening. He truly *was* the fifth Beatle. He had discovered
the group. He had guided them and nurtured them. He had worked
tirelessly to make this a reality, and this, to be sure, was the apex of
both his and the Beatles' careers. Yet all he could think about was
getting them out safely.

"I hope we can get them out of here. I hope we get out of here alive," Brian repeated at least five times while the Beatles were onstage.

"Not to worry, Brian, we have it covered. We'll get you all out." I knew that we had so many lines of defense that, in the end, we could and would control the crowd. I may have lost money at Newport, but what I had learned there about security stood me in good stead here. We were covered.

As far as the music that night is concerned, there's not much I can say. Truth is, the screaming was so overpowering that I doubt anyone heard much of it.

George's fans had a custom of tossing jelly beans onto the stage. Throughout the concert, jelly beans rained down from the upper deck, hitting everyone sitting in the lower deck and on the field.

The security guys were concerned, until someone remembered about George's fans and the jelly beans. Nonetheless, as I was told, "Those damn jelly beans hurt!"

As soon as the Beatles finished playing, the car sped across the field to the stage. I shook hands with the four boys and Brian. I could see that he was relieved. "Great, Sid," he said. "Just marvelous. Thanks again. I'll talk to you soon."

The five of them got into the waiting armored car, and I slammed the door shut. They were in that car and on the move no more than twenty seconds after they stepped off the stage. The back gate of Shea opened, the armored car sped through and they were gone.

The screaming continued, but the audience soon realized that there would be no encore. The crowd began to empty out of the stadium very slowly, as when one departs from a loved one or an object of admiration. I waited until every ticketholder was out of Shea Stadium.

I made my way to the emergency station to thank the doctors and nurses for their services and inquired as to whether anyone had needed medical attention during the concert. When I arrived, about ten or fifteen young girls were lying on stretchers. They were overcome with excitement. As I walked into the first-aid area, one of the young doctors recognized me. "Hi, Mr. Bernstein. It was quite a night."

Suddenly, the girls jumped off their stretchers and besieged me.

"Had I shaken the Beatles' hands?" they wanted to know. Already history was repeating itself.

"Yes, indeed," I replied.

"And did you wash your hands yet?" they asked, almost in unison.

"Not since I shook John, Paul, George and Ringo's hands, no."

"Wow! Can we please shake your hand?"

"Sure," I said. And they all lined up and one after another clasped my hand.

"Look how I cured these kids with just a handshake," I joked to the young doctors. "I should have become a doctor myself!"

The kids walked away, vowing never to let water touch their hands again.

It was beyond amazing.

13

The Rascals Are Coming!

B Y THE TIME I GOT HOME, I was drained. I had been on my feet for over eighteen hours, and in the midst of all the excitement didn't realize how exhausting the day had been. I had no time to reflect on or celebrate what had been accomplished. It was on to the next project: The Rascals.

The next afternoon, August 16, 1965, at Walter Hyman's apartment on Fifth Avenue, Walter, attorney Steve Weiss, the four Rascals and I met. Steve presided over the meeting and represented both sides, which on second thought was not a good idea. We hammered out a deal whereby Walter, as the silent partner, and I, as the active partner, would manage the group. We agreed on a 20 percent commission. I knew that with a break or two The Rascals could be a major act.

We also made a gentleman's agreement that the group would do ten charity events each year. They agreed without missing a step, because they desperately wanted me to manage them. I knew that The Rascals would soon command tremendous amounts of money for their appearances, and I believed that we should try to give something back.

I got to work right away by calling the owners of The Barge in the Hamptons and getting The Rascals an immediate raise of eight hundred dollars a week, in effect doubling their salary. I contacted all the record companies that had shown interest and told them that I was now managing The Rascals and that from that point on they should deal with me.

Jerry Wexler, along with Ahmet Ertegun and his brother, Nesuhi, had built up a formidable record company in Atlantic Records. Specializing in jazz and R&B, Atlantic had well-known artists like Ray Charles, Aretha Franklin, Sam & Dave, Otis Redding, and King Curtis. They did not have any major white pop music acts at the time and were desperate to sign one so that Atlantic could compete with top record companies like Columbia, RCA and Decca. Since Ahmet and Jerry owned homes in the Hamptons, they had witnessed the rise of The Rascals and wanted very much to sign them.

While we were searching for a record label, Phil Spector, the legendary record producer, called from Los Angeles.

"Sid, did you sign The Rascals to anyone yet?"

"No, Phil, but I'm close."

"Sit tight," he said. "I'm flying in tomorrow just to see them."

"Okay, Phil," I laughed. "We're not going to do anything before tomorrow."

The next day, Phil picked me up in his limo, complete with bodyguard, and together we went to The Barge. Naturally, Phil was taken with The Rascals, and the guys were awed that the great Phil Spector had come all the way from Los Angeles to see them, let alone expressed an interest in signing them.

During a break, I explained to the group that Phil was not going to leave Los Angeles. He would be based on the West Coast, and they would be on the East Coast.

"You need a producer to be nearby, especially during the early stages of your recording career," I said. "With Phil, you can never know where he'll be. Let's find someone who's based closer to home."

We turned down the great Phil Spector. He became angry, stormed out and kicked either a stone or a fire hydrant and broke his foot. An ambulance came to The Barge and carted him off to the hospital.

I continued to negotiate with other interested record executives. And there were many. That flashing sign at Shea—THE RASCALS ARE COMING! . . . THE RASCALS ARE COMING!—seemed to have had the desired effect.

As the summer neared an end, I decided to book The Rascals into Harlow's, a small New York City club, and the entire three-week gig was a sellout. There was a celebratory atmosphere. Limos were lined up outside waiting to transport their owners, who had just seen "the next big thing in American music," to their next destination. Every night was New Year's Eve.

From Harlow's, I booked The Rascals into an even smaller club, aptly called the Phone Booth. I was determined that my group would play in only the most intimate clubs until they had a hit record— and you couldn't get more intimate than the Phone Booth. Night after night the place was jammed, and quite a few stars, like Bob Dylan and Bill Wyman of the Rolling Stones, came more than once. Brian Epstein also stopped by several times, invariably dressed as if he had just stepped out of the pages of *Gentlemen's Quarterly*.

One night, I spotted Burt Bacharach and Angie Dickinson patiently waiting on line. I knew how modest and unpretentious Burt was, that he would in no way use his fame to curry favor, so I walked over, took them both by the hand and walked them inside. After The Rascals had finished their set, Angie and Burt came over. "The Rascals are going to be a huge group," they said.

On another night, the great Welsh heartthrob Tom Jones walked in without prior warning. When the ushers spotted him, they brought him right to my table. Tom, whom I had never met, explained that he was in New York on business and that several people had suggested that on his free evening he check out a new group that was playing at the Phone Booth. So, together we sat and watched the boys perform in the packed club. The Rascals were thrilled to hear that a star of the magnitude of Tom Jones found them "awesome," but they were starting to get used to that kind of response.

Finally, we made a decision about a record label. The deciding factor was a statement Ahmet Ertegun made: "Look, Sid. As you know, we don't have any white acts. We need this group. If you sign them to Atlantic, you'll get every possible promotion and production advantage. We will see them through until they make it, no matter how long it takes. I know some of the major record labels are offering you more money, but they don't need you like we do, and I think that's an advantage you should not forgo."

I recommended that the Rascals make a deal with them. They concurred, and when it was announced that the group had signed as the newest Atlantic recording artists, there were many unhappy record execs in town.

Atlantic assigned Arif Mardin, a magnificent arranger and producer, and Tom Dowd, one of the finest engineers in the business, to assist the Rascals. They agreed to allow the group to produce their own records and even granted us free studio time, which was unheard of.

The Rascals were getting press even before their record was released. The buzz that had started at The Barge carried over to Harlow's and then to the Phone Booth. I received a surprising phone call one day from the manager of the Harmonica Rascals, a famous group that had been in movies and on television. This fellow maintained that his group owned the name "Rascals" and that we would be well advised to stop using it. I took this information to Atlantic, whose legal department said that if we preceded "Rascals" with another word we could keep using the name. The executives at Atlantic thought that the "Young Rascals" sounded pretty good, and that became the group's new name.

The boys had not really started to write songs yet, and the most pressing order of business during late 1965 was to find a song everybody thought was a hit. The search was on. Arif Mardin, Tom Dowd and Atlantic were looking, the boys were contacting anybody they knew who could write, and I put the word out to music publishers. We received hundreds of submissions and, one by one, listened to them all.

Songwriters Pam Sawyer and Laurie Burton submitted a tune called

"I Ain't Gonna Eat Out My Heart Anymore," and the consensus was that it would be a hit. There was great enthusiasm and expectation for the record, and we did everything we could to send it straight up the charts.

The most important market for record play and sales has always been New York, with its large, diverse population and its reputation as the media capital of the world. That being the case, New York is also the most difficult city in which to get a new single played. Invariably, a record has to be on the Top 100 charts and have demonstrated its ability to get airplay and sales in other markets before it will even be considered for the New York market.

However, I had some advantages. Through my association with the Beatles, the Rolling Stones, Tony Bennett and many other star acts, I had gotten to know the music programmers and disc jockeys at most of the New York radio stations. Often, when I ran concerts or shows, I would call on local deejays to emcee. Over the years, I had developed many friendships.

One of the personalities with whom I had developed a close friendship was Bruce Morrow, more widely known as Cousin Brucie, who for years was top jock at the leading New York station, WABC. With its fifty-thousand-watt, clear-channel signal, the station could be heard all the way to Florida and even reached parts of the Midwest. The audience was huge. Key to getting airplay on WABC was Rick Sklar, the station's music program director. Rick was highly respected, and if he chose to air a record, other program directors around the country would soon do the same.

It was important to me that Morrow see and hear the Young Rascals. I thought he could be the first to play their record, so we developed a plan. I arranged for the group to meet Cousin Brucie at the WABC offices, and asked him to play along with the gag. It was winter, and they were all wearing muskrat overcoats. I gave the Rascals an extra muskrat coat to take with them to the station. They threw the coat over Brucie, spirited him out of the station and took him to the Phone Booth, where they were appearing. It was a scene reminiscent of Walter Hyman's "kidnapping" of me to hear the Rascals.

It's always great to see radio personality Bruce Morrow, better known as "Cousin Brucie." He currently takes listeners, by way of the airwaves, back to the age of golden oldies on New York's CBS-FM.

This was the first time that Bruce saw the Young Rascals perform live. He had heard the buzz about them from their club dates, and had been onstage at the Beatles' concert at Shea and seen the message board flashing their forthcoming arrival. As Brucie always says, "It was love at first bite."

As a favor to me, Rick and Bruce agreed to air "I Ain't Gonna Eat Out My Heart Anymore" and encouraged other ABC radio stations around the country to follow suit. Through them and WABC, we were successful in getting substantial airplay. However, to get on Bill Gavin's all-important tip sheet, which music program directors consult to learn about hot new records, I had to get play on at least one more credible radio station. The record had to get a Gavin mention.

For years I had been reading in the trades about a great young deejay who worked for the largest radio station in the Buffalo area. His name was Joey Reynolds, and he was so outstanding that he became well-known in national deejay and radio circles. I had met people who had promoted records in the Buffalo area, and they had only positive things to say about him.

I called the station where Joey worked and asked if I could visit, explaining that I had a hot new group in New York called the Young Rascals, that they had a record out on Atlantic Records and that I wanted to discuss playing it for the Buffalo audience. If I came during Mr. Reynolds' radio show, I was told, he would see me. I flew to Buffalo the very next day and went to the station.

While waiting to meet with Joey Reynolds, I was able to watch him work through the studio glass and hear him over the loud-speakers in the waiting room. It was immediately obvious that this guy knew what he was doing. No wonder he was the talk of Buf-falo. At the newsbreak, Joey stood and waved me into the studio.

"Sid, it's a pleasure to meet you. . . .As you can see, I'm on the air, but I should be finished in about thirty minutes. Would you mind waiting? I can spend some time with you when I'm done with the program."

My plane was not leaving for a few more hours. "Sure," I said.

After the show, I told Joey a little about myself and a lot about the Young Rascals. I mentioned nothing about my involvement with the Beatles. I spoke only about the Rascals. Joey listened intently but made no commitment to air "I Ain't Gonna Eat Out My Heart Any-more." A fifty-fifty chance that he would, I thought.

Joey spun the record the very next day and continued playing it until it peaked in the thirties on the station's chart. That earned us a listing in the *Gavin Report* and helped gain momentum for the record, which went as high as fifty-two nationally. A good beginning, but the Rascals still needed a top-ten record.

Even though we didn't have a hit, I was able to keep escalating the price to see them. They were such dynamic performers that before long we were getting two thousand dollars for one show, a high price for a group without a hit record. We played high school and college gyms, social halls and auditoriums. Word was circulat-ing that these four boys could put on a "hell of a show."

Walter Hyman, my partner, came to see me one day. "Sid, I have become very friendly with Dore Schary. He's no longer head of MGM and he's moved back to New York. He's constantly getting projects that people want him to do and he's asked me to come in on one of them, and I want to do it."

"What's the project, Walter?"

"He has a play called *The Impossible Years* that he wants to produce on Broadway. He's thinking we can take it to Hollywood after that and make it into a movie.

"That's good, Walter. What's the problem? Do it."

"Yes, Sid, but I'm involved with you and this Rascals thing. . . . Look, Sid. I'm not crazy about the scene. I'd like you to buy me out."

"What would you like, Walter?"

"Give me twenty-five thousand dollars, and I'm a happy man."

"Okay, let me see what I can do."

I went to Jerry Wexler at Atlantic and told him that I was inclined to buy out Walter's interest but didn't have the money.

Jerry didn't waste a moment. "Sid, we'll lend it to you."

The owners of Atlantic couldn't wait to be rid of Walter. They figured that it would be easier to deal with me than with a tough-minded, rich businessman like him. They were right.

I gave Walter the twenty-five grand, he got involved with Dore Schary's project, and it became a Broadway smash starring Alan King. Later, it was produced as a Hollywood film. Everyone was happy.

THE PRESSURE WAS ON to find another song for the Young Rascals. Material was coming at us from all sides, and one day Felix Cavaliere spoke up. "Sid, I have very strong feelings about 'Good Lovin'.' People are always telling me that we should release it as a single, and I agree. I think it's a hit."

The song, by Rudy Clark and Artie Resnick, had been recorded by the Olympics several years earlier and had been a hit. The Young Rascals performed it in their act, and it was always an audience favorite.

"Felix, if you believe in it so much, let's take it up with Arif, Ahmet and Jerry."

Felix did a convincing sales job, and the bigshots at Atlantic decided to release "Good Lovin'" as a single. The moment they did, it flew up the charts, cracking the top ten in just five weeks. Buoyed by that, I swiftly raised the Rascals' price to five thousand dollars per engagement . . . and we still could not accommodate all the promoters willing to pay it.

I HAD READ IN ONE OF THE trade papers about an interview with Brian Epstein in which he said that he was planning to bring the Beatles

THE RASCALS ARE COMING!

to America during the coming summer. I immediately called Brian in London.

"I read that you're going to take the boys on a tour of many of the major U.S. markets. Brian, I'd love to bring them back to Shea."

"Sid, as long as these boys are together and I am their manager, New York will be your city."

"I appreciate that, Brian. How about if we do the same deal as last time? We'll do everything the same. We had such a great experience, we should try to duplicate it."

"Agreed! Let's do it."

"Great. When are the Beatles available to play in New York?"

"Let's see. Let me review the schedule for a moment. . . . We are going to be in St. Louis on Saturday August 20, and I promised the promoter in Seattle Thursday, August 25. Could we do Shea between those two dates?"

That sounds okay to me, but I need to check on the stadium's availability. In the meantime, I'll wire the fifty thousand dollars to you."

"That's fine, just have the check made out to NEMS, my holding company."

It was as easy as that. No talk about ten bucks a ticket for unsold seats. No gag on advertising or publicity.

"Oh, by the way, Sid, I really have been meaning to talk to you about some of these new acts I've signed, but I just can't find the time. We'll really have to do it soon. I want them to play the States."

"I know what you mean, Brian. I'm so busy now with the Rascals. They're starting to happen, and I've still got some concerts to promote. Let's wait till after Shea and we'll get into it then."

Following the conversation with Brian, I promptly called Jim Thompson at Shea and asked him if the stadium was available for August 23.

"The Mets will be on a road trip," he said.

"Jim, do we still have that stage that Chip built for us?"

"Yes, Sid, it's stored here at the stadium. I kind of figured we would be needing it again."

"Terrific! Can your crew erect it for me?"

"If we took it apart, we can put it back together."

I was licking my chops. I had just saved twenty-five thousand dollars.

"Can we have the stadium for the same price as last year?"

". . . Oh, what the hell, you got it Sid. Just get the insurance."

"Okay, Jim, we're on. I'll talk to you as we get closer to the date. But, it should be much easier this time because we're going to do the exact same thing."

"Good, Sid, we're ready to roll."

AT THE FIRST SHEA CONCERT, the screaming kids had overwhelmed the sound system so that no one could really hear the music. I called Bill Hanley, an audio genius who worked out of Boston. Bill set up a sound system that proved to be a vast improvement over the first Shea concert.

Jerry Rosen, whom I called next, assured me that we could again get Lloyd's to do the insurance. "Why not, Sid, they made twenty-five thousand last time and it turned out to be no risk at all. They'll definitely do it. Don't worry, I'll take care of it for you."

Two days later, I wired the fifty thousand dollars to NEMS and left a message for Brian that the twenty-third of August was confirmed. He could put it on the tour schedule. I was excited about the Beatles reappearing at Shea, but something kept gnawing at me. I knew that Brian was going to book the Beatles into stadiums in Boston, Philadelphia and Washington, and I feared that this might be too much exposure in a relatively small geographic area. I believed that the concert would sell out, but I was not about to count on another P. O. Box 21 miracle. We would promote this concert in the traditional way: posters, handbills, ads and good, old-fashioned public relations.

About a week after I made the deal with Brian, my old friend Norman Weiss from GAC called. He was now the agent responsible for the Beatles.

"Sid, I know that you made a deal with Brian Epstein to pay the Beatles one hundred thousand dollars against 60 percent of the gross, just like last time, but we'd like 65 percent this time."

"You know, I made this deal with Brian, and I could discuss this extra 5 percent with him, and he would probably rescind it. But, I'll agree, Norman, for old times' sake. You can go back to Brian, and tell him you got the extra 5 percent. I don't care."

And I really didn't care. I had picked up an extra twenty-five thousand dollars, because we wouldn't need to build a new stage. But that aside, all I wanted was to get the Beatles back into Shea. A tougher businessman like Abe Margolies or Walter Hyman no doubt would have objected, but I just let it go.

I projected that we would start selling tickets for the event in early July. To that end I began to design posters and handbills, one of which, the official concert poster, has become a valuable piece of Beatles memorabilia.

I attended police and security meetings, but that was all old hat. We were so sure we had taken enough precautions that this time I decided to dispense with the karate black belts. I never heard from Brian about security, either. He knew that uppermost on my list of priorities was to fully protect his boys.

DURING THE PLANNING of the second Shea concert, a call came in from Andrew Loog Oldham about the Rolling Stones.

"Oh, no," I groaned. "Which venue do you want to get me thrown out of this time, Andrew?"

"Don't worry, Sid, I'll tell the boys to really behave this time."

"Right, Andrew. . . . That'll be the day."

"Seriously, Sid, I want to bring them back to New York. How about it?"

Andrew was such a sincere guy, and I knew the Stones were a sure sellout, so I accepted immediately.

"Same deal, Andrew. Ten thousand dollars, two shows, Academy of Music, early May. And this time, I'll double the security!"

"Thank you, Sid. We're on!"

IN MAY, AS PLANNED, Mick Jagger and team played the Academy of Music. They gave their usual, high-energy performance and the kids again went wild. But I was prepared. The "double security" was well worth the expense.

Before the Beatles returned to Shea, I heard from Al Diccio, a vice president at the Singer Sewing Machine Company whom I had met through Tony Bennett. They were old and dear friends.

"Sid," Al said, "Singer is putting a new store at Rockefeller Center, overlooking the skating rink. You could really do me a big favor by making it an outlet for Beatles tickets. The traffic and the publicity would do wonders for the store! And to make it worth your while, Sid, we'll take 25 percent of all the tickets and guarantee their sale. What I mean is, if we don't sell them, we'll buy them."

I did a quick calculation. I had set up a ticket window at Shea and tickets were available at my office. Now I could have a sales outlet in midtown Manhattan, which would certainly be helpful. Remember that these were before the days of Ticketron and TicketMaster.

"You've got it, Al."

"Thanks, Sid. I really do appreciate it."

Even with this positive development, I could tell early on that the Beatles were not going to sell out Shea this go-round. All the publicity could not alter the fact that it was impossible for any act to stay at a frenzied peak indefinitely. Gross weekly ticket sales continually diminished. Perhaps that can be attributed to my original fear that the Washington, Philadelphia, and Boston concerts would drain some of the potential audience.

Interest in the group was still high. A few days before the Beatles were to come to New York, Rick Sklar of WABC called and asked if I could get Bruce Morrow an interview with the Beatles. "Five to ten minutes is all we ask, Sid. Can you set it up?" I promised to try.

I called Rick on the day the Beatles were to arrive at the Warwick. "Listen, Rick, I am going to see Brian and the Beatles at 5:00 P.M. at their hotel. Be in the lobby with Bruce—with your equipment—and I think I can arrange the interview. But you have to be ready to move."

"We'll be there, Sid. We'll be there."

When I arrived at the Warwick that afternoon, I could see that Brian and the boys were exhausted from having performed nine concerts in ten days. I marveled at their ability to withstand such a grueling pace and still be warm and friendly. But now everything seemed to be rather matter-of-fact. I had become a familiar fixture to them.

For his part, Brian looked extremely tired, even unwell, but he was still cheerful. That the Beatles would not be playing to a full house never came up. I was sure that Brian had been informed by GAC that many of the venues on the current Beatles tour had failed to sell out, and that took some of the pressure off me. We sold a little more than fifty-two thousand of the fifty-five thousand seats, so the situation couldn't be called horrendous. I was pleased that we had not made the "ten dollars a ticket for unsold seats" deal. That would have spelled financial disaster.

I asked Brian if it would be possible to get a few minutes for Bruce Morrow to interview the boys. "He's one of New York's top deejays, Brian, right up there with Murray the K. He's a really nice guy, and his boss, Rick Sklar, is the number-one program director in America."

"We know all about Cousin Brucie and WABC. Let me ask the boys."

I stepped out of the suite, and Brian came back almost immediately.

"The boys say okay. How soon can you have the WABC people here?"

"Well, WABC is right across the street from the hotel. They could be here in a few minutes. I can go get them."

"Go get them, Sid."

I took the elevator down. As promised, Rick and Bruce were on the move as soon as they saw the smile on my face. We waited a few minutes, then I took Bruce and Rick upstairs and introduced them to everyone. They set up their equipment and taped the interview in ten minutes. I thanked Brian and the boys and left with Rick and Bruce.

That night, Bruce Morrow went on the air with an exclusive coast-to-coast interview with the Beatles. I had repaid my debt to Rick and Bruce for helping me with the Young Rascals.

I realized once again that Brian Epstein and the Beatles were extremely decent people. After all, Murray the K was the deejay closest

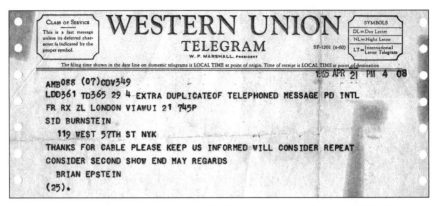

(Above) Before the days of e-mail, this is one way that Brian and I communicated.
(Left) "Ticket(s) to ride" for the Beatles' second Shea concert.

to them, and yet, because I had asked them to see Bruce and Rick as a favor to me, they had agreed.

On Tuesday, August 23, 1966, the Beatles played Shea Stadium for the second and last time. A group called the Cyrkle, who had a hit record called "Red Rubber Ball," opened the show. Jeffrey Katzenberg, the same sharp, smartly dressed kid, again representing the Mayor's Office, was with me in the dugout. We used the identical game plan as the previous year, except for the improved sound system. However, the unabashed frenzy of the fans was absent. There was still plenty of screaming, but what had happened the previous August was a once-in-a-lifetime experience. It could not be duplicated. Brian and the Beatles understood this, too.

As we were standing in the walkway at the entrance to the dugout, Ringo said: "Sid, we hear that your wife is pregnant again. We haven't met her and we hear that she's a very beautiful young lady. This is the third time we're here in New York with you, Sid, and we still haven't met her!"

The overzealous fans are a bit too much for her," I said.

"Ah, Sid is trying to raise a baseball team, Ringo!' John said. "He's going to go for nine!"

George and John have a rollicking good time.

Ringo's drumbeats cause young girls' hearts to beat a little faster.

Everybody had a good laugh, and it signaled to me that the empty seats were not an issue.

As usual, Brian and I stood together on the field during the concert. "Two more dates on the West Coast, and we can go home," he said. "The boys have played almost every day since we got to Chicago eleven days ago. We even had to play two cities in one day on Sunday because of a rain postponement! Everybody is running out of steam, but New York seems to reinvigorate the boys. I, for one, am glad it's almost over."

The pressure was clearly getting to him. The boys sang and played, but Brian did everything else. Too much for one man, I thought.

When the concert ended, just before the Beatles took off, I shook Brian's hand and said goodbye. We both knew that the Beatles' touring days were nearing an end.

Rock historians say that there were about ten thousand empty seats at Shea that night. However, history sometimes gets distorted. The fact is that there were only two thousand five hundred unsold tickets and more than fifty-two thousand satisfied fans.

LOUIS CUTOLO

(Above) Record exec Jerry Wexler and I share a hug when the Rascals' "Good Lovin'" went gold. (Below) And yet another golden moment, this time for "A Beautiful Morning."

LOUIS CUTOLO

"GOOD LOVIN'" REACHED NUMBER ONE. The Rascals were awarded their first gold record and, as their manager, I was entitled to a gold record, too. It was a first for all of us.

We had a small ceremony at Atlantic Records. The company executives handed the Rascals and me our records, and pictures of the event appeared a week later in *Cashbox, Record World* and *Billboard.* I selected a prominent spot in my office and proudly displayed my plaque. This was a milestone, and I was thrilled. But the Rascals weren't through yet. "Good Lovin'" was only the first of ten gold records they were to earn.

TOM MOFFAT, THE TOP PROMOTER and deejay in Hawaii, called me with a super deal for the Rascals. So off we went. The group was booked into a midsize arena for five nights, and although underpaid monetarily, we were compensated in many other ways. All the Bernsteins and all of the Rascals' families enjoyed a fully paid working vacation. From airfare to sightseeing, Tom took care of all expenses. It didn't hurt that when we arrived on the island, two Rascals' records were in the top ten. We were treated like royalty.

DURING THOSE YEARS, the Bitter End on Bleecker Street in Greenwich Village had become a favorite hangout of mine. My friend Freddie Weintraub owned it, and Billy Fields managed it. Billy had traded in his career as a vocalist and sometime promoter for something a little more predictable and secure. The Bitter End showcased musicians and comedians, and a number of big stars like Woody Allen, Richard Pryor and Dick Cavett got their starts there. The Bitter End was also a hangout for show-business professionals and managers. Albert Grossman, who managed Bob Dylan, Peter Paul & Mary and later Janis Joplin and The Band, would come to the Bitter End to relax and see what was new and upcoming.

Albert and I had become friendly, and I considered him the best personal manager when it came to dealing with several acts simultaneously. Albert could maintain his equilibrium and his relationship with his megastar acts, who were subject to jealousies and needs they thought only he could fill. I marveled at his ability to juggle it all.

Across the street from the Bitter End was the Café Au Go Go, where all the underground music groups performed. Alice Cooper, Richie Havens and the Blues Project eventually emerged from there. On Bleecker Street, what the Bitter End was to comedy, the Café Au Go Go was to music.

The Blues Project, five guys from the Village, became a "big buzz" act out of the Café, and I got to know them quite well. Al Kooper, Steve Katz, Danny Kalb, Roy Blumenfeld and Andy Kulberg were bright, educated young men. They were liberal, left-thinking guys with lots of ideas and double the passion. I responded to that, and we became friends. I made it a point to follow their careers and monitor their progress.

I was amazed to learn that the Blues Project, which I considered to be somewhat underground, had managed to secure a booking at the more mainstream Phone Booth. I went to check them out, and after their set they came to sit with me. We talked for a while, and then one of them—Danny Kalb, I think—said, "Sid, we need a manager. Would you consider taking us on?"

It was a request out of nowhere. I considered the guys in the

Blues Project great musicians, and I understood that, at the moment, I was a pretty hot commodity. After all, I was promoting groups like the Beatles, the Rolling Stones, and much of the British Invasion. I still had my hand in some of the pop music promotions at Carnegie Hall . . . and my band, the Young Rascals, had a number-one record.

Nonetheless, although their future looked bright on the surface, I had my doubts. It is a strange axiom of life that sometimes success is intolerable for the successful. As soon as the Rascals achieved a top-of-the-charts hit, the infighting began. Nothing major, mind you, just petty annoyances that had them cursing and berating each other. As a person who disdains foul language and avoids confrontation like the plague, the group's bickering caused me great consternation. Would they eventually self-destruct?

When Danny Kalb asked me to consider managing the Blues Project, I said I would think about it. That night at home I called Albert Grossman, the expert at managing several hit acts simultaneously. I also thought about Brian Epstein, who was handling several acts besides the Beatles. I figured that it was just a matter of building an organization. Perhaps it's within my reach. The Blues Project had all the ingredients for success, and they had paid their dues by playing in small clubs. With the right management and a record contract, they could make it commercially. A few days later, I called Danny and set up a meeting with the group. We had a heart-to-heart talk and made a deal.

Walter Hyman and Jackie Green, a VP at Associated Booking Company (ABC), headed by Joe Glaser, socialized often. When Walter was still actively involved with the Rascals, he strongly suggested that I give the booking responsibilities for the Rascals to ABC. Sol Saffian became the responsible agent and reported to Jackie. I had wanted to give the Rascals to Frank Barsalona, who had worked with me at GAC and had recently opened his own agency, Premier Talent. William Morris and GAC expressed interest, too. But in deference to Walter and his relationship with Jackie, we went with ABC.

So many people knew me from my activities within the music business that they called me to book the Rascals more often than they called Sol Saffian or Jackie Green. I fielded most of the calls, so I was able to convince the promoters who wanted to book the frequently unavailable Rascals to take the Blues Project instead. I wondered why promoters who had sought to book a number-one record act like the Rascals would agree to take a relatively unknown act. After all my years as a manager, agent and promoter, perhaps they trusted me. And I felt comfortable that the Blues Project would not let them down.

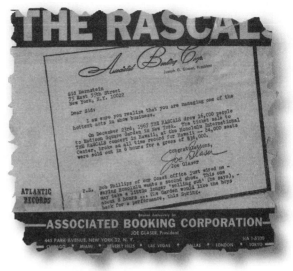

A congratulatory note from Joe Glaser of Associated Booking Company, which scheduled appearances for the Rascals.

The Blues Project had become accustomed to getting one hundred fifty dollars a night. I immediately jacked up their price to five hundred, and in short order I worked them up to seven hundred fifty and then to twelve hundred fifty. They stayed at that level briefly, then I got them a record deal on Verve Records and their price soared to two thousand dollars a night. They were relishing every moment as they watched their careers advance.

The group was on the verge of becoming really hot, and a hit record would put them over the top. Then, Danny Kalb took an overdose of LSD and was arrested in San Francisco. It took a plea from Tom Moffat in Hawaii to Tom Rounds, the top deejay in San Francisco, to get Danny out of jail, but the Blues Project were effectively a thing of the past. Later, Al Kooper and Steve Katz would go on to become founding members of Blood, Sweat & Tears. But for now, drugs had silenced the music.

14

Let's Make a Deal

ONE DAY, I GOT A CALL from Nat Weiss, a successful show-business attorney and close friend of Brian Epstein's. Nat was also the manager of the Cyrkle, the group that opened for the Beatles at the second Shea Stadium concert.

"Sid, I've been thinking . . ." Nat said. "You have the Rascals and the Blues Project, and Brian has the Beatles and some other acts that he's wanted to talk to you about. Robert Stigwood manages the Bee Gees, Eric Clapton and Cream. I think that you, Brian and Robert should meet to discuss a possible partnership arrangement. The three of you together would be formidable."

No one yet knew that the Blues Project had self-destructed. But this nevertheless sounded like an idea worth exploring.

"Nat, when is Brian going to be in New York again?"

"He's going to be at the Waldorf in a couple of weeks. I'll arrange a meeting and let you know the date."

Several weeks later, I went to the Waldorf Towers. Brian told me that his boys were off on holiday. John was making a movie, George had gone to India, and Paul and Ringo were hanging out back home. Nat Weiss introduced me to Robert Stigwood, an Australian, who seemed to be a very nice young man, modest and bright. Nat repeated what he had said to me on the phone: Stigwood had the Bee Gees, Clapton and Cream and was working on some other exciting projects; I had the Rascals and, at that point, the Blues Project. Nat didn't have to repeat who Brian was managing. If we pooled our acts and started a new management company, Stigwood would cover Australia, considered to be a spawning ground for new talent; I would cover America, specifically New York, the home of most of the record companies; and Brian would contribute his mighty reputation and stature in Great Britain and the rest of the world.

"You three together would be an unbeatable combo," Nat continued. "If you pool your resources, there's no telling what you could do."

Brian spoke first. "I'm all for this, and I think it could be very exciting, but I cannot put the Beatles into the partnership. Any other acts I manage will certainly be pooled, but I cannot include the Beatles." There wasn't much argument. Everybody understood that—for personal and business reasons—Brian couldn't share management of the Beatles.

After two stimulating hours evaluating who would do what and where we would maintain offices, Stigwood said he was all for the deal. Brian was too, with only that one Beatles caveat. I told Stigwood, Brian and Nat that I wanted to discuss the plan with my wife and some of my advisers and that I would get back to them in a few days. "But, in principle, gentlemen," I said, "this sounds very good to me."

When I got home, I talked to Gerry. "A great idea, Sid! I think you should give it a try."

"I do, too, Gerry. I'm going to pursue it."

The next day, I went to discuss the proposal with my accountants.

They listened carefully, then one of them said, "Wait a minute, Sid. What are you doing? You're going to put the Rascals in the deal and they are as hot as a pistol! The Blues Project is starting to make a name for itself and you've really gotten their price up. [They were unaware of the Blues Project's imminent breakup.] Also, if you do this deal, the major part of the workload will fall on you. You're the guy in America, by far the largest market, and almost all of the record companies are here in New York. The only way we see this working is for Brian Epstein to include the Beatles. Otherwise, it's not a fair deal."

"Listen, I'm not concerned about the work part of it. I like the action, so I'm happy to take on the responsibility. But if you're telling me that it's not financially sound, I'll back out. I can assure you that Brian will not put the Beatles into the partnership. I can also tell you that Robert Stigwood is very bright and ambitious and the Bee Gees are going to be a gigantic act."

"All well and good, but right now it's not a good deal for you."

I took the accountants' advice. I had been so cavalier about money in the past, had gone through so many ups and downs, that this time I decided to take the cautious route.

With a heavy heart, I called London. "Brian, I would really like to do this. I like Robert, and nothing would please me more than to be partners. You know how much I respect and admire you, but my accountants think that without the Beatles this is a no-go. And Brian, you made it clear that you can't include the Beatles."

"Sid, it's okay. I understand that you don't want to argue with your accountants. I certainly don't want to precipitate anything between you and them. Let's leave it for another time. Maybe things will change."

"Thank's for understanding, Brian. Please tell Nat about my decision. And thank him for trying. He's right. We would be an unbeatable combo."

"Yes, I'll tell him, and he'll tell Stigwood. . . . Talk to you soon, Sid."

"Be well, Brian, and don't work too hard."

He laughed and hung up.

As the years passed, I realized that my accountants rejected the deal because they feared that they might be replaced. I wasn't business-savvy enough to understand the ramifications. Now I do.

AFTER "GOOD LOVIN'" became a number-one hit in the U.S., Atlantic Records decided to push it worldwide, a common practice in the industry. To support Atlantic's release of "Good Lovin'" in Great Britain, I decided to book the Young Rascals into several small clubs in London and across England.

At our first London engagement, at Blazers, I sat at a table smack in the middle of the room. As my boys took to the stage and began to play, I noticed that Paul McCartney, Brian Jones and Bill Wyman of the Rolling Stones, and Keith Moon, drummer of The Who, sat directly to the right of the stage. A few minutes into the set, who should walk in and sit down beside me but Brian Epstein! I had extended the invitation to everyone weeks earlier, and was immensely pleased that they had all come to show their support. After the set, Paul and Brian accepted my invitation to visit with the group backstage. Brian and Paul spent about a half-hour with the group, and both were extraordinarily complimentary and encouraging. The Rascals were very appreciative, especially guitarist Gene Cornish, who had always been in awe of Brian and his dapper mode of dress.

Brian attended another Rascals performance, this time with John Lennon. It was clear that the Rascals could hold their own in the presence of so many great musicians and performers.

During one of the Rascals' first gigs in Britain, Dino's drum was sliding off the stage, so Keith Moon propped himself against the drum to make sure it would remain there. In exchange for that great courtesy, Dino taught Keith how to twirl drumsticks while playing. No one in the world of drummers could twirl his sticks like Dino!

Throughout our stay in England, groups who were achieving popularity in the U.S often came by to visit with us. It was a new and thrilling time. The Rascals and I were navigating unchartered waters of fame and fortune together. We were an extended family of explorers and pioneers.

I wanted to help Atlantic with their worldwide public relations efforts on behalf of "Good Lovin'." Our London trip had gotten the record off to a good start in England, and airplay was beginning in Germany, too. I thought it would be a good idea to take a quick jaunt over to Paris and play the Olympia Theatre, where the Beatles had played immediately before coming to Carnegie Hall. I also wanted to meet Eddie Barclay, Europe's "Mr. Music."

Barclay's Records was the label that released the British and European versions of "Good Lovin'." Sol Saffian, who was the responsible agent for the Rascals at ABC, arranged the date at the Olympia, which would feature the Rascals and a great Spanish band, Los Bravos, who had the hit "Black Is Black."

Felix Cavaliere of the Rascals shipped his Hammond B-3 organ to Paris. The instrument comes in two parts—a heavy keyboard and an equally heavy speaker cabinet—large and unwieldy. But the sound of the Hammond differentiated the Rascals from almost all other groups playing at that time, so the effort was worth it. On the day of the concert, when Felix plugged the B-3 into the available power source at the Olympia, he got the shock of his life. The thing blew up, releasing a mini-mushroom cloud, like something after a nuclear explosion. We had not considered that American and European power setups are incompatible. We had to find an adequate replacement right away.

Everyone searched Paris frantically for a substitute organ, but we could not locate a suitable replacement. What we eventually found was beat-up and broken-down—like a toy, not a B-3. Felix was understandably beside himself, and my brain was in high gear trying to find a solution. As I was sitting in the front row in the Olympia Theatre, I felt a tap on the shoulder. I turned to see Brian Epstein, elegant as ever, with a friend.

"My goodness! What brings you here?"

"I heard you were here, Sid, and just came over to say hello."

Brian had flown to Paris just to say hello and wish us luck. I clued him in on our B-3 dilemma.

"If we had a little more time, we could bring one across the Channel, but we'll never get it here in time for tonight's performance. Have you checked with any other groups?"

"Everybody is out looking for us, Brian. Eddie Barclay's people, the theater staff, but no luck so far."

By then, the Rascals had congregated around Brian.

"Felix, I have been listening to the rehearsal with the substitute organ and can assure you that no one here tonight will know the difference," Brian said. "Don't give it a second thought."

That seemed to calm Felix a bit. Brian wished the Rascals all the best for the evening performance, sat in on the rest of the rehearsal, then leaned over to me. "Sid, I have to catch a flight back to London."

I escorted him out of the theater. "Thanks again for making the trip. You know how much it means to me."

"Not at all, mate. Think nothing of it."

When I took the boys to dinner before the show that evening, all they talked about was how Brian Epstein had flown in for an hour just to demonstrate his support and lend encouragement. Perhaps that's what saved the night and made the Rascals' performance so terrific.

WHEN I RETURNED TO the States from our European trip, I took advantage of the opportunity to promote Ray Charles in concert in Central Park. Dino Danelli had always been a big fan of Ray, and right before the concert I introduced them. I left the two artists alone to talk in Ray's forty-foot trailer, which was, save for a chair placed dead center, without furniture. Precautions were always taken to ensure that Ray, who is blind, would not hurt himself.

When Dino emerged from the meeting thirty minutes later, his face was aglow. I was happy to have made Dino's dream come true.

Keying in on Ray Charles at one of his many performances.

(Above) In 1970, dynamic entertainer Pearl Bailey was appointed Ambassador of Love by President Richard Nixon. (Below) Singer/actress Diahann Carrol made television history in the series Julia, which featured a black actor in a nonstereotypical role for the first time.

ONE OF MY PERSONAL FAVORITES has always been Pearl Bailey. We had met during my Lou Walters days, when I was managing Diahann Carroll and she appeared with Pearl on Broadway in House of Flowers.

Pearl Bailey's singing, acting and comedic talents were outstanding, and I had always wanted to present her in concert. One day, I approached Pearl and her husband and chief adviser, jazz drummer Louis Bellson, to propose presenting Pearl at Carnegie Hall. They nodded to each other and gave me the go-ahead.

Unfortunately, I couldn't clear a date at Carnegie Hall, so we took the Pearl Bailey concert to Lincoln Center's Avery Fisher Hall, home of the New York Philharmonic. Seats were in such demand that we could have done three shows. The house was filled with Broadway artists and Hollywood and record industry execs, and Pearl was magnificent. It was a gala evening. Pearl couldn't have been better.

MONEY WAS COMING IN from many sources. The Rascals were hot, and I was getting a percentage from their personal appearances, record royalties and publishing earnings. The promotions that I did were successful, so the money was flowing from there as well.

I decided to undertake a big project. My attempt to book the Beatles into the old Madison Square Garden didn't come to pass, and I was determined to be the first to present a rock-and-roll concert there. I thought that James Brown, who had become a major artist, was capable of filling the Garden.

I called Ned Irish, the owner of the Garden and basketball's New York Knicks. I knew that Irish was innovative—he had made his reputation by putting college basketball doubleheaders in the Garden.

Calling all stars . . . the lifeline of show business.

"Mr. Irish, it's Sid Bernstein calling."

"Oh yes, Mr. Bernstein! How can I help?"

"Well, Mr. Irish, I would like to present an artist at the Garden. . . . Are there any dates available?"

"Wait a minute, Mr. Bernstein. . . . Who specifically do you have in mind?"

"James Brown. I want to present James Brown."

"What does Mr. Brown do?"

"He sings and performs and has a great following nationwide."

"But I've never even heard of him."

"What can I say, Mr. Irish? He sells a lot of records and is extremely popular."

"Mr. Bernstein, I'm very busy right now and will be out of town for the next few days. I should be back by the end of the week. I'll call you, and if you don't hear from me, give me a holler and we'll continue this conversation."

"Fine, Mr. Irish."

The very next day, Ned Irish called the office.

"Mr. Bernstein, please listen to me carefully."

"I'm listening."

"I want you to make me a hero with my grandchildren."

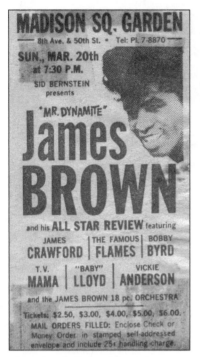

The Godfather of Soul "got on up" and performed the first music concert at this famous New York arena.

"What do you mean?"

"Well, I mentioned to my grandkids the conversation that you and I had about James Brown. They went crazy. 'Grandpa, he's the man!' they said. They wouldn't stop. . . . They want to see James Brown in the Garden, Mr. Bernstein."

"So, let's make a deal."

"Okay, Sid. I'll give you the Garden at a bargain price of twenty-five thousand dollars, and that's only because of my grandkids. You get everything for that money—tickets, ushers, lights, stage-hands. It's all yours."

"Great, Ned. You've got a deal."

I called Ben Bart, James Brown's agent and manager, the same Ben Bart that I used to collude with several times a day at the Paramount when James would refuse to go on for every conceivable reason.

"Ben, I want to present James in the Garden."

"The Garden, Sid?"

"Yeah, you heard me right, Ben. James Brown in Madison Square Garden."

"Sid, you're kidding! James would love to play the Garden."

"Well, you've got it. Everything set. All I need to know is if James is available."

"Don't worry. He'll make himself available. How many shows?"

"Only one. There are seventeen thousand seats, for heaven's sake. . . . I'll offer you guys twenty thousand dollars for the one show. How does that sound?"

"No problem! Of course, I have to check with James, but twenty grand sounds fine."

"Great. Ben, this is going to be the first rock concert ever at Madison Square Garden!"

A few days later, Ben confirmed the deal.

"Sid, James is really excited."

"As well he should be, Ben."

Every seat for James Brown at the Garden was filled. He literally rocked the house. James got the entire audience to join hands and sway to the music. Blacks and whites clasping hands, the chain extending all around the Garden. Such is the power of a great performer, and such is the power of music.

The success of that event confirmed to me the Garden's viability as a concert venue, and next I decided to promote my own group there. The Rascals were becoming a fixture on the charts, first with "I Ain't Gonna Eat Out My Heart Anymore," then "Good Lovin'," followed by "You Better Run." They were ready.

I called Ned Irish: "I'm going to make you a hero again."

"Really, Sid? How's that?"

"Tell your grandchildren that Sid Bernstein is going to bring the Rascals to the Garden."

"Who?"

"Just tell them the Rascals."

"Sid, you were right on the last one. I'll take your word for it."

"Same deal, Ned?"

"Same deal."

Ned Irish was very happy because the James Brown concert had opened up a new revenue stream. I had become one of his favorite people.

The crowd in the Garden were really turned on by the Rascals. There is nothing like seventeen thousand people screaming, whistling and applauding to get the adrenaline going. Sheer energy.

After that concert, I knew that I was dealing with a major act, and I escalated their price from five thousand to seven thousand dollars per show. I couldn't fill even a fraction of the requests for their appearances.

The Rascals subsequently played at the Singer Bowl, on the grounds of New York's old World's Fair, to a sold-out audience of twelve thousand. Many were turned away. The Rascals owned New York.

IT WAS MY HABIT to call Brian Epstein in London from time to time just to chat and find out how he was doing. The Beatles had stopped touring, and I hoped Brian could now enjoy some leisure.

Cordial and considerate, Brian would always inquire about Gerry and the kids. "Any new ones?" he would invariably ask. And there always was. During one such call, in the summer of 1967, Brian told me that he was coming to New York in two weeks.

"Sid, I'm going to be at the Waldorf. Come by and we can talk about some of my new acts and spend some time together."

"I'll look forward to that."

I called Brian at the Waldorf.

"Hello, Sid. How is your day today? Do you have some free time?"

"Sure. I have my wife with me. Your boys always kidded me about never seeing or meeting her. Now you can tell them that she really does exist."

He chuckled. "I'd adore meeting her. Come right on over!"

Gerry and I went to the Waldorf. Brian looked worn out, but he went out of his way to be courteous and solicitous of Gerry, who at the time was very pregnant with Dylan, our second son. We drank tea, and Brian asked her about our other children, Denise and Adam. I inquired about Queenie and the Beatles, of course. Then we devoted an hour to plans he had for some of his new acts and ways I could be involved in presenting them in New York.

After a while, Brian told us that he had to leave for a meeting with Murray the K and offered to drop us at home. We all got into his limousine, and on the surface everything seemed ordinary. But Brian didn't exhibit his customary energy.

"Tell me, Brian, is anything wrong? You don't look well to me."

"Just too much pressure, Sid. It has not been an easy time."

"You have to take care of yourself, Brian. I'm concerned about you."

"I'm trying to do that, Sid. I really am."

Brian got out of the car and told the chauffeur to take Gerry and me home and then return for him.

We shook hands. Brian told Gerry how nice it was to finally meet her. He would send my regards to his mother and the boys and call me from London, he said. Then he left.

That was the last time I saw Brian Epstein.

On August 27, 1967, as I was sitting at home doing paperwork, someone called to inform me that Brian Epstein had been found dead in his London townhouse. I was breathless. True, he had not looked well the last time I had seen him, but he was a thirty-two-year-old man in the prime of life, extraordinarily successful, with no known health problems. We had discussed his future plans. He had everything to live for.

I was shattered. I respected and admired that man, and it hurt deeply to think that he was gone. By saying yes to me, Brian Epstein had allowed me to help make music history.

Later that week, I made a dreaded call to Queenie Epstein. Her pain was immeasurable, but as always she was extremely gracious. "Brian was so fond of you, Sid." Amidst all her pain, she was trying to console me. We had all lost something dear and precious, but she had lost the most of all—a child.

FOR A WHILE FOLLOWING Brian's death, I heard rumors that I was going to be asked to take over as the Beatles' manager. I didn't give that talk much credence, and I was never contacted by the Beatles' organization. The rumors made me think back to when Robert Stigwood, Brian and I had met about a possible merger of our companies. What would have happened if we had indeed joined forces? It's the great "What if . . .?" game at its ultimate.

15

People Got to Be Free

FROM A BUSINESS PERSPECTIVE, as my jazz buddies would say, I was smokin'! My friend Manheim Fox, a folk expert, gave me a call.

"Sid, you've promoted everything . . . jazz, R&B, Latin, pop, the Beatles, the Stones—"

"Stop, Manny. Flattery will get you everywhere. What do you want from me?"

"You've never done a folk concert. Folk is hotter than hell, and I think you should do a festival."

Manny was right. Folk was in. I was far from an expert, but I had been exposed to many folk acts in the Village.

"Manny, I like the idea, but I don't know if I—"

"Don't worry. I'll help you."

With that assurance, and knowing that Billy Fields was great at lining up talent, we booked Carnegie Hall for a four-day festival. Mrs. Satescu wasn't concerned about the demeanor of the audience: they were guaranteed to be well-behaved. So we signed Dave

Van Ronk, Mississippi John Hurt, the Greenbriar Boys, Buffy Sainte-Marie, Phil Ochs and Jesse Colin Young. To spice it up—and for no logical reason—we added Chuck Berry, the Staple Singers, Mose Allison, the Statler Brothers, June Carter and Johnny Cash. In retrospect, the lineup was really an amalgam of country, jazz, R&B and folk.

Manny brought in his friend John Stevens as a copromoter, but I put up the money for the entire four-day festival. It ran in mid-June 1968 and received great critical reviews, but I lost about eighteen thousand dollars. Perhaps surprisingly, I was not overly disturbed. I had the money and chalked it up as a learning experience.

One of the highlights of the festival was visiting Johnny Cash in his dressing room. "Sid, can you please tell me what the hell I'm doing in a festival with jazz and R&B!" The expression on Johnny's face sent me into hysterics.

IN EARLY MAY, MY MOTHER was admitted to the hospital for still another attempt to relieve the pain she had been coping with her whole life. She had the strength to make it through the operation, but fell into a coma shortly thereafter. I visited Mama three or four times a day until, on May 15, 1968, she passed away. It was unexpected, and the anguish was indescribable. My mother had suffered almost all the days I knew her. We buried her and sat shiva.

A short while later, Israeli singing star Shoshana Damari convinced me to do an Israeli all-star show in the Garden. That event, the last I was to promote in the old Madison Square Garden on Fifty-second Street and Eighth Avenue, was dedicated to the memory of my mother.

PETER NERO HAD BEEN the piano player at Jilly's restaurant, Frank Sinatra's hangout. I would drop by there periodically, and Peter and I became friendly. He was making records and they were selling, and my instinct was that he was ready for a concert career.

I approached Peter about performing at Carnegie Hall. He agreed and we scheduled a performance date. We followed the usual publicity routine—posters, handbills—but the concert's success was assured by

Peter's wife, who happened to be a member of the Jewish women's charitable organization Hadassah. She galvanized the Hadassah ladies behind the concert, and they sold a lot of tickets. Had I been able to enlist their aid in selling tickets for every event with which I was involved, sellouts would have been continually assured.

WHEN THE BEATLES CAME on the scene back in 1964, the winds of change started to blow. Clothing, hairstyles, sexual mores, language—nothing was immune. The world I had grown up in was gone. Nowhere was that more obvious than at Woodstock.

In 1969, Artie Kornfeld, John Roberts, Joel Rosenman and Michael Lang had decided to stage a rock festival in that upstate New York town, but when the town fathers canceled the festival permits, the producers took it to Bethel, fifty miles away. The Rascals were invited to perform, but they had a previous engagement. As for me, Gerry was again pregnant and I couldn't leave her and the kids for four days. But I watched the news reports from Bethel and saw the traffic jams and the enormous crowds. The turnout was staggering. Later in the year, in Altamont, California, another megafestival was held, this time featuring the Rolling Stones. I hated that carelessly run event because there was needless violence and loss of life, and I knew the security arrangements had been lax. It was a tragic moment in rock history.

What was coming across loud and clear was that the gamble I had taken by putting the Beatles in Shea had set a precedent. Rock-and-roll had proven that it was capable of drawing huge crowds to very large venues.

The new Madison Square Garden was being built atop Penn Station, bordered by Thirty-first and Thirty-third Streets and Seventh and Eighth Avenues. It was to be a beautiful arena with almost twenty thousand seats and state-of-the-art sound and lighting. Besides the Knicks, the Rangers, college basketball, and the Ringling Bros. and Barnum & Bailey circus—all of which were already in place—music and concerts were contemplated for the new Garden. The appearances of James Brown and the Rascals at the old Garden had cemented that.

Several months before construction was completed, Alvin Cooperman, head booker for the new Madison Square Garden, telephoned.

"Sid, how would you like to produce the first show in the new Garden? We're going to have lots of concerts in this place!"

"Sure, Alvin! I'd love it! . . . Tell me, Alvin, what kind of rental fee will you be asking?"

"Forty thousand a night."

"Okay, I'll get back to you." Forty thousand was a lot, but after all, this Garden was brand new. I wanted the first concert to be a success. I wanted to do something a little different, and I also wanted to make sure that the audience would be orderly.

I called Manny Greenfield, manager for Joan Baez.

"Manny, they've built a magnificent new Madison Square Garden here in New York, and I have been awarded the inaugural concert. I'd love to present Joan."

"Hey, Sid, you know we're getting a lot of money for Joan these days."

"I'm sure you are. But I don't care about the money. I'll give you even more than you're getting! I really want Joan to open the new Garden."

"Well, what's your offer, Sid?"

"How about twenty thousand, Manny?"

"That's good! Let me take it up with Joan."

A few days later, I got the return call. "Sid, I have a problem."

"What's that, Manny?"

"Joan doesn't want twenty thousand dollars."

"Well . . . how much does she want?"

"Five thousand."

"What? Could you repeat that?"

"Five thousand dollars, Sid."

"Manny, could you explain that to me? I offered her twenty thousand dollars."

"Joan wants you to charge only two dollars per ticket for all seats on a first-come, first-served basis, and she and I both understand that at that price you can't make any money. You might even lose money. No preferential treatment for anybody. She wants

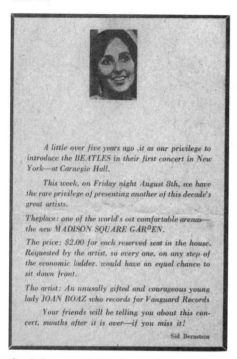

Socially-conscious singer Joan Baez was gracious about the misspelling of her name in this ad.

everybody to be able to afford a ticket."

I did a quick calculation. The sold-out house would gross only forty thousand dollars. Joan would get five thousand, and the Garden would cost forty thousand. I would be losing five thousand dollars. I wanted to be first in Madison Square Garden and Alvin Cooperman liked the idea of Joan Baez. I could afford to lose the five thousand dollars.

"You got it, Manny. Five thousand dollars it is. All tickets, two bucks."

I called the Garden and told Alvin Cooperman the deal. He couldn't believe it. He also explained to me that because of Joan's political leanings, he was going to have to put on extra security in case there was a demonstration.

"Okay, Alvin. Whatever you need . . ."

"No, no, Sid! We'll take care of the security. You're going to lose enough money."

The concert sold out immediately. The combination of Joan, the ticket price and the new arena ensured that. I decided to put Joan on in the round, which meant that she would be right in the middle of the Garden floor. So that everyone would have a chance to see her, I thought it would be nice if the stage rotated ever so slowly while Joan sang and accompanied herself on guitar. She and Manny loved the idea and approved it immediately on the condition that the stage would turn slowly enough to ensure Joan's safety.

The concert was unforgettable. I ordered rose petals by the bushel to be strewn all over the stage and at its base. When Joan walked onstage to a thunderous ovation, she was ankle-deep in a carpet of flower petals. Gerry and Adam sat with me, and this time I chose to sit in the front row, a rarity, so that Gerry and Adam would enjoy those delicious rose petals.

Joan was wonderful, and the audience loved her. Following her first encore, five-year-old Adam, with no encouragement from his parents, walked up onto the stage and gave Joan a rose petal. She leaned down and kissed him, and the Garden erupted. People started to stream downstairs from the higher seats toward the stage. The ushers wanted to stop them, but I told the head usher that I would bear the responsibility. During her second encore, hundreds of people surrounded Joan on the petal-strewn floor, singing along with her while the stage slowly turned. It was a moving sight.

Alvin Cooperman and the Garden hierarchy were so elated with the Joan Baez concert that they cut the price of the house by five thousand dollars.

"We don't want you to lose money, Sid," Alvin said. "You did such a great job! Thanks!"

It was a very nice gesture. I accepted it in the spirit it was given, and in the way I saw it, I came out more than even.

AROUND THIS TIME, Sly and the Family Stone burst onto the music scene. I knew about Sly Stone and his act, and once I heard his records on the radio, I understood why he was gaining momentum like a tidal wave.

David Kapralik had signed Sly and the Family Stone to Epic while still an A&R (Artists and Repertoire) man there. He had quit that post at Epic to become the group's manager when he realized how big they were going to be. I liked David a lot, and I especially admired him for having the guts to quit a successful A&R job to manage Sly.

David called me. "Sid, I'd love it if you could present Sly at the Garden."

"I'd love to, David. I've been watching what's going on. This kid could be the biggest!"

"I know. . . . Listen, Sid, you don't have to put up your own money. I'll take care of that. I just want you to handle the Garden, put together the rest of the bill and put your name on the promotion. And . . . I'll pay you for your time."

"I'd be glad to do it, David."

I called Alvin Cooperman and secured the date of February 13 at the Garden. I explained that I would need the entire room, because three other acts would be on the bill with Sly and the Family Stone, and I needed the arena's full capacity.

"We can't do this in the round like Joan. It won't work, Alvin. We need to set up a proscenium stage, but we need to sell the entire room. I can't help it if some of the fans will see only the performers' backs."

"Anything you want, Sid."

I booked the opening acts, Fleetwood Mac and Grand Funk Railroad. I also decided that I wanted to include a young comedian whom I used to kid around with at the Bitter End, so I booked Richard Pryor.

The concert sold out immediately. I got calls from record execs and music people all over the United States and Canada. Everyone wanted tickets. It wasn't the same level of excitement as with the Beatles, but it was close. Now, it's easy to understand why: Fleetwood Mac, Grand Funk Railroad, Richard Pryor, and Sly and the Family Stone on one bill. I could have sold out a hundred-thousand-seat stadium. People were offering me scalper prices for my reserve tickets, but I refused to be tempted. I was looking forward to the show, particularly because it was a chance to help Richard Pryor.

Fleetwood Mac opened the concert with a great half-hour. They'll be a big act in short order, I thought.

I was sitting in the fourth row on the aisle so I would be available to deal with the constant stream of messages and questions coming my way without disturbing anyone in the vicinity. One of those messages was that Sly had not yet arrived. I hurried to find someone in the Stone entourage and was told not to worry because Sly was at a nearby hotel and would appear onstage as scheduled.

Richard Pryor came on next. I had asked him to do eighteen minutes.

"Good evening, ladies and gentlemen!" Richard began, then

paused for effect and slowly looked around the packed Garden. "I don't know what a kid like me is doing in a fuckin' rock 'n' roll show like this!"

I didn't believe what I was hearing. Alvin Cooperman was sitting in the front row with his two teenage daughters. I quickly glanced over at him. I hoped and prayed that was the end of it.

Richard went on: "I want all you folks to relax and loosen your ties . . ." I glanced at Alvin again, and I could see his head swiveling around, trying to see crowd reaction. "I'm so flabbergasted to be in the company of these great musicians and these great people . . ." Richard stopped and surveyed the entire Garden. ". . . and look at this fuckin' place, it's filled to the rafters!"

The head usher was with Alvin, pointing in my direction. It was only three or four minutes into Richard's set, and I was thinking, *Oh, my God! We're going to have another fourteen minutes of this profanity!*

Just then, the usher rushed over to me. "Mr. Bernstein, Mr. Cooperman wants to see you."

"Tell him that I know exactly what he wants. I'll handle it."

Richard threw another one of his "fuckin'" lines out and, with that, Alvin Cooperman jumped up and rushed his two girls out of the room.

I hurried to the front of the stage and instructed my stage manager to tell Richard to cut the profanity.

"Tell him, Alan, to stop it! And I mean immediately."

Alan called Richard over to the side of the stage, and as he spoke, I could see Richard nodding his head in agreement. Alan hurried over to me. "It's okay now, Sid. I told him what you said and he said he understands."

By this time, the audience was no doubt wondering what was going on. Richard sauntered back to the mike, put his hand over his eyes to shield them from the lights, and began to look the audience over, as if to find one person. Me!

"Folks," he said. "Please forgive me. The show must go on . . . and I was starting to tell you a story that I'll finish in a minute. But I'm sure you want to know what just went on here and why I left the mike to talk to that man." He pointed to Alan. "Well, Sid Bernstein, the fuckin' promoter, asked me to watch my language!"

The audience was laughing so hard that they didn't hear him say, "What's wrong with that man?" You could almost see the waves of laughter. I have always hated profanity, but I must admit that Richard was hilarious that night. He, of course, went on to have a superstar career on stage, screen and television, and I wish him the best in his battle against multiple sclerosis. But, I will never forget those eighteen minutes.

Grand Funk Railroad went on after Richard Pryor. I had to get them to stretch their set to cover for Sly and his family, who showed up an hour and a half late, much to my anger and dismay. However, once Sly started to sing and play, he was astonishing. His movements, his band, his persona just took over. His tardiness became a distant memory. But, that behavior was a tip-off to me. As far as I was concerned, Sly's conduct would limit his career. History unfortunately proved me right.

WHEN THE BEATLES OFFICIALLY broke up in 1970, everyone in the music business was saddened. They had given so much to the industry. Their great talent was no longer going to be heard the same way again. Each would go it alone. It was as if the light and power of the comet had burned out.

America was embroiled in the Vietnam War, and society was in turmoil. Drugs had become a major issue. Respect for authority was being questioned. A feeling of uncertainty was prevalent everywhere. I was vehemently against the war. I had seen war firsthand as a soldier, and the thought of American boys perishing in the jungles of Vietnam was repugnant to me.

Peter Yarrow, of Peter, Paul & Mary, called one day. I knew Peter from the Bitter End and had been a fan of this group. "Sid, I'd like to do a concert for peace, to protest the Vietnam War, and I'd like to ask you to organize it."

Since I shared his view, I considered this a chance to get involved and make a difference. "I'm in, Peter. And I'll ask the Rascals. We'll do it at the Garden."

"Great, Sid!"

In addition to the Rascals, we lined up Judy Collins and Harry

Belafonte. We also got Jimi Hendrix, which was a coup, or so I thought. It was hard to find a bigger star than Jimi Hendrix at that time.

Because some seats were behind the stage, and the sightlines would have been blocked by all the equipment and set-up activities, those seats were not used. Specifically for this event, we had built something akin to a wall to serve as a backdrop for the performers and also help amplify the sound. Hendrix was the second act to go on. He started to play and, after about a minute, backed up, slumped against the temporary backdrop and slid down the wall until he was eventually sitting on the stage. It was obvious that Jimi's weird behavior was drug-induced, and I told the stagehands to remove him from the stage. No one, least of all the audience, was happy about my decision, but I would not allow Jimi Hendrix to make a fool of himself.

WED., JAN. 28
FROM 8 P.M. TO 1 A.M.
(5 HOUR FESTIVAL)
ONE PERFORMANCE ONLY!
WINTER FESTIVAL FOR PEACE
HARRY BELEFONTE
BLOOD, SWEAT & TEARS
DAVE BRUBECK
with McHENRY BOATWRIGHT
JUDY COLLINS
RICHIE HAVENS
THE CAST OF HAIR
JIMI HENDRIX AND
HIS BAND OF GYPSIES
MOTHER EARTH
PETER PAUL & MARY
THE RASCALS
ALL NET PROCEEDS TO MORATORIUM FUND.
CONTRIBUTIONS WILL BE ACCEPTED BY MAIL IF YOU CAN NOT PERSONALLY ATTEND.
NAME_____ ADDRESS_____
SEND ALL CONTRIBUTIONS TO: VIETNAM MORATORIUM COMMITTEE 415 EAST 52 ST 3 B-C NEW YORK 10022
Produced by SID BERNSTEIN
PRICES: $7.50, $6, $5, $4
BOX OFFICE OPENS WED., JAN. 21
madison square garden
Pennsylvania Plaza,
7th Ave., 31st to 33rd Sts.

This ad appeared in New York papers in 1970.

This was one of many occasions when that great talent could not fulfill a professional commitment because of drug use. The combination of fame, money and power was apparently too much for him to handle. How tragic that Jimi Hendrix lost his life to drugs, and at such a young age.

EVEN WITH THE HENDRIX MISHAP, the peace concert had tremendous support, and we were all proud to participate. For me, organizing the event was a labor of love.

I enjoyed organizing events in support of worthy causes, so when Jerry Wexler of Atlantic asked me to organize a benefit for the Martin Luther King Foundation, it was a natural fit. "Atlantic will provide all

NATRA & ATLANTIC RECORDS
Present A
SOUL TOGETHER
for the benefit of the
MARTIN LUTHER KING FUND
and the
NATRA SUMMER PROGRAM

starring

**ARETHA FRANKLIN
THE RASCALS
SAM & DAVE
SONNY & CHÉR
JOE TEX
KING CURTIS & THE KINGPINS**

THE NEW MADISON SQUARE GARDEN, NEW YORK, JUNE 28, 1968
Entire Production Supervised and Produced by Sid Bernstein

CREDITS:
NATRA and ATLANTIC RECORDS want to thank the following
for their contributions to the "Soul Together" Show:

Publicity: Dick Gersh, Major Robinson
Producer's staff: Dave Brigati, Sherry Arber

We also wish to thank Radio Stations WABC, WLIB, WMCA, WNEW, WNJR,
WOR-FM, and WWRL, for their public service announcements for the show.

PHOTO CREDITS:
ARETHA FRANKLIN/David Gahr   THE RASCALS/Ira Mazur
KING CURTIS/Stephen Paley   JOE TEX/Don Bronstein
SAM & DAVE/Flair Photography Ltd.   SONNY & CHER/Andy Leo

the acts, Sid. You just run the concert." I did not want anyone to think that the concert was a commercial venture.

As promised, Atlantic involved most of their acts in the benefit. On the Garden bill were Sam & Dave, Sonny & Cher, Aretha Franklin, the Voices of East Harlem and the Rascals. The place was jammed, and at the end of the evening I proudly announced from the stage that we had been able to raise seventy-three thousand dollars for the King Foundation.

IN 1968, THERE WAS A super group called Blood, Sweat & Tears on the rise. I wanted to present them in concert at the Garden, so I called Bennett Glazer, their manager, and his response was enthusiastic.

Bennett and I negotiated a price of forty thousand dollars for the band, and the Garden wanted its usual forty thousand. I also allocated fifteen thousand dollars for advertising and promotion. In addition, I decided that I wanted Miles Davis on the bill. Blood, Sweat & Tears was a horn band, and who better to pair them with than Davis, king of the horn?

Miles agreed to make the appearance for five thousand dollars. This was going to be a dream show. Of that I was certain—so much so that I had tentatively reserved the Garden for the following night to accommodate the expected overflow audience. Before anyone had bought a single ticket, I had put out a hundred thousand dollars.

An unfortunate circumstance preceded the concert. During the spring months leading up to the event, Blood, Sweat & Tears went out on a U.S. State Department-sponsored tour. Many of their fans felt that the group had sold out by associating with the Nixon White House, and they boycotted the performance. I don't know if Blood, Sweat & Tears had sold out politically, but I do know that they did not sell out for me at the Garden. Because of the negative publicity surrounding the State Department tour, I had to cancel the second reserved day and hoped that I wouldn't lose a bundle. There was a lot of money at stake . . . and all of it was mine.

On top of that, we began to get threatening phone calls

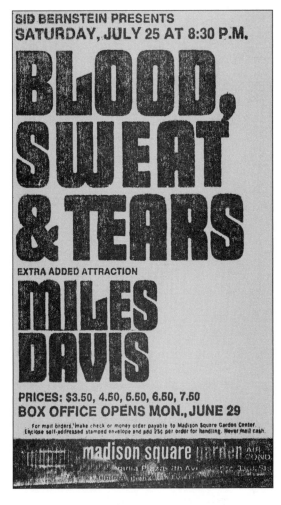

SID BERNSTEIN PRESENTS
SATURDAY, JULY 25 AT 8:30 P.M.

BLOOD, SWEAT & TEARS

EXTRA ADDED ATTRACTION

MILES DAVIS

PRICES: $3.50, 4.50, 5.50, 6.50, 7.50
BOX OFFICE OPENS MON., JUNE 29

For mail orders, make check or money order payable to Madison Square Garden Center. Enclose self-addressed stamped envelope and add 25¢ per order for handling. Never mail cash.

madison square garden

and letters stating that people were going to throw bags of horse manure on the stage to protest the group's participation in the State Department tour. In response, I immediately increased security, which in turn increased expenses.

We sold somewhere between 60 and 65 percent of the tickets. As I sat in the audience and listened to the great music, I knew that I was going to lose approximately twenty thousand dollars.

Blood, Sweat & Tears finished their set, and I immediately left my seat to congratulate them on their performance. David Clayton Thomas, their sensational lead singer, came offstage, stopped and shook my hand.

"Sid, don't worry. . . . You're not going to lose any money," he said.

I returned to my seat, and Blood, Sweat & Tears came back for an encore. After the show, I went to the dressing room to say goodnight and pay the band. All of the band was there, and so was Bennett Glazer.

"Why the long face? You broke even," Bennett said.

"What do you mean?" I asked. My calculation was that I had lost twenty grand.

"We're reducing our fee by twenty thousand dollars. You broke even."

Those were young guys with great sensitivity and a manager with a lot of heart.

IN APRIL 1970, Billboard invited me to speak at their annual convention. That year the magazine's conference was to be held in Mallorca, off the coast of Spain. Gerry was quite pregnant with our fourth child, but she was given medical permission to travel, so we decided to go together.

Mallorca is beautiful, and Gerry enjoyed herself immensely. I spoke on a program with Bill Graham, the legendary manager and West Coast impresario who was involved with Jefferson Airplane, Santana, the Grateful Dead and others. Also on the panel were Paul Marshall, a top show-business attorney, and Lee Eastman, a leading labor lawyer whose daughter Linda was a big Rascals fan and Paul McCartney's new wife. A huge group attended our panel. Bill Graham, whom I had never met, was a dynamic orator. I was the last speaker on the schedule, and I chose to discuss music as an international language.

After my remarks, the head of a major German record and publishing conglomerate approached me. "Mr. Bernstein, if we had more gatherings like this and more speakers like you, we wouldn't have to worry about the brotherhood of man and peace in the world. I will not forget what you have said here."

Nor will I forget that moment.

OUR THIRD SON, BEAU, was born on June 13, 1970. I was working constantly, but all I wanted was to be with my family. In fact, the Rascals often tell stories of my attending sessions at the recording studios and falling asleep shortly after my arrival. I remember thinking that if I fell asleep often enough, the Rascals would stop asking me to come to the studio.

On one of my visits, I was enjoying a nice snooze when I was awakened by a commotion. The four Rascals were in the studio with Arif Mardin and Tom Dowd. Felix Cavaliere was angry and berating Eddie Brigati, as usual, for his tardiness in completing a lyric. Gene, Dino, Arif and Tom stood apart from the fray and looked on. I watched the scene from the darkened control room as the debate between Felix and Eddie escalated. After a few minutes, I decided to diffuse the tension. I stood up and removed my loafers and trousers, revealing a pair of underwear that I refused to discard because my mother had darned them for me many times in threads of many colors. With my ample belly hanging out, I proceeded to tiptoe into the small area between the control room and the studio. I then burst through the door and streaked across the studio floor in my socks and underwear. If anything would break the tension, that would! The fellas started laughing so hard that the animosity quickly evaporated. . . . Eddie completed the lyric, and everyone returned to work.

A temporary reprieve. . . But all was not well in the land of the Rascals.

PETER YARROW WANTED TO do another peace concert, this time in an outdoor stadium to attract as large a crowd as possible.

"Sid, we did so well last winter at the Garden. Let's do it again this summer."

The war was on everyone's mind. Street protests were increasing, and the college kids were becoming more and more agitated. I felt even more passionately that this war was not ours to fight and that we should get out of Vietnam.

"Peter, this time we'll do it at Shea and have fifty-five thousand people."

"Great, Sid! Great! We're on!"

We had to organize the concert in eight to ten days. In my entire career as a promoter, I never had to organize such a big concert in such a short amount of time. The bill featured Richie Havens, Miles Davis, the Staple Singers, Paul Simon, Janis Joplin, Steppenwolf, Creedence Clearwater Revival, the cast of *Hair*, Peter Yarrow and, of course, the Rascals. Murray the K was the emcee. We started at noon, and the concert ended at 9:30 in the evening. That place was rocking!

During the Rascals' rendition of "People Got to Be Free," a number-one record worldwide, Murray the K had to stop the boys midsong. Shea Stadium management requested that we halt the concert because the fifty-five thousand concertgoers were jumping up and down so hard that the stadium was actually shaking. (The lower stands at Shea are built on rails, underpinned by springs so that they can be moved for football games.) It was thrilling to actually see the stadium palpitating, but I understood management's concern. We found a solution: Peter Yarrow got up and sang "Puff the Magic Dragon" and asked everyone to stop jumping on the seats. That did the trick.

Janis Joplin showed up as high as a kite, and I was trying to talk her out of going onstage. She insisted that she wanted to go on but would not make her entrance until it was dark, to heighten the drama. Finally, I had to inform Janis that she would not be allowed to perform. I wasn't about to watch her fall off a stage fifteen feet high.

GRAND FUNK RAILROAD was one of the opening acts I had booked for Sly and the Family Stone at the Garden. Terry Knight very capably managed Grand Funk, and they had become huge since their Garden appearance. I considered Terry one of the brightest and best managers I had ever met. One day, he called.

"Sid, I need your help. I want to put Grand Funk Railroad in Shea Stadium. You don't have to put up a dime; I'll pay for everything. All I want you to do is handle the arrangements with the people at Shea and let me use your name as the concert promoter. If you agree, I'll give you twenty-five thousand."

Grand Funk was a happening group. I thought it would be the easiest twenty-five thousand dollars I would ever make.

"Why not? You got a deal."

"Oh, yeah, Sid. One more thing. I want to break the Beatles' revenue record for a single concert, which you set in 1965. Can you please scale the tickets so we could gross a little more than they did?"

"Sure, I'll do it. With my name on the posters and in the publicity, it'll look like I'm breaking my own record. I love it! No problem!"

I made three times as much from that promotion as I did from both Beatles concerts. And it was easy; I made all the arrangements in three days. We filled Shea Stadium, and the place was jumping. We took in around three hundred and thirty thousand dollars. Everyone thought that I was responsible, but it was really Terry Knight and Grand Funk Railroad.

WILLIAM MORRIS IS ONE OF the leading talent agencies in the world, with an impressive client list. The tradition at William Morris was to put all the newly hired and aspiring agents in the mailroom and see if they could work their way up. The thinking was that if someone had the drive and creativity to get out of the mailroom, they would probably make a successful agent. One day, I got a call from David Geffen, an agent who had recently graduated from the mailroom. I had seen him at clubs and concerts, and we became friendly.

"Sid, we just signed Laura Nyro, who's a fantastic singer/songwriter. She has an album that's going to be released on Columbia Records soon, and she needs a manager. I'd like to recommend you. I think you'd work well together."

"Where can I hear her?"

"She just moved to the city. She's got no furniture in her apartment, but she does have a piano and some folding chairs. Why don't you meet me there later today?"

I went over after work. David introduced me to Laura, who was quite shy. I sat on one of the folding chairs, and the young woman sat at the piano with her back to us. When she started to play, I could tell immediately that she was something special. I was very tired after a long day at the office, and it didn't help that I couldn't see her face. Before long, I fell asleep. It's not easy running one of the hottest bands in the world and raising four young kids at the same time. I wasn't getting much rest. David jabbed me in the ribs. "Hey, Sid!" he whispered. "You're snoring, and she can hear you. She's getting angry. Come on! Stay awake!"

"I'm sorry," I whispered back. "She's really great. I must apologize—"

"No, don't say a word."

When Laura finished singing, I told her how much I had enjoyed listening. Then David and I left.

Unbeknownst to me, Laura and Felix Cavaliere of the Rascals knew each other. Laura confided in Felix that I had fallen asleep while she was playing for me and that she never wanted to speak to me again. Felix tried to defend me, but to no avail.

The next time I spoke to David, he told me that he believed in Laura so much that he was planning to leave William Morris to manage her. My slumber, which so angered Laura, gave David Geffen the opportunity to become Laura Nyro's manager and subsequently develop his own fabulous career. This extremely talented man, along with Jeffrey Katzenberg and Steven Spielberg, started DreamWorks. I have no doubt that he would have found another way to initiate his success, but I'd like to think that my untimely nap helped him get there a little faster.

THE RASCALS' RECORDING CONTRACT with Atlantic was up for renewal. and I began to negotiate with Jerry Wexler and Ahmet and Nesuhi Ertegun. I explained that I wanted the Rascals to remain with Atlantic and that we had upheld our end of the original agreement, even though we probably could have renegotiated when the Rascals started to produce one hit after another. I expected that Atlantic would want to reward our loyalty.

When Jerry Wexler got back to me, he was less than encouraging. The last Rascals album, he said, had done poorly because Felix had become a disciple of the Swami Satchadananda and the music had gone off on a spiritual tangent. The brass at Atlantic was not sure that the group could recapture its winning ways. Jerry's counteroffer was not what I had in mind. I told him that I needed to think it over, but I really wanted to test the waters elsewhere.

I was annoyed with Atlantic. When the label was desperate for a white act to help it become more mainstream, the Rascals had filled the bill. In fact, the group had put them on the map to such a degree that Atlantic now had many white acts and had become one of the major record companies in the world. I felt that Atlantic should show its appreciation.

Word spread that the Rascals were looking for another record company, and I got many calls. Rocco Laginestra, head of RCA, offered a million-dollar advance. That was tempting. Then, Clive Davis, a former lawyer who had the magic touch for Columbia when it came to songs, artists and records, offered me the same basic deal that Rocco and RCA had. I recommended to my boys that we sign with Columbia because I felt that Clive and Columbia would be a perfect fit for a group like the Rascals, whose members wanted to produce their own records with minimal supervision. I loved Rocco and respected his business acumen, but Clive Davis was a music guy, and the Rascals needed a music guy. The boys agreed.

I called Atlantic and told Jerry Wexler that the Rascals were going to sign with Columbia. He wished us luck. I then called Clive and told him of our decision.

"Sidney," Clive said, "we should try to keep this between us. Next week we're having the Columbia Records International Convention in Freeport, the Bahamas. We bring in Columbia people from all over the world to talk business and have some fun. I'd like to fly the Rascals in secretly and surprise everyone at the convention with news of the signing. We'll put them behind a curtain while I make my opening remarks. After I finish, I'll introduce them as our newest artists. It will be very dramatic!"

"Sounds great to me, Clive. And you can be sure we'll keep things mum."

The Columbia lawyers worked feverishly, and the Rascals contract was finally ready for signing just three days before we were to leave for Freeport. We scheduled a meeting to review the contract. The attorneys, accountants, members of the Rascals and I sat around a conference table. Steve Weiss took the floor.

"Fellas, I'm going to give everyone around this table a copy of the Columbia Records contract. We're going to read through it paragraph by paragraph. You may ask questions at any time. I worked very hard on this with the attorneys from Columbia. Sid has negotiated a terrific deal for you, and we need to have this finished before you take off for Freeport."

Steve began to read, and we breezed through the agreement quickly. Everyone seemed happy. The boys liked the idea of signing with Columbia and were enthused about working with Clive Davis. And the million-dollar advance didn't hurt, either.

Steve passed a pen to each of the guys, and they were poised to sign. Then, with his pen raised in midair, Felix said: "I want to know just one thing. Are we going to give value for value received? This is a lot of money we're getting, and I just want to know if all of us are going to give value for the money."

I knew that his remarks were directed at Eddie, and I immediately became nervous.

Felix looked at Gene and asked him if he was okay with the deal. Gene was already envisioning the new car he was going to buy; he looked at Felix and nodded his okay. Felix then asked Dino, and he nodded his agreement. Eddie gave Felix a searing look.

"Felix, what the hell are you talking about?" Eddie said. He then stood up, dropped his pen and stormed out of the conference room. Everyone was motionless. I raced out after Eddie, who was waiting for an elevator.

"Eddie, what are you doing? There's a million dollars on the table! Come on back. We'll work it out."

Eddie took an album he was carrying and blocked his face. I think he was crying. He was still a kid, just twenty-three or so at the time. The elevator doors opened and Eddie got in. "Forget it, Sid. Just forget it," he said. And the doors closed.

I went back to the conference room. The remaining Rascals were discussing what to do now. We wanted to sign the contract and show up in Freeport as we had promised Clive.

Gene had friends in a Rascals cover band, the Brass Buttons, based in Rochester, New York. Their lead singer, Jay Capozzi, looked like Eddie. Gene suggested that we get the lead singer of the Brass Buttons as a replacement. I was pleased to see Gene thinking on his feet. Still, I felt that I had to call Clive and explain the situation.

"Sid," Clive responded, "get those contracts signed and over to me ASAP! We're prepared to make the announcement at the convention. I want the band there!"

"Fine," I said. I was relieved, but hoped Eddie would return to the band.

The day before our scheduled appearance, we arrived in Freeport undetected. I found a remote rehearsal studio, and the boys immediately began rehearsing with Jay Capozzi. Jay was a very good singer and eager to please.

On the convention's opening night, we sneaked into the hotel. The ballroom was packed. As Clive began his remarks, the boys got into position behind the closed curtain. They waited patiently until Clive concluded: "This has been a wonderful year for Columbia. We have reached new heights in sales and revenues. And, ladies and gentlemen, behind this curtain we have our latest talent acquisition. They will lead us to even greater heights. It is my pleasure to present them. Ladies and gentlemen—the Young Rascals!"

The curtain parted, and the audience went wild. The Rascals went into their first song. I sat near the front, and Tony Orlando, who was running Columbia's publishing company at the time, slid over to me. "Hey, Sid. Is that Eddie Brigati up there?"

I placed my fingers over my lips.

"Sid," he whispered again, "is that Eddie?"

"Tony, be quiet, please!" Tony Orlando, who a few years later became a star with "Tie a Yellow Ribbon Round the Ole Oak Tree," was so attuned to the music world that he knew something was amiss.

Jay Capozzi did a great job, but I could see the handwriting on the wall. The Rascals were in free fall. Eddie Brigati was gone for good, and Felix would never find another lyricist who could lock into his music. I was the captain of a sinking ship.

MY FONDEST MEMORY OF the Rascals' time at Columbia actually has nothing to do with the group. Shortly after we began working together, I went to the Columbia recording studios on East Fifty-second Street to see how things were proceeding. The building housed many studios and rehearsal rooms, and even though I had directions to the studio where the Rascals were working, I got a little lost. I randomly began opening door after door, until I came upon a room that was in semidarkness. Seated on a blanket, I saw two adults and two children having a picnic. Not wanting to disturb, I quickly turned to leave.

"Hello, Sid," said a familiar voice. I turned back to see Linda and Paul McCartney and their children taking a break from recording. We chatted briefly, and they wished me luck with the Rascals' new deal.

I walked away in amazement. What a wonderful scene I had just witnessed! Linda and Paul were big stars in the show-business universe, but to their children they were just Mom and Dad.

CLIVE DAVIS WAS TRUE to his word. He took the Rascals into the studio, and they began to record with their new lead singer. But the chemistry was gone. Despite the rancor and animosity, Eddie and Felix had been able to turn out hit songs. Without Eddie, there would be no more hits. The long, slow decline of the Rascals had begun. The requests for appearances diminished, and so did their price. Twenty months later, it was all over.

Although the Rascals did not achieve the kind of longevity that I had envisioned, for two-and-a-half years in the late '60s they were the number-one band in the U.S. and a favorite of other great bands around the world. I was proud to have been their manager and grateful for all the success they had enjoyed.

What, people ask, happened to those guys?

Felix Cavaliere is an extremely intelligent man. During the Rascals' heyday, he was the musical soul of the group. Felix had a strong social conscience and insisted that black acts open their concerts. I was especially proud of his enlightened views. Years later, he demonstrated a natural aptitude for business and made some shrewd real-estate acquisitions using some of the money that he made with the Rascals. He now lives in Nashville, where he writes and is involved in the music business.

Eddie Brigati is a good-natured, gregarious soul with a great sense of humor. He went out of his way to provide for his family. I identified with him as far as family and relationships were concerned. He has energy to spare and was a wonderful lyricist and front man for the group when things were going well. Eddie currently lives in New Jersey. We haven't spoken in years.

Dino Danelli, the quiet one, is a great drummer with a unique style and sense of showmanship. With his erect posture on the drumstand and his ability to twirl the drumsticks, Dino provided a solid steady beat and brought energy and excitement to the act. He lives in New York and is now a record producer, as well as a fine painter. We talk from time to time.

Gene Cornish came from Rochester and his ambition brought him into the Rascals. Gene was attracted to the finer things in life and had a penchant for fancy cars. He was great in a crisis. Gene lives in New Jersey and is still involved in the music business. We have stayed in touch over the years.

In 1999, the Rascals were inducted into the Rock and Roll Hall of Fame in Cleveland. I was happy and proud to see them receive such a well-deserved honor. I always knew that the Rascals and their music would stand the test of time.

BY THE TIME OUR FIFTH CHILD and second daughter, Casey, was born, on November 25, 1971, the Rascals had broken up. I was beginning to reevaluate my business life. My overhead was high, the financial burdens enormous, and the Rascals' breakup caused conflict within my family. I had put all my financial eggs in that one basket, and we certainly had had a great run. The Rascals had made many hit records and generated considerable amounts of money. We were all living the great life.

Gerry and I had acquired a large, expensive apartment in Manhattan to accommodate our growing family. We had household help. All the kids were enrolled in private schools. I had a car and driver.

During those great Rascals years, I had pulled back from concert promotion and had turned down all other acts that approached me about management. I was quite content with my life, both personally and professionally. The most important thing to me was spending time with Gerry and the kids. The Rascals' success enabled me to be an ever-present father and husband, and I was most grateful for that.

However, when the Rascals parted, the cash flow dried up almost immediately. While my income was decreasing, our expenses were increasing.

16

Sinatra, Elvis and . . . Claudy

ABE MARGOLIES WAS CLOSE with manager-promoter Jerry Weintraub and his wife, the lovely chanteuse Jane Morgan. Jerry was an extremely powerful person in the music business. In addition to Jane, he handled John Denver and held the rights to promote Frank Sinatra, Elvis Presley and the Moody Blues. Abe had long thought that Jerry and I would make a good team.

I knew Jerry Weintraub from the business. He was handsome and extraordinarily persuasive, a super salesman with personality to spare. When Bernie Brillstein and Marty Kummer—Jerry's partners from Management Three—decided to leave, Abe told him that now would be the time to approach me about joining the company. Jerry and I had an immediate meeting of the minds . . . and he offered me a generous salary and benefits package.

Marvin Zolt, head of business affairs at Management Three, said, "Listen, Sid. We all know you're coming in as a partner, but it's my feeling that we should wait before we put the partnership agreement into a contract. Why don't you and Jerry have a trial period, sort of like a courtship? You'll get a heck of a salary, but let's wait to do the contract."

Marvin was a decent guy and so convincing that I agreed to wait up to a year before signing a contract. Also, I assumed that Abe would always be available to mediate any dispute I might have with Jerry. I went to work and was able to bring Billy Fields with me.

With acts like Sinatra, Elvis, John Denver and the Moody Blues constantly needing attention, there was never a dull moment. I was working in my office one day when my secretary, Marilyn, buzzed me. "Sid, there's a lady on the phone who says she's Shirley MacLaine."

"Great, who's this loon?"

"No, Sid, she sounds serious."

Still skeptical, I told Marilyn to put the call through.

"Hello. Is this Sid Bernstein?"

"Yes."

"This is Shirley MacLaine and I was told to call you."

"Who *are* you?"

"Shirley MacLaine!" she laughed.

I was Sid the Music Man. Why would the movie actress Shirley MacLaine be calling me? I decided to play along.

"Okay, Shirley. How can I help you?"

"Sid, the people at the Garden said that you're the guy to call."

"For what?"

"Well, I'm planning a show called *Women for McGovern*. It's all about and for women who support George McGovern for president. The people I spoke to at the Garden said that you could help me put the show together."

"What would you like me to do, Shirley?"

"I was hoping, Sid, that you would coproduce the concert with me."

"What would we be producing?"

"I can get some really interesting women to appear, but I haven't the faintest idea how to deal with the Garden, the unions, tickets, staging, everything. I need help, Sid. Would you be interested?"

"Yes, I support the senator. I'd be glad to help you."

"Good. Would you like to have dinner with me this evening at my apartment so we can discuss the details?"

"Shirley, I'd be happy to." I wasn't about to turn down an invitation to dinner at Shirley MacLaine's apartment.

That evening, I walked the few blocks from my office to Shirley's building. When I arrived, Pete Hamill, the columnist and author, was standing in the kitchen in an apron, cooking soup. Pete and I were acquaintances. After a sumptuous meal, Shirley listed the performers she had lined up for the concert: Dionne Warwicke, Tina Turner, Mary Travers of Peter, Paul & Mary, Judy Collins, Mama Cass Elliot of the Mamas and the Papas, Marlo Thomas, actress Melina Mercouri, Broadway stars Gwen

Can you imagine what a star-studded lineup like this would bring in today? The ushers alone were worth their weight in gold!

Verdon and Chita Rivera, the legendary Bette Davis and Mrs. Rose Kennedy, mother of the slain president. To add a little extra zip—as if that were needed!—Shirley had recruited her brother, Warren Beatty, Senator Gene Tunney, Robert Redford, Eli Wallach, Jack Nicholson, Paul Newman, Alan King and James Earl Jones to be celebrity ushers. Not a bad group to be associated with.

Since Shirley had already lined up all the talent, making the arrangements was a breeze. During the planning, Shirley and I had only one bone of contention. Who was to receive the top promotion credit on the posters and programs? She wanted my name to appear first, but I insisted that she have the honor. I won.

Women for McGovern played to a packed house. It turned out to be an amazing night of entertainment.

"How could you do this to me?" wailed Jerry Weintraub, a life-long Republican. "This is embarrassing! My friends are lambasting me!" I just turned my palms heavenward.

I DIDN'T HAVE MUCH TIME to worry about Jerry's embarrassment over the McGovern concert because I was preparing to speak at *Billboard* magazine's annual convention in Geneva. Gerry wanted to take the kids to the sunny beaches of Hawaii rather than the cold, snowy Alps, so I traveled to Switzerland alone.

The time in Geneva was terrific. I enjoyed catching up with many friends from the record business, and my talk about concert promotion and the potential concerts have as vehicles for charitable fundraising was very well received. Somehow, everything at the convention was running late, and my speech ended later than scheduled. I had to rush to the airport immediately after the presentation.

Bob Altshuler of Arista Records and I jumped into a cab and made a mad dash to catch the last plane to Paris. I was eager to begin my journey to Hawaii to join Gerry and the kids. I hadn't given her an exact date for my arrival, but since I had finished my business in Europe, I was ready for a vacation. The cab made its way to the airport a bit too leisurely, and we missed our flight. Bob proposed an alternative.

"C'mon, Sid, I can't be stranded here. I have to get to Paris for business. Let's take the train together and spend the night in Paris. You can catch an early flight back to the States."

I definitely wasn't interested in spending the night in Geneva, so I agreed to take the four-to-five-hour train ride with Bob. Without advance reservations, it was impossible for us to get a private compartment, so Bob and I shared one with a lovely French couple returning home to Paris after a Swiss holiday. Perfect! I seized on the opportunity to converse in French.

As we proceeded into France, the conductor began calling out the names of the upcoming station stops. The names all sounded wonderfully familiar. . . . And then I heard "Dijon!" My heart stopped. I thought of Claudy. Whatever happened to Claudy?

"Bob, did you hear the conductor call out Dijon?"

"Yes, I believe he said Dijon."

The French couple nodded in agreement. "*Oui, monsieur, Dijon.*"

I told them in French about my experiences during the war. I related the story of Claudy. "My first real sweetheart," I said. "*Ma première cherie.*"

A debate started raging within me. Should I get off the train at Dijon? I decided to share my dilemma.

"Go, Sid." Bob said. Do it. *Carpe diem!*"

"*Allez-vous! Allez-vous!*" the French couple said.

The conductor entered our compartment, and my traveling companions explained my dilemma. "*Oh, monsieur, allez-vous! Allez-vous! C'est très romantique!*"

By that point, I had the feeling that if I didn't get off the train on my own steam, Bob, the French couple and the conductor would have thrown me off.

WHEN I DISEMBARKED AT DIJON, it was pouring rain. The two-block walk from the train station to the Grand Hotel, where I had stayed twenty-seven years before, left me drenched. As I filled out the check-in card, I asked the concierge if he would be so kind as to look up the name Vilfroy in the local telephone directory.

"Yes, a Vilfroy is listed, but not at the address you have given me, sir." I had given him the address I had etched in my memory from 1945.

"Would you please dial the number for me?"

"*Certainement.* . . . Nobody is answering. Here is the number and address, sir. It is late. Perhaps they will be returning soon."

"*Merci beaucoup, monsieur.* I do appreciate your efforts."

I went up to my room, peeled off my soaking wet clothes and took a hot bath. Relaxed and refreshed, I tried the number again. Still no answer, so I decided to revisit the streets I had not seen since I was a soldier.

By now the rain had let up, and I started walking to the site of the GI nightclub. As I approached, I could see that it was now called Café Central and—much to my surprise— was still a nightclub. It was 10:00 P.M., and the cinemas were letting out. People began filtering toward Dijon's main street. Wandering among them, I began looking for a nineteen-year-old girl and her mother whom I had last seen in 1945. No sign of Claudy or Madame Vilfroy among the moviegoers, so I began looking in the windows of the restaurants around the town square. Memories were everywhere.

I returned to the hotel and tried the phone number once more. Again, no answer. Disheartened, I went to sleep. The night was fitful, but I awoke to a warm and sunny Saturday in Dijon. I ate breakfast and then decided to go to the address the concierge had given me the night before.

As I walked along that summer morning, I could see how much Dijon had changed in the postwar years. The town had virtually doubled in size. I found the address and looked at the building directory on the front door. "Madame Vilfroy" was clearly printed next to a bell. I pressed it several times, but there was no response. Perhaps Madame Vilfroy was on holiday. Even though it was getting hotter with each passing minute, I wanted to inquire further. After about ten minutes, a young man carrying trash walked down the stairs and opened the front door.

"*Excusez-moi.* My name is Sid Bernstein, and I am an old friend of Madame Vilfroy. I was wondering if you might know her."

"*Certainement, monsieur.* She is a friend of my mother."

"I have been unable to reach her. . . . By chance, would you know where she might be?"

"Wait here, *monsieur,* and I will be right back."

The young man ran up the stairs and returned a few moments later with a woman he introduced as his mother.

"Madame Vilfroy recently fell and is away convalescing," she explained.

"Oh, I am so sorry to hear that. Would you possibly know Madame's daughter, Claudy? Does she live here in Dijon?"

"*Mais oui, monsieur.*" The woman turned to her son. "Michel, please run back upstairs and get Madame Bonheur's address."

"Claudy is married to a doctor, *monsieur.*" My heart was pounding.

Michel returned and handed me a slip of paper on which was scribbled Claudy's address.

Deeply grateful, I thanked mother and son for their assistance. "*Au revoir. Merci beaucoup. A bientôt!*"

"*Au revoir. Bonne chance!*"

I glanced at the piece of paper and began walking toward Rue Liberté. The morning had grown considerably warmer, and my shirt was soaked with perspiration. When I reached 38 Rue Liberté, my stomach was churning. I rang the bell and heard the door click in response. I pushed open the door, walked up the two flights to Apartment 2C and rang the bell next to a frosted glass door. A red-headed woman in her forties answered.

"*Bonjour.* How may I help you?"

"*Madame*, I have not been in Dijon for a very long time and I am looking for some friends I had made as a soldier here at the end of World War II. I went to Madame Vilfroy's building and a neighbor kindly informed me that she was recuperating out of town from a fall. The neighbor told me that her daughter, Claudy, lives —"

"I am Claudy, Sidney. Please step inside. I want to call my husband."

Visions of my youthful self and thoughts of what might have been overcame me. I stepped inside the apartment, and as Claudy turned away to call her husband, I began to sob.

A few moments later, Claudy returned, followed by a tall, handsome man resembling the movie star James Stewart.

"*Bonjour*, Sidney. It is a pleasure to meet you. Please make yourself comfortable in our home."

"*Merci.* How very kind of you."

"We are waiting for our two sons to return for lunch. Then we will all be leaving for our country home."

The table was set for four.

"Would you please join us for a sandwich, Sidney?" Claudy said.

Claudy, Dr. Bonheur and I took seats around the mahogany table.

"I have heard so much about you," the doctor said. "I even know what you looked like in 1945."

Claudy produced a photo album on the front page of which was a picture of me and nineteen-year-old Claudy at the fountain in the center of Dijon. As I looked up and gazed at Claudy, I did not see a middle-aged wife and mother, but the beautiful young woman I knew and had left behind.

As Claudy and I sat around the table and talked about our families and what had transpired over the last twenty-seven years, Dr. Bonheur listened raptly. We were interrupted by Claudy's two handsome blond teenagers bounding into the room.

"An old friend," Claudy explained to her sons.

We made room for the boys at the table and continued talking. I told them about my three sons and two daughters and extended an invitation to them to come to visit New York. Their eyes sparkled in anticipation. Perhaps my sons could visit them in Dijon, I said. A Bernstein-Bonheur exchange program.

It was time to say goodbye. Claudy explained that they had a long drive ahead, and I realized that I needed to start thinking about getting to Paris and catching a flight home. I walked Claudy and her family to their car.

"Claudy, please remember me to your mother and tell her how disappointed I was not to see her. Please convey to Madame Vilfroy my gratitude for her wonderful treatment, those many years ago, of a young soldier far from home."

We exchanged addresses and phone numbers, and they drove off.

As I walked back to the Grand Hotel, I reflected on life's ironies. I had not answered Claudy's letters because I had concluded that since she was not Jewish, nothing would come of our relationship. A poor excuse, I thought. After all, I had ultimately married Gerry.

I CHECKED OUT OF THE HOTEL and caught the next train to Paris. When I learned that I could not get a flight to New York until the next morning, I checked into the Georges V, one of the finest hotels in Paris. I changed clothes and decided to visit my favorite café on the Champs Elysées. As I walked inside, there was Larry Uttal, the president of Bell Records. Larry had attended the *Billboard* convention and stopped in Paris before heading back to New York. I was happy to see a familiar face.

"Sid!" Larry said. "Come sit with me."

I joined him and ordered a hot chocolate and my favorite chocolate éclair. As I savored the delectable pastry, I related my odyssey of the last day and a half.

Tears welled up in Larry's eyes. "I'm glad you went back to Dijon, Sid. If you ever want to make a movie about this and need backing, count me in."

Unfortunately, Claudy and I did not keep in touch. Her sons never came to visit us in New York. My children never went to Dijon. I never called or wrote. But this time, neither did she.

DURING MY TIME AT MANAGEMENT THREE, I watched Jerry Weintraub deal with Elvis's legendary manager, Colonel Tom Parker, as well as Sinatra's lawyer and adviser, Mickey Rudin. Jerry had a certain finesse, and observing how he interacted with clients taught me another way to deal with people.

One of the reasons Jerry had asked me to join Management Three was because he was stretched thin, as both Colonel Parker and Mickey Rudin always expected to deal directly with him. Whenever one of them called demanding to speak to Jerry, I had to keep them occupied until he became available. As a result, I began to develop a working relationship with both the Presley and Sinatra organizations.

We were responsible for the Elvis tours whenever they arose. Tom Parker had a unique relationship with Elvis. He got half of what Elvis made and kept everyone—except a few people known as the Memphis Mafia—away from the star. Though he was born in Holland, Parker had affected a southern accent after living in the South for so many years. He was a consummate professional and saw to every detail. Colonel Parker had an inordinately large ego, and as much as I tried, I could not warm to him.

One day, the Colonel showed up at the office unexpectedly. Jerry was on the road with one of the other acts, so I had to host our guest.

"Sidney," he said to me in his adopted accent, "would you like to go to lunch?"

"Sure, Colonel. Have anything special in mind?"

"How about the Blue Grotto? I know you like Italian food, and I love that place."

"Yes, I know that restaurant from way back. It's excellent."

We drove to Little Italy in the Colonel's limo and were welcomed as kings upon our arrival. The Colonel loved Italian food almost as much as I did, and the gastronomic experience we had that afternoon—spaghetti with a great marinara, meatballs, garlic bread—was *molto delizioso*.

The Colonel expressed his delight. "Best garlic bread in all of New York," he said between mouthfuls. Then, out of nowhere, he leaned across the table: "Hey, Sid. You don't really like me, do you?"

"What did you say, Colonel?"

"Let me put it to you this way, Sid. You're not very fond of me. I've seen you with others, and you seem to be more guarded and reserved in my presence. What is it?"

I tried to formulate a tactful response. "You're right, Colonel. I don't really like you as much as I—"

"C'mon, Sid, tell me the truth. What's the problem between us?"

What had started as a simple lunch had turned into a potential disaster for me and Management Three. The Colonel was Elvis Presley's manager and an important client. I didn't want to be responsible for souring what had been a successful business relationship.

"I respect you a great deal, Colonel—"

"C'mon, Sid. Tell me. Please tell me."

". . . I don't know, Colonel. I'm usually very open with people, but with you, well I find it difficult. I usually become close to the people I work with, but I can't seem to do that with you. I don't know what it is. I have to think about it."

"Okay, Sid. Would you think about it? I really like you and it would mean something to me to know why you hold back with me."

That night, I thought about what I had said to the Colonel at lunch. He had been open and honest, yet I felt unable to reciprocate. I recalled a recent trip I had taken with him to check out a venue for an Elvis appearance. Parker looked at the manifest—the report on ticket sales, seats sold, scale of the house, etc.—and commented, "Sidney, look at this. You and I just walked through the orchestra section of this arena and you saw me stop and make a notation. Do you remember me saying that I thought the space we stopped at could hold another fourteen to sixteen seats?"

"Yes, Colonel. I do."

"When I stopped there, Sid, did ya' wonder why the space was open?"

"No, I didn't."

"Well, when Elvis comes in here to do this concert, there will be seats here with people in them. Somebody is tryin' to steal seats from us, Sid."

Then I remembered once seeing the Colonel actually selling program books at an Elvis concert, and I asked him why he was doing that.

"The reason I'm here, Sid? You probably think I'm an old, foolish man to be sellin' dollar programs. We sell so many of these programs at a concert that I want to make sure they don't slip some of the nonlicensed ones in with the official ones. I also want to get a look at the folks who buy these things. I want to see their style and what they're like. It helps me do my job better if I have a picture of the fans."

I remembered how countless people resented that the Colonel never let them get close to Elvis but that he had once granted me access to one of the greatest stars in the history of show business—as a favor.

There was that time that I had been pushing Jerry to use his relationship with the Colonel to persuade Elvis to hold a press conference before his next New York appearance. I had gotten numerous phone calls from the media—and also from young Elvis fans—requesting access to The King.

"Sid, you know how the Colonel is about the press. He won't do it. You want him to allow local high-school and college newspapers to interview Elvis? You're crazy, man! *The Times* is one thing, but this is ridiculous!"

I wouldn't give up. "C'mon, Jerry. It'll be a wonderful opportunity for these kids to see Elvis. We'll rent a big room, and you and the Colonel can control everything. It'll be terrific. You can handle *The Times* and the rest of the media. But let Elvis talk to the kids."

I bugged Jerry so much that he finally relented. A few days later, he came out of his office with a big smile. "You win, Sid."

"What did I win, Jerry?"

"The Colonel agreed to do the press conference. Set it up!"

"Great. I have a list of the names of the kids who have been calling us. I'll start contacting them immediately."

"Remember, Sid. You wanted this. You asked for it, right?"

That sounded ominous. "What do you mean, Jerry?"

"Well, Sid," Jerry laughed. "You are going to see *the* Elvis press conference."

WE SET UP THE CONFERENCE in a large room at a hotel on Long Island. Jerry Weintraub introduced Colonel Tom Parker, who emerged in an outrageously large cowboy hat.

"Hi, y'all," he waved as he sat before the assembled audience of three hundred budding high-school and college journalists. The Colonel talked endlessly. He was a captivating speaker and had the kids howling. Then, he took some questions. He was a master show-man, just like the man he represented.

After about forty minutes, Tom Parker slapped his forehead. "Why, y'all, I've been goin' on and on, and I completely forgot that Elvis is waitin' back there. I do appreciate that y'all came, but I suppose you're waitin' on Elvis!"

The Colonel motioned to one of the road crew. "Could y'all get Elvis out here? Tell him it's time for the press conference."

Dressed in black from head to toe, his eyes hidden by sunglasses, Elvis came out from behind the curtain and waved to the crowd.

"How y'all doin'?" he drawled. "It's nice to see y'all here, and I thank you for coming. I really appreciate it. I love New York City! It's such a fantastic place. I suspect that y'all be at the concert, so why should I take your time now? We'll have a real party."

Then Elvis gave them two raised hands with the peace sign and waved: "Been fun talkin' to y'all. Thankya vera, vera much. God

Elvis in all his glory—hips, lips and rock 'n' roll!

Even without a whole lotta shakin' going on, The King ruled.

bless." And poof! He was gone. It took all of two minutes, but the kids loved every second.

The Colonel returned, did an additional ten-minute monologue, and then he was gone, too.

That night, thinking about the Colonel, I concluded that he was not the egomaniac I had previously thought. He was incredibly intuitive and clever, and the fact that he had picked up on my reservations about him made me lament that I had not been warmer toward him. We spoke several times after our lunch at the Blue Grotto, but I never got to tell him in person how much I had come to respect and admire him.

ONE DAY, JERRY CAME INTO my office with a big grin.

"Sid, listen to this. I just got a call from Warner Brothers Records. They're offering us one hundred thousand bucks if we can do an album on how to play chess. . . . Wait! Don't faint. I'm not done yet. . . . They want us to go to Reykjavik, Iceland, to sign Bobby Fischer to make an instructional chess album. Fischer's in Reykjavik now, competing in a world title match against Boris Spassky, the Russian champion. What do you think? Should we give it a shot?"

Bobby Fischer, one of the all-time great chess whizzes, was also known to be quite an eccentric. I could tell that Jerry didn't want to go to Iceland alone; he enjoyed having me as a traveling companion.

"Sure, Jerry. Let's go. A hundred thousand dollars is easy money if we can get Bobby Fischer onboard. Paul Marshall is his attorney. I'll see if he can set up a meeting for us with Bobby."

I called Paul, a well-known entertainment attorney, and explained why we wanted to meet with Bobby. Paul thought it was a great idea and offered to try to arrange something with Bobby, Jerry and me. "But, remember," Paul warned, "this kid is a little strange. You might make the trip and never get to meet him."

When Jerry and I arrived at Reykjavik, we thought, *What an incredible place!* The sun was still blazing at 11 o'clock at night. Kids were playing in the streets. The men looked like Vikings, the women like Nordic goddesses. Of course, I quickly discovered all the great restaurants. Jerry and I stayed in a four-star hotel where the hot water was supplied by underground thermal springs.

But, try as we might, Jerry and I never got near Bobby Fischer. It was impossible to make contact with him. I even tried to enlist Bobby's sister to help us get an audience, but she couldn't arrange it. After about five days, we packed our sunglasses and headed home.

Although I was working at Management Three mainly as a talent manager, I still had a reputation in the industry for staging benefit concerts. I enjoyed that, particularly if I felt I was supporting a worthy cause. One day, Geraldo Rivera called and asked me to work on a benefit for Willowbrook, a home for the mentally challenged. At the time, Geraldo was married to Edie Vonnegut, daughter of author Kurt Vonnegut. Through our work together on the concert, I could see how talented Geraldo was and that he would likely achieve great success as a TV journalist.

I thought that Management Three should manage Geraldo. Jerry Weintraub concurred, and when I suggested it to Geraldo, he was enthusiastic.

Geraldo was working for ABC television. He had a penchant for getting into mischief, and I would have to visit ABC from time to time to bail him out. The first executive I met there was Marty Pampadour. He and I worked out a good system of communication, and we were successful keeping Geraldo out of trouble. After Marty moved on, I had to develop a similar relationship with the new executive, Michael Eisner, who today is the chairman of the board of the Walt Disney Company. Mike and I were able to keep Geraldo on the straight and narrow and negotiate a deal that got Geraldo a nightly show, a major step in his career.

I also got Don Imus to join the roster at Management Three. I thought that he was a unique talent with something interesting to say. My early confidence in Imus and what he was doing was right on target. I am happy to see he's achieved success with his nationally syndicated radio and TV show. I particularly admire the valuable work that Imus does on behalf of Tomorrow's Children. He demonstrates through action how star power can be used to help the less fortunate.

JERRY HAD DISCOVERED JOHN DENVER while visiting the Bitter End. He signed him to Management Three and got him several appearances on *The Merv Griffin Show*. John's television work and appearances in many important clubs around the country fueled his recording career, and soon he was selling records by the carload. I began to think about John Denver, his career, and the best way to take him to the superstar level.

I suggested to Jerry that it was time for John to have a breakthrough engagement in New York. Jerry agreed, and we arranged for a concert in Carnegie Hall. We got tremendous support from RCA, John's record company. Management Three and RCA pulled out all the promotional stops: posters, ads, handbills. John Denver got the first-class treatment he deserved, and the concert was a huge success.

Jerry threw a post-concert party at his apartment for "just a few" of his friends. I arrived to find the place so jammed that people had spilled into all the rooms, including the bedroom. There, sitting on Jerry's bed, which was the only spot left, I had a nice conversation with a couple from Texas who were Jerry's neighbors each summer in Kennebunkport, Maine. That was my first encounter with Barbara and George Bush.

After John's big event in New York, we booked him into the Greek Theatre, an important L.A. venue. I went to our office in Beverly

Monday, August 28, 1972

THE Hollywood REPORTER

TARGET JOHN DENVER AS NEW SUPERSTAR

By Glenn Lovell

During a period in which few contemporary singers have proven much more than weekend sensations on the small screen and only the most versatile vocalists have managed to maintain a significant following, Sid Bernstein, president of Management III Ltd., believes his promotion company has found the answer to this bleak situation in singer-composer John Denver.

Bernstein told The Hollywood Reporter that Denver possesses "those unique, seldom found qualities which will make him tomorrow's television superstar."

Though Management III, composed of a team of four agents, is involved in handling such merchandizable talents as Mary Travers and Silverbird (a new all-Indian singing family), and has just finalized negotiations with chess-master Bobby Fischer to record a how-to record for Warner Bros., it is pouring most of its efforts into grooming Denver for future TV, film and concert spots.

Bernstein noted that the singer-composer's sudden ascendency to wide acclaim is not an unexpected overnight rise to stardom, but rather the resultant windfall from a carefully calculated campaign, masterminded by Jerry Weintraub chairman of Management III.

The strongest indication of Denver's possibilities in show business, particularly in TV, came when he hosted his own three-hour variety show entitled "The Midnight Special" on Aug. 19 from 1-2:30 a.m.

Though politically oriented to "get out the vote" and hastily negotiated by Management III, this unusual venture proved an unprecedented success since it found a mass audience for an early morning time slot heretofore considered impossible to fill. The NBC special managed to gain a rating of 5.7—high beyond NBC's expectations.

About the possibility of a permanent latenight series in the near future, Bernstein is uncertain though he mentioned that Denver recently completed a 45-minute special for BBC which proved so successful in Britain that agent Harold Davason is negotiating a variety series there and producer Ed Scherick has approached Denver about a movie scoring assignment. "It is my hunch," Bernstein said, "that Denver will come off beautifully in a variety show geared to the 18-25 year age group. When he arrives in his own American TV series, which is inevitable, he will sustain a following as long as Andy Williams and Perry Como."

The evolving or grooming of the Denver image which is geared to appeal to a massive cross-section of the American public without estranging social or age groups has been Jerry Weintraub's formidable task. This endeavor is labeled by Bernstein as "creative management," or a method of linking a singer's special attributes with carefully chosen situations tailored-made for the artist.

Speaking of the four-year union between Weintraub and Denver, Bernstein said "this union will have the same kind of longevity, in my opinion, as the Presley-Parker relationship has enjoyed." He added that the association between agent and performer has resulted in the type of serious, sincere, logical planning which very few show business people receive these days.

"In the last 10 years the record business and quality of television variety shows have suffered from the lack of proper agency representation and legal counciling," Bernstein said.

"Today TV appearances for new young talent are extremely hazardess because the right elements rarely come together at the right time," he continued. "There is seldom the union of the perfect script, showcase, and performer."

As coordinated by Weintraub, the promoter who finally clinched the much-coveted deal with Elvis Presley to tour the U.S., Denver has been carefully introduced to the public by well-timed degrees through fastidious selection of live performances and television spots.

In this article, rumors of finalized negotiations with Bobby Fischer were just that—rumors.

Hills and did the Bernstein Special: posters, handbills and carefully placed ads. We took Jerry's convertible, hired two young guys and started our hit-and-run poster campaign. Thank God that Caddy was fast—faster than the police, that is. We came close to seeing the L.A. County Jail more than once!

John Denver was a big hit in Los Angeles, and that catapulted his career skyward.

PETER, PAUL & MARY WERE doing eight specials for BBC television in London, and they invited John to make a guest appearance. Upon hearing John Denver, the BBC brass flipped and immediately offered him his own eight-show series. Jerry Weintraub didn't like the paltry sum being offered and he procrastinated in getting back to the BBC. Eager to make a deal, they invited us to London to see if we could reach an agreement. Jerry again dragged his feet, but I convinced him that we needed to get to England and finalize a deal quickly. "England is the gateway to continental Europe," I said, "and John needs the exposure so that his records can become as successful there as in the States." I was so persistent that Jerry finally agreed to a deal with the BBC.

To celebrate John's first appearance on British television, Jerry and I decided to go to England with our wives. After the first television broadcast, Jerry threw a party for clients, friends in the music business and industry executives. I had brought the Moody Blues to America for their first visit, and ten years later Jerry became their American manager, so we invited them to the party. Mike Pinder, a member of the Moody Blues, brought Ringo Starr. I was happy to see Ringo and we embraced. Then, for the next hour and a half, Mike Pinder and Ringo Starr talked about the colors of the sky, the shape of clouds and the end of the rainbow. I didn't know what those guys were on, but I do know they were seeing things that escaped me.

I was deeply saddened when John Denver lost his life in a plane crash. He was an extraordinary singer and songwriter—and a fine man. I am grateful to Jerry for allowing me to play a pivotal role in John's journey to stardom. It takes many qualities to be a really big star, and John Denver had them all: talent, commitment, sincerity, heart, belief, love and warmth. John had the ability to connect with his audience and touch their souls.

WHILE I WAS AT MANAGEMENT THREE, I got a call from John Lennon and Yoko Ono's office requesting that I come to a film studio in New York to have my knees filmed. John and Yoko were working on a project in which they would film prominent people in the music industry walking past a camera with their pants rolled up above their knees. Although I thought the project was a bit odd, I agreed and set up a time for them to film me.

On the day of the shoot, I showed up at the studio in the West 60s and was greeted by the Lennons. They instructed me to roll up my pants, expose my knees and walk down a line on the floor. I never knew what the film was for and I never asked John or Yoko for an explanation. Truth is, I don't know if it was ever completed or released.

You might be wondering why I consented to place my knees on public display. It's simple: because John and Yoko asked me to. I could never refuse John. He was very special to me. I regret I never had the chance to ask him what the film was for. I can just see it now: "And the Academy Award for Best Knees goes to . . . Sid Bernstein!"

AFTER WORKING AT MANAGEMENT THREE for more than a year without any mention of the promised partnership, I began to get antsy. To be sure, I was well-paid, and the action was steady, fun and interesting. But with the birth of Etienne on January 25, 1973, there were eight of us in the Bernstein family. Gerry in particular was worried about having financial security for herself and the kids, and that would be assured if I got the partnership. I started dropping hints around the office. I tried to be subtle, but Jerry clearly realized what was on my mind. One day, I sat down with him.

"Listen, Jerry, I've been thinking about this partnership thing. I really need to get it resolved."

"Sid, why don't we see how we get along?"

We were getting along beautifully. Jerry had surprised me several times with generous salary increases, and that was very welcome.

But sufficient time had passed for him to evaluate our compatibility. Jerry was just stalling. He didn't really want any partners; he had dangled the partnership possibility just to lure me to Management Three.

I went to Marvin Zolt and voiced my concerns. "Sid," he advised, "you've come a long way here, and you know how much Jerry respects you and how generous he is. Let it go for a while."

I explained that I needed to take this step for my family's financial security. I needed to know where I stood.

"Marvin, I'm asking you to find out from Jerry whether he's going to come through with a partnership or not."

"Okay, Sid. I'll try to talk to him."

A week or two passed with no reply, so I called Jerry myself. He was on a yacht somewhere with Frank Sinatra and Mickey Rudin. I didn't want to be put off anymore.

"Jerry, I have decided that I'm going to leave. I want to give you notice. I'm not in a rush, though, so how many weeks would you like me to stay to tie up loose ends?"

Jerry Weintraub is subject to quick decisions and pulls no punches. He gets hot quickly. "Leave today. Right now," he blurted out.

Jerry didn't speak to me for three years after that.

Perhaps my phone call was ill-timed. Perhaps we should have had that talk face-to-face. The bottom line is that I was promised something and never got it. I had upheld my end of the bargain, but there had been no reciprocity. So I left. I was disappointed, hurt and frustrated, but I didn't have time to dwell on it or wallow in self-pity. I had made my decision and it was too late to retreat. It wasn't easy to leave, but I had to secure my family's future.

Had I made a big mistake? Abe Margolies said yes.

PART FOUR

Destiny Calls

17

Bouncing Back

J ERRY WEINTRAUB'S DISMISSAL OF ME was a blow, but I immediately established Sid Bernstein Music, took an office at 505 Park Avenue and went to work. Slowly but surely, I was reestablishing myself as an independent promoter and manager.

In the late sixties, a wonderful R&B group, the Stylistics, was formed. By the seventies, they were gaining popularity with their soft, romantic ballads like "Betcha By Golly, Wow" and "I'm Stone in Love With You." I booked them into Carnegie Hall and, of course, they sold out. It was great to be back in the game.

On the heels of that successful promotion, I decided to run with another hot R&B group, Harold Melvin and the Blue Notes. They were headed up by a great frontman, Teddy Pendergass, and had such hits as "If You Don't Know Me By Now" and "The Love I Lost." I liked the music and knew it would be another slam dunk. It was. I was back in action.

Out on my own again, it was time to start taking on some of my own clients. I had a good relationship with Bruce Morrow, who

SID BERNSTEIN
presents

THE STYLISTICS

plus

DEODATO
AND HIS BAND

CARNEGIE HALL
THURSDAY, JUNE 20 AT 8:00 P.M.

Tickets Now At Box Office
Tickets Also Available At Over 150 Ticketron Outlets.
Call (212) 541-7290 For Location Nearest You

THE STYLISTICS NEW AVCO ALBUM

Cousin Brucie to NBC

■ NEW YORK—Bruce Morrow has ended a thirteen year association with WABC Radio, and effective August 19, will join WNBC as the 6-10 p.m. announcer. The announcement of the new deal was made by Sid Bernstein, Morrow's manager, who negotiated the arrangement with NBC radio general manager Perry Bascom, on Morrow's behalf. Bernstein, while not giving terms of the deal, called it "one of the most beautiful contracts in radio history."

Morrow, who is presently on vacation, will fill Wolfman Jack's slot on WNBC when he returns to the air. Wolfman, meanwhile, is leaving WNBC to return to the west coast.

wanted off WABC radio, where he had worked for years. I gave him a call, we struck a representation deal, and I helped Bruce land a job at WNBC with a big raise and occasional appearances on NBC television news shows reporting on pop music.

My roster was diversified and expanding. In one particular case, my eldest son, Adam, attended the same school as the son of Deodato, a famous Brazilian pianist and award-winning conductor and arranger. He had a hit record with a version of "Also Sprach Zarathustra," better known as "The Theme to 2001: A Space Odyssey." Deodato and I became friendly after seeing each other at PTA meetings and school functions. Soon I was managing his career and giving a boost to my own.

BILL GRAHAM CALLED from San Francisco.

"Sid, I got the George Harrison/ Dark Horse tour. Since you first brought the Beatles to the States, you should present George at Madison Square Garden."

Naturally, I agreed, and the sold-out show was a dynamic musical evening.

Walking around the Garden during the performance, an usher informed me, "Sid, some friends of yours are twelve rows from the stage. The guy is wearing a big black hat. Take a look, but be nonchalant about it. We don't want a riot."

I casually walked up the aisle and spotted a young woman sitting there with the man in the black hat. She gave me a big smile and a wave. The guy winked and gave me the thumbs-up sign. I waved, smiled and kept walking. Paul and Linda McCartney were enjoying the music of their buddy George Harrison.

When I went backstage to see George after his concert, he was chanting, burning incense and seemed to be praying. I didn't want to disturb him, so I waved, he waved and I went home. That was George—the quiet one.

FELIX CAVALIERE HAD FINALLY managed to reduce the ill will that Laura Nyro felt toward me as a result of my falling asleep as she sang. David Geffen was no longer her manager, and she needed a new one. She was extremely talented, and I was more than happy to add her to my growing client roster.

Because of that earlier negative experience, I wanted to do a super job for Laura. I prided myself on professional conduct, and my untimely nap and the fallout from that had always disturbed me. Laura was highly musical and had assembled one of the best bands I had ever heard. I decided to present her at Carnegie Hall. Everything was thought out and executed in a first-class manner. The lighting, staging, publicity and advertising all had my undivided attention. I was determined that this concert be triumphant for Laura.

As an extra little touch, upon presentation of a ticket, each female concertgoer would receive a long-stemmed daffodil. I enlisted a well-known florist to supply the flowers, and I hired additional staff to stand behind the ticket-takers and distribute one to every woman who walked into the hall. The daffodils were beautiful, the finest that money could buy.

Every seat in Carnegie Hall was filled. Laura was unaware of what I had planned, and I made sure that she stayed in her dressing room for an extra fifteen minutes so that everyone would be seated before her entrance. First the band members came onstage, and the

CARNEGIE HALL/79th SEASON

SID BERNSTEIN

presents

LAURA NYRO

THE RASCALS

ALICE COLTRANE
and
PHAROAH SANDERS

In Concert

For the benefit of the

Integral Yoga Institute

500 West End Avenue, NYC, N.Y. 874-7500

227 West 13th Street, NYC, N.Y. 929-0585

After Laura let sleeping dogs lie, I promoted her at Carnegie several times.

surprise on their faces brought a smile to mine. Finally, Laura Nyro—a quiet, unassuming person, gentle and demure, the quintessential "flower child"—was introduced.

She was met with thunderous applause. Ever modest, she walked out with head bowed and eyes downcast. When she got to the microphone, she looked up to acknowledge the ovation. As she caught sight of the yellow waves of daffodils, her mouth fell open in wonderment.

"Thank you! Thank you!" she said. The women in the orchestra were waving the flowers, those in the upper balconies were standing and waving theirs, and Laura was nothing short of overwhelmed. It was already an event—and she hadn't yet sung a note.

Lovely, sensitive Laura Nyro became a very dear friend to the Bernstein family. Sadly, she died several years ago after battling breast cancer. Now, as then, her poetic soul lives on through her beautiful lyrics.

I LOVED BEING ON MY OWN again. I thrived on the independence. The financial pressures were enormous, but I was getting by and having fun.

Abe Margolies introduced me to Joe Taub, a born salesman with eyes like Paul Newman's and a striking mane of white hair. Joe, his brother Henry and Frank Lautenberg had started Automatic Data Processing, which became a huge business. Eventually, they sold ADP and walked away with a lot of money. In addition, Frank Lautenberg went on to be elected a U.S. senator from New Jersey.

Joe became very friendly with the great vocalist Enzo Stuarti, a New Jersey neighbor of his, and when Joe wanted to help Enzo, he came to me for advice. Enzo had been on *Ed Sullivan* and other TV shows, but he had never appeared in concert. I recommended that we do my Carnegie Hall formula and invite reviewers and press. Joe agreed and helped sell out the house. As a result, Enzo began to get more concert dates, and Joe Taub and I had a budding friendship.

Joe found out about my departure from Jerry Weintraub and stopped by my office. "Sid, how could you leave? You've got six kids! How could you just walk away? He has Sinatra and Elvis! How in the world could you do it?"

I explained what had transpired and what I was planning. During the course of our hour-long talk, calls came in from several famous people. That impressed him considerably.

"Sid, you have oil flowing right alongside your desk. It's in your territory, right under your chin, but you don't have a ladle to pick it up. You're not taking full advantage of the opportunities in front you. I'm sitting here, listening to you talk on the phone, and well-known people are constantly calling you. *They're* calling *you!*"

"You're probably right, Joe. What do you suggest?"

"You need to take advantage of these opportunities. I want to come back and spend some time with you."

For the next month, Joe sat in the office or came to lunch with me, trying to get a handle on how the entertainment business was run and what he could bring to the endeavor. He gave me advice, and I liked what he had to say. We decided to become partners. I was excited to have an associate who dressed like a king, looked like a movie star and had substantial financial resources. Before long, Joe Taub was pumping money into my new company.

Joe had weekly massages as part of his exercise routine, and he believed so strongly in their power to keep mind and body in balance that he insisted that I have a massage before any important meeting or event.

One day, as Joe and I were sitting in the office, a young lady walked in. "Mr. Bernstein, you won't remember me," she began. "When I was a young girl in my early teens, I lived in Teaneck, New Jersey. My name then was Phoebe Laub, and my friends and I would go to your shows at the Academy of Music. I saw the Rolling Stones, the Moody Blues and other groups there. My friends all had money and could buy tickets, but I couldn't, so I just went along for the ride.

"You had a little office at the Academy of Music, and my friends and I would come by and say hello. Often, after my friends would rush to get to their seats and I would turn to go home, you would produce a ticket from your pocket so I could attend the concert. 'This seat is not with your friends,' you would say, 'but it will get you into the concert.' I would call my mom to tell her that you had given me a ticket and that I would be returning home with my friends. I have never forgotten that. And now, Mr. Bernstein, I am looking for a manager."

"Really? Have you been to see anyone else?"

"I saw Jerry Weintraub just yesterday."

"He's great. He's marvelous. He has Sinatra, Elvis, the Moody Blues. . . . Why are you here?"

"I don't want him. I want you because of the way you treated me when I was a kid."

"I understand—"

"Mr. Bernstein, I have an album that was put out by an independent label, and it has sold seven hundred thousand copies. Now, I'm moving to Columbia Records. My new name is Phoebe Snow."

Now I knew who she was! It wasn't often that an indie label sold seven hundred thousand copies of anything, so blue-eyed soul singer Phoebe had been featured in the trades. Was I interested in managing her? Of course! Joe, Phoebe and I began to discuss a formal business relationship.

After signing Phoebe, Clive Davis invited her to appear at Columbia's convention, to be held in Toronto that year. Phoebe asked me to accompany her, and Joe Taub urged me to go even though we hadn't yet signed her to a contract.

When we arrived in Toronto, Clive wanted to introduce Phoebe around and have her sing for all the industry people. She was reluctant because she had no one to accompany her on the piano, but a young Columbia artist volunteered his services. I'll never forget the night that Phoebe Snow and Billy Joel dazzled everyone at the Columbia Records convention in Toronto.

Joe Taub took Phoebe under his wing, but she had so many problems that we couldn't get her career off the ground. We would book an engagement, and she would cancel. She would have a date for a recording session and not show up. It was an impossible and discouraging situation. I had seen this erratic and unprofessional behavior with Judy Garland, Jimi Hendrix and Sly Stone.

Phoebe had amazing talent. She had two great friends willing to help her—Joe and me. But she couldn't help herself.

A MUSICIAN BUDDY OF MINE called one day.

"Sid, I just got off the phone with Melba Moore. She heard that I knew you, and she was asking me about your qualifications as a manager. Of course, I gave you a glowing recommendation. If she calls, listen to her story. Her marriage has just ended, and she has some career problems—no record label, no agent, no manager. But, Sid, you know she's enormously talented."

"Yes, she had great success on Broadway in Purlie! and I've seen her sing on TV. She's got an incredible range. But, I've also heard some industry rumors that spell trouble."

"They're untrue. Give her a chance. If she calls, talk to her."

Melba called the next day, and we made an appointment to meet. Only a half-hour elapsed before I concluded that she was a lovely, genuine human being. All the stories about how temperamental she was were soon forgotten.

"Melba, what would you like to do?"

"Sid, I'd like to start fresh. I'd like to start right from the beginning, and I need the guidance that a manager like you can provide. I know that resurrecting my career will be a challenge, but I hear that you're the man who could do it."

"I'd like to think about this. Let's meet again tomorrow."

The next day, Melba came to my office. "Yes," I told her. "I'll accept the challenge! But I don't want to sign a contract yet, Melba. Let's see how we get along."

"Sid, you would be willing to work with me without a contract?" She couldn't believe it.

"Yes, I'm prepared to do it that way."

My efforts on behalf of Melba bore immediate fruit. I called Art Kass at Buddah Records, and he made a recording deal right on the phone. Then I called Nat Lefkowitz, chairman of William Morris, to see if he'd consider Melba. We set up a lunch date, and I could quickly see that Nat had heard the same stories I had. I would have to resort to salesmanship.

"Nat, this is a new and improved Melba. A different lady. She's unattached, and her major problems are behind her. She's really a sweet, shy, modest, gentle person. I think she's going to be a star again soon."

"Sidney, if you can guarantee that she'll behave professionally, we'd be willing to sign her and give it a shot."

Melba must have thought that I walked on water. Within two weeks of coming to my office, dejected and with seemingly few prospects, she now had a manager, a hot record label and a top booking agency. We went to work, and in a slow, steady progression her career was revitalized. As soon as Melba began to make some television appearances, her price for live shows began to escalate. I decided to put her in a benefit with Alan King, Carol Channing and Frank Sinatra. Gradually, we were earning back her respectability. Melba Moore was on the upswing—big time.

But Melba had to have a man in her life . . . and shortly after we met, she fell in love with Charles Huggins, the entrepreneur/owner of Frank's Restaurant, a famous Harlem eatery. Charles was a handsome, bright guy, and Melba married him.

About a year into the marriage, she came to my office: "Look, Sid, Charles wants to be in the music business, and he wants to manage me."

I can't say that I was shocked, but I had a feeling that this was not going to be the best thing for Melba. We were on a roll, and she was threatening the chemistry.

"Melba, are you sure you want to do this?"

"He's my husband, Sid. He really wants to be in the management business. He wants a change from the restaurant. What do you think?"

"Melba, you have become very dear to me, and I consider you my friend. If this is going to bring you happiness, and if you're sure it's the right thing to do, then go and do it. You have my best wishes."

Having her husband double as her manager didn't help Melba, but it sure helped Charles Huggins. He used it as a stepping stone to sign and manage record producers, and he became very successful. Unfortunately, his marriage to Melba wasn't as successful. They eventually divorced.

ONE DAY IN THE SPRING of 1974, I ran into my friend Arthur Aaron on the street. Arthur had been a big fan of the Rascals and had gotten friendly with a couple of the guys. I would see him from time to time at their appearances. After exchanging family information, we got into a discussion about the Beatles.

"Sid, do you think the Beatles will ever perform as a group again?"

"I don't know, Arthur. But I sure would like to have an opportunity to try to get them back together."

"What do you think it would take?"

"Probably ten million bucks," I laughed.

We chatted for a few more minutes and went our separate ways. The next morning, Arthur called to tell me that he had spoken with his wife's uncle, who happened to be Arlen Specter, the senior senator from Pennsylvania. "He thinks that the First Pennsylvania Bank might be interested in putting up the money for a Beatles reunion. Should I ask him to pursue it?"

"Sure, why not? We'll never get it done without the money. Ask him to proceed."

That afternoon, Arthur called again. "Sid, we have a lunch appointment with the chairman of the bank on Thursday, in Philadelphia."

The following Thursday, Arthur and I took the Metroliner to the City of Brotherly Love. We picked up Arlen and walked to the bank, where I was introduced to John Bunting, chairman of First Pennsylvania Bank. We were ushered into the chairman's private dining room and met by an executive vice president of the bank. We spent the next forty-five minutes enjoying lunch and chatting. The chairman and his vice president loved Beatles stories, so I served up some interesting ones. After dessert and coffee, the chairman looked at me intently. "Mr. Bernstein, what can we do for you?"

"Well, Mr. Bunting, as you know, there is still great interest in the Beatles. Everywhere I go, people ask whether the group is going to reunite. As you are also aware, it has been years since they played together, so it's a longshot at best. I think, however, that money might be the catalyst needed to bring them back together. I would like to offer them ten million dollars for a one-time, closed-circuit concert to be broadcast worldwide."

"Where would you present the performance, Mr. Bernstein?"

"It should be in a time zone that would maximize viewership."

The chairman posed some more questions, then he stood and extended his hand. "It's an interesting idea, Mr. Bernstein. Let us think about it, and we'll get back to you."

We exchanged goodbyes, and Arthur and I headed back to New York.

The very next morning, the phone rang. "Sid, it's Arthur. Arlen just called from Philadelphia. The bank says they'll put up twelve million dollars—ten million as an advance against whatever you negotiate with the Beatles and two million for infrastructure. All we have to do is get the Beatles to agree."

"That's great news, Arthur! I'll get to work on it right away!"

"One more thing. The ten million dollars is open-ended. As long as Bunting and his team are running the bank, the money is there."

"Thanks, Arthur. Tell Arlen I appreciate his efforts, and we'll keep him posted."

I decided early on that I would not go directly to the Beatles. Industry etiquette dictated that I deal with their representatives to initiate any business dealings. Thus ensued a flurry of letters and phone calls and more letters and phone calls between layers of law-yers, accountants and advisers. It was impossible to get any defini-tive word about anything. On top of that, the Beatles—particularly John and Paul—were dealing with issues of their own. We couldn't even get them together as a group to present our proposal. It was a sad thing for me, because I knew that millions of Beatles fans were yearning for a reunion. I wanted to see it myself. I vowed to keep trying.

I'd always had some kind of plan to orchestrate a Beatles reunion, but as the realization of the enormous difficulty of facilitating one sank in, I put it on the back burner. I yearned for the days when a phone call to Brian Epstein could get something done.

THEN CAME ABBA.

Lou Levy, who had discovered the Andrews Sisters and founded the highly successful Leeds Music Publishing Company, called from London. "Sid, I just came back from the Eurovision Song Contest in France. There was an act there that won the contest unanimously. Two guys and two girls from Sweden who call themselves ABBA. You have to get on a plane immediately and go see Stig Andersen. I've already told him about you, but don't wait for his call. I'll give you his number in Stockholm. Call him! Immediately! He's the group's manager, publisher and producer. He's the guy, Sid."

Lou knew his stuff, so as soon as I hung up, I called Stockholm. Stig Andersen knew exactly who I was.

"You fit in with my plans, Sid. When will you be free to come to Sweden?"

"Stig, Lou is so enthusiastic about what you and ABBA are doing that I would like to visit as soon as possible. I can leave New York in two days."

"Fine, Sid. Make your reservations and let me know when you will be arriving. I'll meet you at the airport."

Three days later, Stig Andersen, a man in his thirties, met me at the Stockholm airport. I had been around long enough to know the real thing when I saw it, and I could tell almost immediately from our conversation that this was a guy with smarts. We went to his offices, which housed one of the biggest music publishing companies in the country.

"Sid, the group is not here in Stockholm. They're vacationing at their summer home. I am going to see them tomorrow; I bring them provisions weekly."

"Provisions?"

"They live on a little island in the Baltic Sea. It's quite secluded. It's the only way that they can escape the scene that goes on around them when they're here in Stockholm. They've become so popular that it's hard for them to get any privacy." What Stig said reminded me of what had happened to the Beatles in England.

The next morning, the sky was ominously cloudy, but Stig and I drove to the edge of the sea, the car fully loaded with food and beverages. We transferred the stuff onto a boat and took off. The weather grew increasingly threatening. We kept passing the many islands in the Baltic. After a while, the sky turned black and the sea became extremely choppy. Stig must have seen my expression. "Want to turn back, Sid?"

I swallowed hard. "No, Stig. I've come this far. Let's go. If you have an oar, I'll row so we can get there faster."

He laughed. "No oar, Sid. Just the engine."

We finally reached the island, and as soon as the boat touched shore, the clouds parted and the most beautiful sun appeared. As we alighted, the two B's in ABBA, handsome young men named Bjorn and Benny, came forward to greet us. We unloaded the boat and carried all the food to a cabin. One of the B's said, "Stig, we're glad you're here, because we have to move the baby grand up the hill to another cabin, which we rented to use as our music room."

I had come to sign a group, and in a short period of time had become a sailor, a deliveryman and now a mover. I pitched in, and we lugged that baby grand piano up the hill and into ABBA's new rehearsal room. Oh, my aching back!

Upon arriving at the new cabin, we were met by the two A's of ABBA, a gorgeous blonde and an equally beautiful redhead, Anna and Anni-Frid, wives of Bjorn and Benny. If these young people can sing as good as they look, I thought, we really have something here.

One of the girls smiled. "So they enlisted you to help with the piano, ya?"

"Did they ever!" I pointed to my back.

"Does your back hurt? We'll rub it down." We were all laughing by now.

We sat up there in their music cabin, talking and listening to their music for several hours. It was super. We made a deal right on the spot for me to be their American manager.

During our return boat trip, Stig said, "Sid, you really made an impression on ABBA. They thought you were this very important man from the States. Your willingness to help with the piano made it for you with them!" I quickly forgot about my aching back. Just shows you what a little shlepping can do!

Stig asked me to stay in Stockholm for an extra few days. because ABBA was going to perform and the press was eager to meet the man who had brought the Beatles to America and would now do the same for ABBA. The next day, I met with the media at Stig's offices. Naturally, most of the questions were about the Beatles.

On the day after the press conference, one of Stig's assistants came rushing to the hotel. "Mr. Bernstein!" she said, holding out one of Stockholm's daily papers. "Look! You are on the front page!"

Indeed. There on page one was a picture of ABBA and me. "Sid Bernstein—the American manager of the Beatles—has arrived in Stockholm," the caption read. Of course, that was a mistake. I was the Beatles promoter, not their manager. Perhaps Stig had intentionally misspoken to a reporter because he thought that title added weight to my signing ABBA.

I attended ABBA's concert the next night. They were fabulous, and I went home with great expectations.

The men and women of ABBA were superb writers, terrific singers and positively stunning. They could have been one of the all-time great acts were it not for a decision by Stig Andersen to wait until the group had back-to-back number-one records before breaking them in the U.S. Few acts strike gold twice in a row, but Stig kept waiting and waiting, and he wouldn't let me present ABBA even in New York. His hesitancy dissipated the group's momentum.

When ABBA finally did make a few appearances in America, they were extremely well-received, but they never achieved the superstardom I had hoped they would.

In the long run, however, the story turned out well for ABBA. Stig took them to Australia, where they broke every attendance record and became megastars.

In April of 1999, *Mamma Mia!*, a musical featuring twenty-seven ABBA songs, opened in London. Hits like "Dancing Queen," "Money Money Money" and "Knowing Me Knowing You" are woven into a story about a mother and daughter preparing for the daughter's wedding. Enormously popular in England, in the fall of 2001 *Mamma Mia!* opened on Broadway, where it also became a runaway smash.

SHORTLY AFTER MY ASSOCIATION with ABBA ended, John Lennon called.

"Sidney, I'm taking some friends out to dinner. They say they want Italian food. You're the expert. Where should we go?"

I had a reputation to uphold. "Paolucci's, John. Paolucci's is the best. It's on Mulberry and Grand Streets, in Little Italy."

"Oh, yeah, I remember that. You told me and my mates about that place the first time we met you."

"You're probably right, John. I had completely forgotten. There are two items on the menu that you have to order: shrimp fra diavolo as an appetizer, then the veal parmesan—"

"Wait a minute, Sid!" John interrupted. "I won't remember these names and for sure I can't spell them, so I'm going to put Harry on."

Harry Nilsson, John's buddy and a great songwriter and artist, took the phone. "Sid, how the hell are you? How are all your kids?"

"Great, Harry! Everybody's fine. I hope you're behaving yourself!" We laughed. John and Harry had become notorious in the press for their overexuberant partying.

"Listen, Sid. The Englishman here can't spell his own name. What are those dishes again?"

I repeated the names to Harry, then John took the phone back. "Thanks, Sid. We're going."

Two days later, two messengers brought me two of the largest fruit baskets I'd ever seen. The card read: "Thank you ever so much. We had an incredible time. Harry and John."

The next time I went to Paolucci's, Dominic, the owner, told me that the group of famous rock-and-rollers I had sent to the restaurant were "all so well-behaved and courteous! And, they left the biggest tip in the history of the restaurant!"

LEE GUBER, WHO RAN the Westbury Music Fair and a circuit of in-the-round summer theaters, also produced Broadway shows. At the time, he was married to Barbara Walters, the TV journalist and daughter of my old boss at the Latin Quarter, Lou Walters. Lee approached me one day with a request that I help him stage a big rally at Madison Square Garden for Congressman Hugh Carey, who was running for governor of New York. Lee also asked if I could persuade Melba Moore, who was then still my client, to open the show for Frank Sinatra, a friend of Carey's. Lee explained that Carol Channing also had agreed to appear, and that Alan King was set to emcee.

"Sid," Lee said, "we need you to deal with the Garden, the unions, the tickets, etc. You know the Garden better than anyone else."

"Lee, I'll do it." I wasn't about to turn down a bill with Alan King, Carol Channing and Frank Sinatra. I was also interested in giving Melba the exposure.

I made all arrangements in two days. The night of the concert, I went to the Garden early to make sure that everything was running smoothly. All seemed to be in order except that Congressman Carey's plane was delayed in upstate New York, where he was attending a fundraiser. I received messages saying that he would be about a half-hour late. Not great, I thought, but not uncommon.

I asked Alan King to stretch his routine a little and to tell the other performers likewise. About twenty minutes after I took my seat in the orchestra section, Jilly Rizzo, Frank Sinatra's good friend, came to me. "Sid, The Boss would like to speak to you."

"Okay, Jilly, I'll be right there. I just want to watch the end of Melba's set."

"No, Sid, I think you ought to come right now. It's getting a little hot in his dressing room."

"All right, we'll go now." I rose to follow him.

I had my arm around Jilly, and we were sharing a joke as we walked toward the dressing room. Halfway there, he slipped out of my grasp. "Sid, I forgot something. Why don't you go see Frank, and I'll meet you there in a few minutes."

Jilly was abandoning ship. When I got to the door of Sinatra's dressing room, Tiny, his bodyguard, said, "The Boss is a little hot."

I opened the door and walked in, introducing myself.

"Mr. Sinatra, I'm Sid Bernstein, the producer of this event."

"Hi, Sid." He extended his hand. "I've heard a lot about you from Jerry Weintraub."

Sinatra turned to the mirror to straighten his bowtie. He was in shirtsleeves, and I was amazed to see that he had a potbelly. I had always thought of him as slim. He stared at my image in the mirror. "Sid, what's holding up the show? It looks like we're twenty-five minutes behind already. What's up?"

"Mr. Sinatra, Congressman Carey was attending a fundraiser in Rochester and his plane was delayed. As soon as he gets to La Guardia Airport, we're going to get him here as quickly as we can. My information is that the congressman's plane should land soon."

Turning from the mirror and looking directly at me, he said, "Jilly tells me that you are an expert on Italian food. Jilly says you're the man. . . . You know your pasta and pizza. . . . Tell me, Sid, where's the best pizza in New York?"

For years, I had gone to Patsy's in Harlem, and often I would hear that I had just missed Frank Sinatra. I also remembered hearing that the Warner Brothers plane would transport pizza from Patsy's to Los Angeles just for Frank.

"Patsy's, Mr. Sinatra. Patsy's has the best pizza."

"Man, that place is great. I still go up there sometimes when I'm in town."

He was flexing his suspenders. We were now buddies in food. I could see that Sinatra was no longer bothered by having to wait for Hugh Carey.

"But, Mr. Sinatra, the pizza I remember best was made at a little restaurant in the South Bronx that had a coal oven like Patsy's. It's the only pizza that could even dare to be compared to Patsy's."

"Knock off the 'Mr. Sinatra' business, Sid. You can call me Frank." He leaned forward conspiratorially. "So which restaurant is that?"

"It was on Cortland Avenue, about ten blocks from Yankee Stadium, but it's been gone now for some time. It was called Delli Venneris."

"What did you say?" His eyes widened. "Did you say Delli Venneris?"

"Yes, Frank, Delli Venneris."

"Sid, you have just hit me square—and I mean square—in *la pancia*." And he smacked his stomach with clenched fists. "I haven't heard that name in twenty years! That place was a masterpiece!"

Frank was born in 1915 in Hoboken, New Jersey. From heartfelt singing to rat-pack swinging, he did it his way.

I did not want to tell him that years ago, after a veterans' meeting, Milt Pollack and I drove to Delli Venneris one winter night. It was about 11:30, the streets were desolate, and the wind was blowing up the canyon of apartment buildings. A solitary limousine was parked in front of the restaurant. Milt and I parked behind the limo and went inside. Al Delli Venneris greeted us and motioned us to sit.

"Sid, I'll be right with you! I have something in the oven." And he went into the kitchen.

I called after him. "Al, take your time."

I looked around the darkened restaurant and whispered to Milt, "Don't be too obvious, but if you look behind you, in the rear of the place, I think you'll see faces you recognize."

Milt turned slowly and whistled through his teeth. "Wow, Sid! That's Ava Gardner and Frank Sinatra!"

"That's right, Milt!"

As I stood in front of Frank Sinatra in the Garden, I wondered if he remembered going to Delli Venneris with Ava Gardner.

"Do you remember how they used to drop the cornmeal on the paddle before they put the pizza into the oven?"

"I sure do, Sid. That place was great."

All of a sudden, he changed topics. "Sid, do you know the prime minister of Israel?

"No, Frank, I don't. You're probably not going to believe this, but I've never been to Israel."

"You've never been there?" he asked incredulously. "You gotta go, Sid! That place is marvelous. The spirit is unbelievable, and the generals that I know there are some of the toughest guys I've ever met. I've done some work there. They love American music in Israel. You gotta get over there sometime soon, Sid."

"I know, Frank. I plan to go when I get some free time."

There was a knock on the door and someone announced that Congressman Carey was in the building. I turned to leave as Frank put his jacket on.

"Sid, take care. Maybe we'll run into each other someday at Patsy's."

With Frank's passing, I am saddened to think that it is now an impossibility. Suffice it to say that Frank Sinatra left an indelible mark on the American cultural landscape. He was an original. And he knew his pizza!

I HAD SEEN WOODY ALLEN in one of his early comedic performances at the Bitter End. I thought that he was so funny and clever, I vowed that one day I would put him in one of my shows. The opportunity arose when I presented Count Basie and Mel Tormé at Carnegie Hall. For some reason, I felt that Woody would fit on the jazz bill. I paid him the princely sum of seven hundred fifty dollars, and he put on a great show, never questioning his inclusion in that lineup.

It takes great courage and confidence for an act to appear on a bill that's a little offbeat. There's no assurance that the crowd will respond favorably. The audience for this Basie/Tormé show came to hear jazz and got the bonus of seeing one of the comic geniuses of the twentieth century. I knew they would love Woody and accept him, but I'm sure he wasn't convinced of that when he took the date. Ironically, Woody went on to become a terrific jazz clarinetist.

Courage is a hallmark of live performers. No matter how good you think you are, no matter how much confidence you possess, you still have to get up in front of a live, paying audience sitting there thinking: "Show me." That's why we call it "show business" and why the good ones make the kind of money they do. Failure and humiliation in front of a crowd is just a missed step, missed note or missed line away.

Allan Stewart Konigsberg, aka Woody Allen, was born in New York City on December 1, 1935. His work, though often comic, is filled with human insight.

Woody Allen bases his entire shtick on insecurity. Yet he plays to the audience time and again. That's courage!

HELEN REDDY AND JEFF WALD, her husband and an agent at William Morris, called to ask if I would organize a concert at Lincoln Center's Avery Fisher Hall to benefit Ramsey Clark's U.S. Senate campaign. I agreed to do it and was excited with the star lineup: Paul Newman, Joanne Woodward, Harry Chapin, Neil Simon, Julie Harris, Harry Belafonte, Adolph Green, Dustin Hoffman, Tom Paxton, Dave DeBusschere, Phyllis Newman, Jack Gilford, Patrick O'Neal, Dick Shawn, Marlo Thomas and Kevin McCarthy. In addition, Avery Fisher Hall is magnificent.

It had become easy for me to put on an event like this. I had produced so many shows that I could arrange the entire event in just a few days. I enjoyed the action and could always take a memorable experience or anecdote away with me.

On the day of the Helen Reddy & Friends event, I got the opportunity to work with Paul Newman. We spent four hours arranging

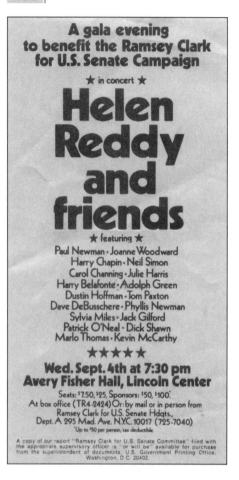

the schedule: who would open, the order of the performers, how long each act would be onstage, and so on. We did the runthrough on paper, because not everyone was able to attend rehearsal.

I had heard that Paul Newman was a prodigious beer-drinker but that it didn't affect him. In the time we spent together, he drank beer as if it were water, with seemingly no effect on his mental capacities. I was amazed. Paul Newman has movie-star looks, as most any woman would tell you. I was impressed with his manner and style. He has an indefinable glow.

EVEN THOUGH MY ASSOCIATION with ABBA did not work out as hoped, I was still interested in bringing European groups to the States. David Stein, a friend who was on the cutting edge of what was happening in music everywhere, called one day to tell me about a Scottish group called the Bay City Rollers.

"Sid, this band is the hottest group in England now! They have some hits and they are causing Beatles-like hysteria. Their gimmick is that they wear tartan plaid. The kids are buying Rollers merchandise faster than it can be manufactured. And I have the newspaper articles to prove it."

"Send me the articles, David. I'll take a look."

I read the press clippings and started to pick up some English magazines on my own. David was right. Kids were waiting hours to get a glimpse of the Rollers. Their concerts were selling out. Again I saw that magic word—"hysteria." I decided to see for myself.

In the U.S., the Rollers were on Bell Records, which was headed by Clive Davis, who was also president of Arista. I decided to contact my old buddy Clive.

"I'm thinking of going over to Scotland to meet with the Bay City Rollers. What do you think, Clive? I want to bring them to America."

"Please, Sid, don't do it. They don't play their own instruments. They use studio musicians. You're known throughout the business for your integrity, Sid. If you bring these kids to New York, you'll absolutely lose your credibility. Leave it alone."

I knew that Clive was a purist. For a group to feign playing instruments was not kosher with him.

"I appreciate what you're saying, Clive, and I'll think about it, but I can't promise you I won't check it out. I really feel like I have to see them." I knew that they were about to kick off a thirty-eight-city tour of the British Isles. Nothing could deter me. I had little to lose and maybe everything to gain.

When I got settled on the plane to Glasgow, I was surprised to see Barry Reiss, a mutual friend of mine and Clive's and business affairs manager for Arista, seated nearby. Hilarious! He had been dispatched by Clive to influence me not to bring the Rollers to America. Barry and I were staying at the same hotel, so we drove there together from the airport. Looking out the car windows, we saw that the streets were full of kids wearing tartan plaid.

"Look at this, Barry. Look at what's going on here."

"Yes, Sid, something is definitely happening."

When we got to our hotel, several hundred kids were milling about. Although they no doubt thought that the Rollers might be staying at the hotel, the finest in Glasgow, they actually were coming from their homes in nearby Edinburgh. All night long, I heard Roller's songs outside my window, and I knew then that I was on to something. The next morning at breakfast, I asked Barry if he had heard the kids.

"Allllll night!" he said groggily.

Tam Paton, manager of the Rollers, had been expecting me and left my ticket to the first of two shows that day at the front desk of the hotel. As I walked to the nearby theater, I could see hundreds of youngsters, accompanied by their parents, heading in the same direction. Across from the theater, a huge trailer with three windows cut into the side was selling Bay City Rollers caps, vests, scarves, kilts, shirts—you name it. They were doing big business, and everything was in tartan plaid. Barry and I exchanged glances, and I could see that he was beginning to grasp just how popular the Rollers were. There was no longer a question that bringing the Rollers to America would make good business sense.

The performance was about what I had expected. The kids were on their feet the entire time—screaming, swaying to the rhythm of the music, tartan scarves held above their heads. It wasn't the Beatles, but it sure did bring back memories. The Bay City Rollers were five good-looking young men who sang reasonably well.

After the show, I went backstage to see Tam Paton. He wanted the Rollers to play America soon, so I invited him back to my hotel to discuss the possibilities.

No back-and-forth. No protracted negotiations. Paton and I made a deal right then and there. We signed a one-year contract granting me the right to represent the Bay City Rollers in America, then returned to the theater for the second show. Whereas the first audience had been predominantly eight- to twelve-year-old boys and girls, the evening show consisted overwhelmingly of female teens who, out of excitement, kept jumping on their seats and screaming. It reminded me of the first and only time that the Rolling Stones played Carnegie Hall.

On my return to New York, the first person I called was Howard Cosell, the sportscaster and television personality, who was preparing to launch a variety show that would be almost a carbon copy of Ed Sullivan. Abe Margolies had introduced me to Howard at Abe's Steak House, which Abe opened after Les Champs closed.

"Howard, I just came back from Scotland, where I signed a very exciting act that I think you should put on your first show. The Bay City Rollers could help put your program on the map."

"Sid, I appreciate your calling me with this opportunity, but you need to talk to the producers, Alan King and Rupert Hitzig. They handle that aspect. You know Alan. Call him and discuss it with him.

I have no objection whatsoever. If they say it's okay, we'll put the Bay City Rollers on our first show."

I called Alan King and set up an appointment to see him at his office. Howard attended the meeting along with Roone Arledge, who was Howard's boss at ABC and producer of the immensely successful *Monday Night Football* telecasts, which had catapulted Howard to stardom. I began the meeting by passing around pictures of the cheering crowds in Scotland.

"This, gentlemen," I said, "is by no means the Beatles. But not since the Beatles has there been a hysteria and reaction to a group like this by the young kids in Britain. I stayed in a hotel in Scotland and was kept up all night by kids wearing Bay City Rollers clothes and singing Bay City Rollers songs. It's my prediction that if you put the group on your show, you'll need to have police barricades around the theater and kids will be lined up for days waiting for tickets. It'll get you tremendous press coverage. I'm suggesting that you do a remote from Great Britain featuring the Rollers for your first show. You'll televise, via satellite, a concert in London that I will arrange with the group's manager."

"This is Howard Cosell!" During his twenty-nine year career, the famous sportscaster added pizazz to the games with his strong opinions.

New York-born comedian Alan King wears many hats and always comes out on top.

I took a breath and continued my sales pitch. "You'll show your audience the hysteria, the kids wearing tartans and the whole scene surrounding this good-looking young group. The following week, you'll telecast the Rollers live from the Ed Sullivan Theatre. I guarantee you'll need those barricades and police security. The Rollers will put Howard Cosell's show on the map."

They bought it on the spot. Everyone in the production group was excited. The deal was made just as I had outlined it: the remote first, then the Rollers live the following week.

On the night of the first Cosell show, the Bay City Rollers played a concert to a small packed theater in London. Tam Paton had set it up, giving instructions that the kids in the audience be allowed to rush the stage. The group sang "Saturday Night," which was then in release in the U.S., and the kids overran the stage and knocked down the lead singer. Security was purposely lax. The result was that American television viewers saw pandemonium.

The following week, as promised by Cosell, the Bay City Rollers came to the U.S. to appear on his show. Several busloads of kids and members of the press were at the airport to greet them. On the Saturday morning prior to the show, the Rollers went to rehearsal at the Ed Sullivan Theatre. From there, I called Gary Smith, with whom I had worked as talent coordinator on Hullabaloo.

Gary was producing a TV show in England, and I told him I was at a rehearsal with the Rollers at the Ed Sullivan Theatre in New York.

"What's that screaming I hear, Sid?"

"The kids screaming for the Rollers, who just got here. They're appearing on Howard Cosell's show live this Sunday. Last week, they were on via satellite from England. Gary, they'll be back in Britain next week. Is there any chance you can use them for one of your shows?"

"Sid, you're not going to believe this, but I'm here preparing to do an Ann-Margret special. The Temptations, who were supposed to appear, just canceled. Can you get the Rollers here within the next four days?"

"I sure can, Gary."

The Bay City Rollers kicking up their heels on the streets of New York. The British group went on to release five straight U.S. gold albums.

"You've got a deal, Sid."

We had the Rollers on TV so often in those few weeks that their record "Saturday Night" soared up the charts and went to number one. I was booking them all over the U.S. and getting twenty-five grand a night. Clive Davis was a happy man. He momentarily forgot that the Bay City Rollers didn't play their own instruments.

Tam Paton worked with me for the year, as contracted. After that, he chose to go with ICM, a large booking agency, because he thought he could save money in commissions. What he gained financially, he lost in drive and creative involvement. An agent is not a manager. This was not surprising, because Tam never seemed to have the boys' best interest as his top priority. He kept them on a payroll. While he lived in the splendor of a mansion and drove a Rolls Royce, they lived in comparative poverty.

I was the Bay City Rollers' manager in America. From me they got specific skills, dedication and experience. When they made the change, they got agents who wrote orders. The group lost the momentum that I had brought to their team. Their star dimmed . . . and soon they were gone.

In 1976, the Boat People were a major issue. Many desperate Cambodians and Vietnamese were braving unknown seas in rickety boats to find refuge in other lands. The pictures of men and women with young children, miserably adrift on the water, were heart-wrenching. No one wanted to take these people in. It reminded me of the Jews fleeing Hitler's Europe thirty-five years earlier.

I wondered if I could do something to help alleviate the suffering of the Boat People. To be sure, I could donate money, which, of course, I did. But, as only one concerned citizen, I knew that whatever I could do would not begin to address the tremendous needs of these refugees.

Taking sixty thousand dollars of my own money, in addition to contributions from Felix Cavaliere, Laura Nyro and my childhood friend Jerry Rosen, I wrote and placed a full-page ad in the Sunday edition of The New York Times and the Paris edition of the International Herald Tribune, imploring the Beatles to reunite and perform at a concert to raise money for the Boat People. I knew that these ads would be seen by millions. I got many calls and letters thanking me for having taken the initiative.

On the Monday after the ad ran in the Times, Hans Janitchek, assistant to the secretary general of the United Nations, called and asked if I would come to see him. As we sat in his sun-drenched office overlooking the gleaming East River, he said, "First of all, understand that everything we say in here is being heard by someone out there. They are always listening." And he pointed out the

THE NEW YORK TIMES, SUNDAY, SEPTEMBER 19, 1976

Sunday
September 19, 1976

Dear George, John, Paul and Ringo,

You have made the world a happier place to live in. Your music has found its way into the hearts of millions of people in every corner of the world. For almost ten years now, your dedicated old friends, and countless new friends—have hoped, have waited, and patiently watched for a signal from you—that you might play from one stage, just one more time, individually, or together.

In a world that seems so hopelessly divided, engaged in civil war, scarred by earthquakes, and too often living in fear of tomorrow's encore of tragic headlines—more than ever, we need a symbol of hope for the future. Simply by showing the world that people can get it together.

Let the world smile for one day. Let us change the headlines from gloom and hopelessness to music and life and a worldwide message of peace. You four are among the very few who are in a position to make the dream of a better world come together in the hearts of millions in just one day.

The burden of the world is not on your shoulders—we all share that responsibility. This proposal is made for your consideration—only if you can find the time—and the strength to put it together.

We out there would welcome your return.

THE PLAN: Your appearance on one stage; whether you play individually or collectively, or both, would be seen by an audience of millions Moderately priced tickets would be sold in advance, at every theatre, auditorium, concert hall, and arena—where closed circuit television cables could be placed.

On the day of the event, ticket holders would be required to bring, in addition to their ticket of admission—a can of food, or an article of new or useful clothing, to be deposited in boxes at each facility. These gifts could feed and clothe an impoverished nation for years.

A 'volunteer' foundation or worldwide organization such as CARE or UNICEF could lend their resources to pick up these life-giving gifts, the day after your concert, and distribute them five days later to an area, changed over-night into a nation of hope and life.

*
THE POSSIBLE
REVENUES: $100 million from the sale of an album recorded 'live' of this event...$40 million from the sale of seats at a moderate ticket price to every closed-circuit venue around the world...$15 million for TV rights around the world; to be shown the next day, or the next week, free, to all who couldn't buy tickets; the night of the concert...$60 million from a movie of the event itself, and an equal amount of footage devoted to each of you—to talk, play, or share in your own way, your lives as individuals—with your friends who want to see you...$15 million from the sale of program books and souvenirs.

THE TIME: New Year's Day or Easter 1977.

THE PLACE: Bethlehem! Liverpool! Or wherever it is right.

Respectfully,

Sid Bernstein

window. I didn't know who "they" were, but I could imagine. It was very cloak-and-dagger.

"Mr. Bernstein," Hans continued, "you have no idea what an impact your ad has made here at the UN. The halls are buzzing. For quite a while now, the secretary general has been exploring the possibility of reuniting the Beatles for the benefit of UNICEF. He has met with no success. Because of your association with them, you probably stand as good a chance as anyone to effect a Beatles reunion. The secretary general would like you to know that he and the entire UN community will help in any way we can."

Hans told me that members of the UN would probably be calling and that I should be careful.

"They will try to use you," he warned.

Our meeting was long and exciting. I hoped that the UN's influence might help make the benefit concert for the Boat People a reality. No one could predict what would happen, but I could not have been more gratified that my ad made such an impression on the members of the United Nations.

In the days following my meeting with Hans Janitchek, I fielded many inquiries. The British and Israeli ambassadors to the UN called, the British ambassador explaining that his government had attempted to reach out to the Beatles and convince them to reunite for a worthwhile cause, meeting with no success. The Israeli ambassador pledged to help in any way he could to get the Beatles to agree to perform at a benefit concert. As an aside, it is interesting to note that the country that ultimately took in the most Boat People was Israel. The Jews remembered what it was like to seek asylum and be turned away.

Despite everyone's efforts, absolutely nothing could convince the Beatles to reunite for this cause. They continued to have internal problems, and none of them responded directly to my ads. Paul McCartney, in an interview with the Paris bureau of the *International Herald Tribune*, said that I was heaping too much responsibility on him and his mates. No matter how hard they tried, he said, they could not save the world. John Lennon told a reporter from *Playboy* that the ad was just "Sid with his Yiddish schmaltz, on bended knee doing Al Jolson." John's comments really stung.

I believe that the good Lord granted those four boys something special and that they never really understood the influence they had, how beloved they were and the full extent of responsibility that went with it.

ONE DAY SOON AFTER, my daughter Denise and I were walking on Lexington Avenue. We were about to cross Eightieth Street when a huge limousine abruptly pulled up. The door flew open and a thin, well-dressed man jumped out of the car.

"Sid! Hello!"

My daughter, about fourteen at the time, was startled.

"Hi, how are you? This is my daughter Denise."

"Hi, Denise," he said and took her hand. "It's nice to meet you."

"Sid, I wish those guys had accepted your offer in the ad. The ad was beautiful."

Mick Jagger doing his famous strut.

"I wish they had, too. It would have been quite an event. I'm sure you would have been there."

"Oh, yes, Sid. We would have been there."

We talked for a few more minutes, then the fellow looked at his watch. "Got to run along. I'm late for an appointment with Ahmet. Goodbye, Denise." He shook Denise's hand and jumped back into the limo.

Denise was enthralled. "Oh, my God! Mick Jagger!"

After the car departed, I chastised myself for not asking Mick to spearhead the event for the Boat People. After all, he was friendly with each of the Beatles. Perhaps he could have galvanized them into action.

JOHN LENNON AND YOKO ONO lived in The Dakota, a stately old apartment building on the corner of Seventy-second Street and Central Park West. Some of my favorite restaurants and bakeries were nearby, so I was often in the neighborhood. Periodically, I would meet John and Yoko on the street as they were going about their daily lives. We had a standing joke: Every time we met, John would introduce me to Yoko, who would invariably say, "John, how many times are you going to introduce me to Sid?"

Several weeks after I had heard about John's interview in *Playboy*, I ran into John and Yoko.

"Sid! Sid!" John shouted. We hugged, as always, and he introduced me, yet again, to Yoko. We spent just a few minutes talking. The schmaltz comment was not mentioned, but I walked away from our conversation convinced that John's statement was made in jest. A joke, nothing more. I felt that our relationship was intact and would continue forever.

18

Branigan Shenanigans

I HAD BEEN GOING IT ALONE at Sid Bernstein Music for several years. I liked the independence and range of projects, but remained open to other possibilities.

In the early and mid-1970s, when the New York Knicks basketball team was in its heyday, I would often take my two eldest sons, Adam and Dylan, to Madison Square Garden to see the games. Our seats, given to me by Don Kirshner, creator of the Monkees and a legend in the music business, were fabulous—right behind the Knicks bench. In the row in back of us sat a fellow named Al with his two boys, who were a bit older than mine. Al was such a big basketball fan that when we won a close one, he would throw his arms out and kiss me.

One day, my secretary buzzed. "Alton Marshall on the phone."

"Who? Never mind. Put him through."

"Hello, this is Sid Bernstein. How can I help you?"

"Sid, this is Al from the Garden, the guy who sits behind you and your basketball maniacs!"

"Alton, I'm sorry. I just knew you as Al."

"No problem. I also happen to be the president of Rockefeller Center. Sid, I would like to talk to you about a business proposition. Would you come over to my office when you have a free moment?"

The next day I walked to Rockefeller Center and made my way to Alton Marshall's lavish suite of offices.

"Make yourself at home, Sid. Perhaps you've been reading in the papers that the Rockefeller family wants to close Radio City Music Hall. Don't believe it. Nothing could be further from the truth. We want to do everything possible to keep it open. Your reputation as a promoter is well-known, and we would like you to consider coming in as producer and promoter of our live shows."

"Al, that's very flattering, but what you have in mind will be very costly."

"Yes, but we'll put up the funds to pay for the acts you think are appropriate. We'll give you the money for advertising and promotion. We'll even provide you with office space right in the building. The salaries for your staff, union labor costs, rental of the Music Hall facility and other operating costs will come out of your gross take from the shows. . . . In essence, we'll be your partners, Sid."

My interest was apparent.

"When would you like to start?"

I smiled. "How about today?"

We shook hands, and I rushed back to my 505 Park Avenue office, eager to tell Billy Fields, Marilyn Rubenfeld and Barbara Davies that we were moving to Radio City Music Hall.

I THOUGHT IT WOULD BE EASY to book acts into Radio City, one of the most famous venues in the world. As home of the Rockettes and the world-renowned Easter and Christmas spectaculars, it had over the years become as popular a New York tourist attraction as the Empire State Building and the Statue of Liberty. I had the money to buy any act I wanted and to pay for advertising. It should have been easy, but I had the most awful time.

In the years since I had stopped promoting, Ron Delsener had moved in and become a promotion powerhouse. While I was busy managing acts, Ron had established allegiances everywhere. Every time I inquired about the availability of an act for the Music Hall, I was told that "Delsener has that."

I spoke to Lee Guber about my predicament. He offered a solution: "Sid, I'm always booking performers for my summer theaters. I think that if I ask to book them into Radio City, no one will refuse me. Let's be partners."

I had no choice. I wanted to do this on my own, but the cards were stacked against me. Lee had the leverage. If the agents and managers wanted to keep their clients working at the Guber theaters in Westbury, Long Island, and Valley Forge, Pennsylvania, during the key summer months, they would have to honor his requests to appear at Radio City.

The first act we presented at the Music Hall was the great British rock band Jethro Tull, which had exceptional musical ability and was known for its unique sound and the mysterious, surreal imagery in lyrics. The group sold out the three weekend shows, and many people were turned away. It seemed as if Radio City had become a pop music venue overnight.

Lee Guber demonstrated his clout. In short order, we had Marvin Gaye, David Soul, Patti LaBelle, Sammy Davis, Jr., Linda Ronstadt, Frankie Valli, Buddy Rich, Nancy Wilson, Sarah Vaughan, Stan Getz, Maynard Ferguson, Paul Anka, Arthur Fiedler and the Boston Pops and others. Our relationship with Radio City and Alton Marshall was top-of-the-line. We received first-class treatment, but . . . and it's a big BUT . . . we couldn't make any money. As producers, we had to pay the Music Hall's rental fee from the first proceeds. Then, of course, there were all the operating costs, which were extremely high. The partnership was great for Radio City because they got their fees, but no matter how hard we tried, we couldn't turn a profit. After two years, Lee and I threw in the towel. But those two years were not wasted.

I MOVED SID BERNSTEIN MUSIC to offices near Lincoln Center. John Jackson, our production manager at Radio City, wanted to help me arrange a Beatles reunion. The proper way to reach John, Paul, George and Ringo was through their representatives, I told him. I was reluctant to buttonhole the boys individually. I also mentioned that I had a twelve-million-dollar financial commitment that Senator Arlen Specter had helped arrange with a bank in Philadelphia, but that I had run into a brick wall.

John suggested that I call his best friend, Gary Stevens, who among other things was the press agent for Johnny Carson and could reach practically anyone on the planet. Gary came to my office, and we kicked around some ideas. He believed that we needed someone with unquestionable credentials and a worldwide reputation to penetrate the insular world of the Beatles.

"Someone like Prince Philip," he said.

"You mean the husband of the Queen of England?"

"None other."

I put Gary on retainer so he could explore the possibility of having Prince Philip intercede with the Beatles' representatives on my behalf. Gary contacted a friend at the United Nations, who gave him the prince's number at Buckingham Palace. Gary dialed and explained to an assistant to Prince Philip's aide that I was the promoter who had first brought the Beatles to the U.S. and that it was my desire to stage a Beatles reunion, with all the proceeds earmarked for various charities. The assistant's interest was piqued, and he assured Gary that the prince would hear our proposal. He also stated that the prince's favorite charity was the World Wildlife Conservation Fund.

About a week later, Prince Philip called Gary from Buckingham Palace. At first, Gary had a hard time believing that it was really royalty on the phone.

"Old chap, what's this all about and should I get involved?" the prince asked.

"Prince Philip," Gary said, "a successful Beatles reunion would mean millions for various charities, including the World Wildlife Conservation Fund."

"That sounds sensible. What exactly are you instructing me to do?"

"Prince Philip, if you could call all four of the individuals—Paul McCartney, John Lennon, Ringo Starr and George Harrison—and request that they bring about this reunion for charity, it would be a beginning."

"Yes. But I don't know their addresses or phone numbers or who their agents are. . . . Tell me about this chap Bernstein."

"Sid Bernstein is the man who initially brought the Beatles to America. He is also the man who presented them at Shea Stadium in the first stadium concert in U.S. history."

"Just one moment," the prince said. "S-H-A-Y—." He was taking notes.

"No, please excuse me, but it's S-H-E-A."

"Tell me, Mr. Stevens, does Mr. Bernstein have a date in mind for this concert?"

"Not yet."

"Well, let me look into it. I'll call you back, or you can call my assistant."

Two or three weeks passed. Not a word. Gary called the palace and a rather abrupt female assistant to the prince told him, "If we have any news for you, sir, we will call."

Two weeks later, Prince Philip called Gary personally, about midnight London time.

"Mr. Stevens, I have been working on this, and frankly I am running into a stone wall. There are so many layers of people—lawyers, accountants and the like—shielding the principals."

"You understand, Prince Philip, how much money this could mean for charity?"

"I know, and I wish I could assist you. You're a good man, and I'm sure Mr. Bernstein is a good man, too, but I cannot make any headway. If you have any further ideas, please call me, Mr. Stevens."

The timing was wrong. The Beatles still had many issues among themselves, and nothing would get them back together until those were resolved. I never got a chance to thank Prince Philip for his help, but I deeply appreciated his taking the time to try.

THOUGH OUR EFFORTS TO EFFECT a Beatles reunion never bore fruit, I didn't take it personally. Every encounter I've ever had with the Beatles as a group or individually has been comfortable and warm.

One day after school, Gerry took some of the kids for ice cream. As they were ordering, Paul McCartney came into the store with two of his children. Gerry and Paul had never met, so she introduced herself and they chatted for a bit while the kids enjoyed their ice-cream cones.

As Gerry was leaving, Paul asked her to send me his best regards. He added: "Mrs. Bernstein, your husband is one of the most decent men in our industry."

Paul's words meant a great deal. I will never forget them.

IT WAS DURING OUR STAY at Radio City that I discovered Laura Branigan. The weekend that Linda Ronstadt was to play there, I decided to go to the Music Hall very early to sit in on Linda's rehearsal and sound-check. I wanted to consult with the stagehands and other crew members to make sure that everything was perfect.

As I approached the backstage entrance, a group of people were walking in the opposite direction. I made eye contact with a tall, beautiful young woman with long, flowing hair. She smiled, but I kept walking. As I reached the stage door, I heard a voice.

"Mr. Bernstein! Oh, Mr. Bernstein!" I turned around, and standing before me was that gorgeous creature.

"Do we know each other?" I asked.

"You don't know me, but I know who you are. My name is Laura Branigan. I've been meaning to call you for weeks. I'm a singer, and I need a manager."

"So why didn't you call?"

"I didn't think you'd take my call, Mr. Bernstein."

"I understand, Laura, but you should have called. I speak to everyone. All you have to do is call the switchboard at Radio City and ask for me."

"I'll call you soon," she said.

I proceeded backstage to see to the arrangements for Linda Ronstadt. When I got to my office, I told Marilyn, Barbara and Billy that I had met this absolutely ravishing girl who said she was a singer in need of a manager. "I hope she calls. If she can sing half as good as she looks, watch out!"

The very next morning, Marilyn buzzed. "Laura Branigan on the phone, Sid. Let me put her off. We're getting hundreds of calls for tickets to see Linda! We're sold out, and it's too hectic. What do you need this for right now?"

"Wait a minute, Marilyn. She's the girl I met yesterday. I want to talk to her."

I chatted with Laura briefly and made an appointment to see her the next day. When she arrived, everyone in the office stopped working. She was stunning. Laura and I talked for a while in my office, then she asked if she could sing for me. As I showed her into the rehearsal room next to the office, Marilyn whispered, "Sid, really, there's no time for this right now!"

"It's okay, Marilyn. Just twenty minutes is all I need."

We entered the rehearsal room, and Laura sat at the piano. "This is a song I wrote. It's called 'Memories.'"

She began to play, then closed her eyes and started to sing. Sheer magic. I hadn't experienced such powerful feelings from a performer since Judy Garland. Tears were streaming down my face. Laura finished and opened her eyes.

"Are you ready for the next song?" she asked.

"No, Laura. I've heard enough."

"Don't you want to hear more? I have two more songs that I think are pretty good."

"No, Laura, not necessary. What would you like me to do for you?"

"I'd like you to manage me."

"You got me, Laura. You got me. I'll manage you. Speak to Barbara Davies, my business manager. Tell her who your lawyer is and we can begin working out a deal."

Several weeks later, we signed a five-year contract. I had discovered the next Judy.

LAURA HAD STAR QUALITY, but because her performing experience was scant, I felt that she needed to sing in front of small groups to get feedback and gain confidence. So, I began to invite friends and acquaintances—seven to twelve people at a time—to the rehearsal room during lunchtime to hear Laura. Everyone seemed to love what she was doing, and she was developing poise and self-assuredness.

Eight or ten weeks into this regimen, I invited Shirley MacLaine to a lunchtime concert.

"I'll come," she said, "but I can't stay long. My editor is in town."

"Fifteen minutes is all, Shirley. It'll take only fifteen minutes."

When Shirley arrived dolled up in a fur coat and matching hat, people were already in the rehearsal room. She made quite the entrance and caused a bit of a stir. When everyone settled down, Laura began to sing.

An hour later, everyone had gone their separate ways, but Shirley was still offering encouragement and support to Laura.

I walked Shirley out of the building. "Sid, this girl is going to be a star. You really have something here."

"I know, Shirley, I know."

WHEN I FELT THAT LAURA BRANIGAN was ready to be heard by the record companies, I began to invite the A&R men and other record execs to our musical lunch events.

Bob Summer, president of RCA, attended one session. He loved Laura and sent his Artists & Repertoire people to have a listen. They reported back that none of her originals had hit potential. RCA passed. One after another, record companies came, listened, loved her and passed. All the A&R folk issued the same verdict.

I was puzzled. After all, the R in A&R stands for repertoire. It's the A&R person who's supposed to find a hit song for the artist. That's what great A&R men like Clive Davis do for talent they believe in. I was frustrated and furious. Does no one have the patience to do the work necessary to find the right song for Laura?

Furthermore, although I was promoting Laura as a singer and a songwriter, that didn't mean that Laura and I would refuse to record someone else's material. No one even asked us to.

Not one of the labels I had invited pursued Laura, and I was amazed. But, then again, almost every record company had rejected the Beatles.

I refused to give up. There were other options. For one, I had not invited anyone from Atlantic Records to the lunchtime presentations. I knew they were still a little peeved because I had moved the Rascals to Columbia, but I bit the bullet and called Ahmet Ertegun. He was charming and cordial, and invited me to bring Laura up to Atlantic.

"Ahmet, I'm not going to bring her to the office. You're going to be conducting business, fielding phone calls from Mick Jagger and who knows who else. This girl is a terrific torch singer. She deserves your complete attention. It won't work at your office."

"So how can I hear her, Sid? You don't have any tape on her. Where can I hear her?"

"At your home, Ahmet."

"I don't have a piano at home."

"Are you kidding me, Ahmet? One of the world's preeminent music mavens and you don't have a piano? Wait till I tell everyone that!" We both laughed.

"Sid, it's true, but my brother, Nesuhi, has one. We can go there. Let me ask him. Hold on."

I heard him on his other line speaking to Nesuhi in French. In a moment, Ahmet came back on the line.

"Sid, Nesuhi thinks I'm crazy, but because it's you, he's agreed. When can you bring her up?"

The following Friday, Laura and I made our way to Nesuhi's Fifth Avenue apartment. Mica Ertegun, the famous interior decorator and Ahmet's wife, was there with Ahmet and Nesuhi. A butler was offering drinks. I introduced Laura, and she began to sing. Almost immediately, everyone was tapping their toes and swaying to the music. As Laura sang "Memories," Mica's eyes looked misty. When Laura finished, Ahmet abruptly said that he wanted to talk but that he had to go home to change into his tuxedo. He and Mica had another engagement that evening.

"Let me get a cab for you, Sid," he said. "You can drop me at home, and we can spend a few minutes talking."

We talked as we rode. "Sid, what's the deal? What do you want to do?"

"Two albums the first year, if the first one doesn't hit. Four more albums after that, an advance of one hundred thousand dollars and big budgets for the recording sessions. I'm not sure about the percentage. We'll discuss that later."

"We'll let our attorneys work that out. You have a deal, Sid." We shook hands, and that was it. I was demanding, but it worked.

I called Laura, and when I told her about the deal, she started screaming. We had gone from nowhere to almost everywhere in the course of one hour at Nesuhi Ertegun's Fifth Avenue apartment.

Atlantic assigned Arif Mardin, its number-one producer, to work with Laura. He loved her singing and worked very hard on the album. Three singles were released, but none of them made it, so the album was shelved. The recording and release of the three singles took up almost two years, and still we had no hit.

Laura and I were in the recording studio one day when Mick Jagger came strolling in wearing, jeans, a T-shirt and sneakers.

"Sid, I hear you have quite an artist recording here. People have been telling me that she's marvelous. I'd like to hear her."

"By all means, Mick. Be my guest."

He sat near me on a bench in front of the recording console. "Hey, Mick. Remember when you and the Rolling Stones got me rolled right out of Carnegie Hall? Remember when your lunatic fans tried to jump over the orchestra pit at the Academy of Music? Hard to believe that was ten years ago. Mick's eyes rolled upward in memory, then he concentrated on Laura.

"She's marvelous, Sid. I think she's going to be a big star. I wish you luck."

With that, he left.

I ORGANIZED A BAND FOR LAURA and she did a few club dates, primarily at Reno Sweeney's, a trendy Greenwich Village club. Audiences were enthusiastic. It was just a matter of time.

Atlantic brought in a German with the Americanized name of Jack White to work with Laura. Jack owned the publishing rights to "Gloria," which had been a hit in Italy and Germany. As soon as he played the song for us, I turned to Laura. "That's our hit!" Of that, I was certain.

Atlantic flew Laura and Jack to California to record "Gloria." While there, Jack White's partner evidently planted seeds of doubt in Laura's mind. The day before the projected release of the single, I got a call from Larry Krutek, Laura's husband. "Sid, you have to raise one hundred thousand dollars to promote 'Gloria' for Laura."

"What, Larry? What are you talking about?"

"You have to do it, because if you don't, the record will go nowhere. We need to hire independent promo men, and they're expensive."

"Larry, I believe in the record and I think that Atlantic, with their crack promo team, can break 'Gloria.' I don't think we need one hundred thousand dollars' worth of indie promo men.

I thought about Larry's "plea" and tried but was unable to raise the one hundred grand. Was it because my heart wasn't in it? Was it the undue pressure coming from Larry? Whatever the reason, I didn't do it.

Soon after, Jeff Grinstein called and said he had heard that I was no longer Laura Branigan's manager. I knew Jeff when he was the president of the Bay City Rollers fan club. When Tam Paton, the Rollers' manager, pulled the group from me, Jeff quit in protest. Then I began to manage Laura, and Jeff became the president of her fan club. I respected Jeff, but when he related this rumor to me, I thought he was smoking funny cigarettes.

"Forget it," I said. "It's ridiculous. We still have a year to go on our contract."

Just a half hour or so earlier, I had gotten off the phone with Laura and everything seemed in order.

At Sid Bernstein Music, everyone had to pass my door en route to their office. It was customary to exchange quick hellos, but on the day that Jeff relayed that rumor, Mitch, our promo man, walked right by without a word. That was odd. A while later, he called me from three offices down and asked if I was sitting.

"Yes, Mitch, I'm sitting."

"Okay, I need to come in and tell you something."

As he walked in, I could see by the look on his face that "something" was terribly wrong.

"What is it, Mitch?"

"I just came from Atlantic Records and everybody was asking where you are and what's going on. They said a rumor is out that you're no longer managing Laura Branigan and that a woman named Susan has taken over."

"That's absurd, Mitch. Who's Susan? I just spoke to Laura in our usual morning call, and she ended it as always: 'I love you, Sid.' This is nonsense. Forget it."

It was now about 12:30 or 1:00 P.M. in New York. The call from Jeff Grinstein had alerted me that something was rotten in L.A. Initially I had discounted it, but no longer. Gerry had warned me about Laura's husband many times. "Sid, that guy Krutek is going to be your undoing." Now her words were haunting me.

This was rock bottom. Laura was like family. I had nurtured her career for five years, and she had become a big sister to my kids. I had turned down opportunities to manage other artists, some of whom had become susperstars, so I could devote all of my energy to pushing Laura. She was on the verge of hitting it big. Could she possibly be the voice behind the rumors?

Around 2:00 P.M. New York time, I received a call from an agent at William Morris. "Sid, there's a story all over L.A. that—"

"Discount it." I refused to believe what was happening. It was just too shocking.

I left the office to pick up Adam, Denise and Dylan at school. I took them to Baskin Robbins for ice cream, then we went to sit in Central Park. Adam and Denise asked me what was wrong. "Just tired," I said.

The truth was that this was one of the worst days of my life. After dinner that evening, I told Gerry what had transpired.

"I'm not surprised, Sid. Not a bit."

I HAD BEEN IN THE BUSINESS for more than thirty years. I had always tried to deal in good faith and fairness. Doing the right thing had always been paramount. Shenanigans were not for me. I felt heartsick. I needed a change.

"Sid," my friends said, "you are always willing to sit and talk to just about anybody. You dispense advice based on forty years' worth of experience, and you never ask for anything in return. Stop giving it away! Hang up a shingle as a consultant and start getting paid for the advice!"

I decided to heed their words and see what it would be like to get paid for the guidance I had so freely dispensed for so many years.

After he heard how the relationship with Laura Branigan came to an end, Abe Margolies encouraged me to return to promoting. He was ready to fund anything I wanted to do, but since promoters like Ron

Born Sheldon Greenfield, Chicago native Shecky Greene was a major Las Vegas attraction for decades.

Delsener and Bill Graham had basically replaced me, I didn't want to return to promoting full time. I had lost contact with the venues, agents and acts. I told Abe that I wanted to try my hand at consulting.

At Abe's bidding, I did, however, make an exception and agreed to promote Shecky Greene at Carnegie Hall. He was a terrific comedian and a frequent customer at Abe's Steak House. I worked out the details, and as a favor to the man who had always told me to "DO IT!," I presented Shecky at Carnegie. The engagement was successful, and I felt better. Then I made another exception and presented country star Mickey Gilley in a successful run at the Copacabana. Was I on a roll? For a minute, I considered going back into the promotion business. But no dice. No more promotion for me.

IN TIME, ABE ACCEPTED my decision not to resume my career as a promoter. However, he insisted that I take legal action against Laura Branigan.

"I know, Sid, that you don't like confrontation, but I will not allow you to walk away from this. Get the toughest, most aggressive lawyer you can and sue this girl. This is a gutter fight, and you need a lawyer who will get down in the trenches with you."

I retained Barry Slotnick, who later became famous defending Bernhard Goetz, who had protected himself with a gun when four young men tried to hold him up in the New York subway system. Barry is a great attorney, but he wasn't a music attorney and, combined with his increasing workload, found it difficult to move my case along. Abe suggested that we find another lawyer, so we switched to Roy Cohn, whose national reputation as a tough, no-holds-barred street fighter had been made in the 1950s during the McCarthy era. Again, it was delay after delay.

Finally, I told Abe that I thought an entertainment attorney could get the case settled quickly. He agreed, and Marty Silfen, a young litigator, came aboard. I was awarded a satisfactory settlement, but no amount of money could make up for the heartache and hurt that Laura Branigan had caused. She had a disco hit with "Gloria," but her second hit, "Solitaire," paled in comparison.

Laura Branigan's career has been spotty. She hasn't approached the stardom that I believed was in her grasp and might have attained had she remained in mine. That is something neither I nor Laura will ever know.

19

Un-Imaginable

O N December 8, 1980, I was at Fine & Schapiro's restaurant on Manhattan's Upper West Side, having a leisurely dinner with David and Sandy Brokaw, the West Coast-based publicists for Mickey Gilley. We were celebrating Mickey's highly successful run at the Copa. Celia Matthau, former daughter-in-law of Walter, came into the restaurant to pick up a takeout order. Celia was a singer from California, so I asked her to join us.

As usual, the conversation turned to the Beatles, and everyone wanted to hear inside stories. Time passed swiftly, and before long the busboys were preparing the restaurant for closing. We walked outside and turned left to make our way to Broadway. I hailed a cab for the two PR men from Los Angeles and instructed them to go east on Seventy-second Street and through Central Park to their hotel.

"On the last corner before the park, look to your left and you will see The Dakota," I said. "That's where John Lennon and Yoko Ono live." I bid them goodbye and hailed another cab to take me to an appointment downtown.

After dropping Celia off en route, I proceeded to SPQR, a famous Italian restaurant on Mulberry Street, in Little Italy. I had promised that I would look at the nightclub that was about to open above the dining room. Lou, the owner, took me upstairs to show me the new club, and we discussed the best time for the grand opening and which artist should be the first to appear.

All of a sudden, I heard a shriek. "Oh, no. Oh, no! Oh, my God! Sid! Sid! Come here, come here!" It was Lou's wife, Luba. "You won't believe this! My girlfriend just called and said that John Lennon has been shot and taken to a hospital."

Who would want to shoot John Lennon?

"It can't be right," I said. "It must be a mistake."

Lou and I finished our conversation and he offered me a lift. Since they lived in New Jersey, Lou and Luba dropped me off on West Seventy-second Street so that I could make my way east.

I hopped a cab and asked the driver to go through Central Park. The radio was on, and the talk was about John.

"Señor," I said to the cabbie, "is this true what they're saying about John Lennon?"

"Yes, and this has been going on all night, every station. He's gone."

"*What?!?* John Lennon is dead?"

"Yes, they could not save him. He's gone."

By now we were approaching The Dakota. From the distance I could see flashing police lights and people milling about. It was 1:30 in the morning, and the scene was surreal. Photographers and satellite trucks were everywhere. What seemed like thousands of kids holding candles were standing vigil. I was numb. The cab crawled through the traffic and finally made it through the intersection and into the park.

It was hard to believe that I had been a block away, at Fine & Schapiro's restaurant, talking about John Lennon, when he was gunned down.

Gerry was waiting for me when I got home.

"Sid, you heard?"

"Yes, Gerry."

"The phone hasn't stopped. They're calling from everywhere. You have more than twenty-five messages. Sid, it's so late and you have a lecture at Hunter College first thing tomorrow morning. Please get some rest."

I had forgotten that weeks earlier I had committed myself to speaking to the students in the music department at Hunter. I looked at all the messages: the BBC, Paris radio, The New York Times, Daily News, New York Post, NBC, CBS, ABC, Time, Newsweek—the list went on and on. Everyone wanted a statement about the terrible tragedy that still didn't seem real.

"I can't answer these tonight, Gerry. I'm heartsick. The only one I'm going to respond to is Good Morning America, because of Alan Cohen. Alan, one of the show's producers, had been a friend for many years.

"Oh, Sid, thank you for phoning back. I wish this call was about something else, and I'm sure you're getting bombarded. It's devastating . . . but I've got to have you on Good Morning America tomorrow. Could you please do it as a favor to me?"

"Alan, I'm bushed. This is a terrible day, and I really have nothing to say. Besides that, I'm committed to doing a lecture at Hunter College early tomorrow morning." I looked at my watch and realized that it was already tomorrow.

"We'll put you on first, Sid. No more than ten minutes, I promise. I'll send a limo and have the car drive you home as soon as you finish. I'll even give you a wake-up call at 6:15."

"Okay," I said. "Only for a good friend."

Promptly at 6:15, the phone rang. The limo was at the front door when I emerged from the building. The ride to the ABC studios took but a few minutes, and before I knew it, my time on air with David Hartman went by. I don't remember what he asked or how I responded.

The limo took me home by way of Seventy-second Street. When we reached The Dakota, I heard throngs of mourners with candles singing John Lennon songs. Radio, television and newspaper people were everywhere. It was a repeat of the scene I had witnessed at 1:30 in the morning. It was if no one had moved all night. Pat Collins, a New York news personality, saw me through the car window, and I cracked it open to say hello.

"Sid, you've got to say a few words, please."

"Pat, I'm exhausted and overwrought and I don't want to get out of this car."

"Okay, I understand, Sid," she said graciously.

I went home and tried to sleep. Gerry turned off the phones. About an hour into a doze, the insistent apartment buzzer woke me with a start.

"Mr. Bernstein, a camera crew is here asking for you," the doorman said.

Then another voice came over the intercom. "Can we have a statement from you in front of the building, Mr. Bernstein? It'll just take a few minutes."

"I don't want my building or my home photographed. There are lunatics out there shooting people. I'm scheduled to give a talk at Hunter College in about an hour and you're welcome to attend. I'll answer any questions you have at the college."

"All right. We appreciate it. Could you use a ride to Hunter?"

"Sure, we can drive over together, and I'll do the interview there. Thanks."

When we arrived at the college, the professor who had arranged for me to speak was there to greet me.

"Mr. Bernstein, thank you so much for coming. I wasn't sure if you would show up. I know how traumatic these last twenty-four hours must have been for you. Would you mind if we moved your talk to a larger room than previously scheduled? There are so many people who want to hear you speak this morning."

"Of course. That would be fine," I said.

While arrangements were being made to change lecture halls, I was taken to an office in the music department and given a seat with a footrest. I promptly fell asleep. In a few minutes, there was a knock at the door.

"We're ready for you now, Mr. Bernstein. Please follow me."

As I entered the hall, I was dazed. It was packed with sad faces. People were standing along the walls and squatting in the aisles.

Newspaper reporters tried to nudge their way to the front. Only the Beatles could generate this kind of reaction so quickly. It was the incredible Beatles grapevine at work. They had found out about my talk at Hunter and passed the word. The professor introduced me.

Sitting behind a desk crowded with microphones, I began slowly. "I was all prepared to talk to you as students of the music business. But, in view of the events of last night, that has to change. . . . I don't know if I can speak about music right now, because the tragedy that happened not far from here has changed everything. A wife has lost her husband; children have lost their father; I have lost a friend; the world has lost a champion for love and peace. The voice of John Lennon will be sorely missed."

My own was breaking. From the corner of my eye, I could see one of the older newspapermen remove a handkerchief from his breast pocket and dab his eyes.

"The world will sorely miss John Lennon," I continued. And then I stopped. There was nothing more to say. I went home to escape into the oblivion of sleep.

THE NEXT DAY, I went to The Dakota with my sons Adam and Etienne. A huge crowd stretched completely around the block, waiting to leave cards, flowers and gifts at the entrance to that stately old apartment building. My boys got on line and placed their offering on the iron gate that surrounded the building.

The following Saturday, New York City Mayor Ed Koch declared a day of commemoration for John. In the cold, tens upon tens of thousands moved en masse in the direction of Central Park. I made my way to the ABC-TV truck to find Ernie Anastos, a respected news anchorman, with whom I agreed to do a live interview.

"Cousin" Bruce Morrow helped me climb onto the truck platform. There we stood, surveying the crowd of almost one hundred thousand people as a light snow began to fall. Bruce leaned over to me. "Look at the snow, Sid. It's like angels falling from the sky."

How befitting the occasion, I thought. And how appropriate that Yoko Ono had arranged for John's ashes to be spread in the park where she, John and son Sean used to walk.

Ernie asked me to make a statement.

From my vantage point, I could see my daughter Denise and two of her friends in the crowd. Through the loudspeaker, I could hear the song "Imagine." Denise and her friends were sobbing.

I looked out at the sea of sadness and said, "Our tears are falling on this hallowed ground that now holds John Lennon's ashes."

As I left the park that day, I reflected on what had just happened and remembered the glorious past. There would be no more chance meetings on the street. No more requests to see my knees. No more frantic calls for restaurant recommendations or tickets to events. How do you replace that part of your heart? You don't.

NINETEEN YEARS LATER, on December 31, 1999, word reached me that a crazed man with a Beatles obsession had broken into George Harrison's estate outside London and attacked both George and his wife, Olivia.

Not again! I thought. How frightening that George, the most re-clusive and security-conscious of the group, had not been immune from the act of a madman. This time, however, the news reports had a different ending: George and Olivia were expected to recover. I breathed a sigh of relief.

Once again, phone calls poured in from all over the world. My statement was simple: "I am thankful that George will be okay, yet terribly sorry that he has to go through this physical and emotional ordeal." I explained that although my relationship with George was not as close as that with John and Paul, I sent him my love and wishes for a complete and speedy return to health." And I truly meant it.

I had developed a close bond with John, since he had become a fellow New Yorker, and with Paul and his wife, Linda, who also spent a lot of time in New York with their family. George, on the other hand, shunned the limelight. He was introspective and re-served, yet highly spiritual. But I liked George from the moment I met him at the Plaza Hotel so many years earlier. He is a gentle man and a gentleman.

George Harrison's sensitivity was demonstrated during one of the Rascals' trips to Great Britain. The group was in London to perform, and George invited them to a studio where he was recording. After only a few minutes, he received a call regarding an emergency at his home and left immediately. Later, he called to apologize profusely and the next day sent his limousine to bring the Rascals to his home for a visit. The group spent several hours with George, hanging out and listening to music. Even though it was a tough time for him, George extended his hospitality. That's just the way he is.

MORE THAN THIRTY YEARS AFTER the Beatles broke up, it is still impossible for George, Paul and Ringo to find peace and privacy. They must continually protect themselves from the unrelenting interest, curiosity and adoration of their fans. They began as four unknowns from Liverpool and now, in a sense, they are prisoners of fame.

What would Brian Epstein say of this?

20

Here, There and Everywhere

I N 1981, CLIVE EPSTEIN, Brian's brother, came to New York. He called to extend best regards from his mother, Queenie. Clive and I hit it off immediately. He had a wife and three children, so we talked about our families. Of course, we also spoke about Brian. I told Clive how Stigwood, Bernstein and Epstein almost became partners.

"That would have been great for Brian. Too bad it didn't happen," he mused.

Clive was surprised to learn that I'd never been to Liverpool. "I'd like for you to meet my family, and my mother would be especially thrilled. Come visit, Sid."

After some months, I accepted his invitation and with my son Adam flew to Great Britain. Clive insisted that we stay at his home rather than a hotel. When at last I met Queenie for the first time after all these years, we spent hours talking about Brian. "I miss him terribly," she confided. "I can still hear his footsteps around the house."

With Queenie's permission, the rabbi of the community took

me to Brian's gravesite in the synagogue cemetery. As I stood before the tombstone bearing Brian's Hebrew name, I said a silent prayer: "Thank you, Brian, for what you did for me. I will always treasure your memory. May your soul rest in peace."

WHILE IN LIVERPOOL, Clive got us tickets to a repertory theater production of *Lennon*, a wonderfully acted play about John's life. It ended with the sound of three shots. There wasn't a dry eye in the room.

After the show, Clive took me aside. "Sid, the cast knows that you're here and would love to meet you. Do you think you could spare some time?"

"Clive, take a look at me. It's a tribute to the performers and the production, but the show really got to me. I don't think I'm in the mood to meet the cast."

"It's okay, they'll understand. Please don't disappoint them."

How could I say no? I collected myself and together with Adam made my way to the dressing rooms. On the way, I stopped in the loo, as they call it, and splashed cold water on my face. A bit later, after speaking with the cast, Adam and I were introduced to Bob Eaton, the play's director. It was then that an idea hit.

"Bob, I'd love to bring the play to New York."

"Mr. Bernstein, it would be a realization of a lifelong dream for me to be able to direct a play in New York. Of course, I am very interested."

It was a quick and simple negotiation, and I returned home with a compelling new project. But bringing the play across the Atlantic was more complicated than I had anticipated. Union rules made it impossible to import the cast and director intact, so I had to choose one or the other. I knew that without British actors and their instinctive feel for Liverpool's language and milieu, it would be tough to do justice to the material. But on the other hand, I believed that Bob Eaton would be able to achieve an excellent result with American actors. And, after all, it was Bob to whom I had first proposed a New York production. I chose the director.

It took two years before *Lennon* opened at the Entermedia, a six-hundred-seat theater on Second Avenue at Twelfth Street. The American cast—

That's me in front of the Lennon *marquee. Though the show was not a commercial success, it was a much-deserved and wonderful tribute to John.*

including the versatile Greg Martin, a Brit who had been living in the States for a while—was superlative. The audiences rose to their feet night after night. But the critics were less kind, some erroneously stating that the actors weren't actually playing their instruments. Perhaps it was just too soon after John's passing for fans to deal with the reality of his murder. Whatever the reason, audiences did not come in sufficient numbers to warrant our keeping the show open. We closed in nine weeks.

Throughout my association with the Beatles in the 1960s, I had never had the opportunity to meet their legendary producer, George Martin. Several years after *Lennon* opened in New York, at a luncheon in the Grosvenor Hotel for the British version of the Grammy Awards, I finally got to do so.

I was in London to introduce Perry Muckerheide, an American friend, to Cynthia Lennon, John's first wife. Perry wanted to stage a tribute to John in Milwaukee, and I was doing some consulting for him. He wanted to meet Cynthia to get her feedback and support. While we were at the Grosvenor, Perry heard about the awards luncheon and wanted to go. It was too late to call for tickets. Still, Perry and I went to the entrance of the hall.

"My, how crowded," I said. "No way we're going to get in without tickets."

"Just sit for a minute, Sid."

Perry approached two ladies collecting admission tickets, and he explained who I was and that we had just arrived in England and were surprised to find out about the awards luncheon. He called me over and introduced me, whereupon these extremely solicitous women told us to take any two seats we could find. Perry and I found two empty ones at a table near the back of the room, next to a set of stairs. As we sat there eating, Perry grabbed my arm.

"Sid! Look! There's Linda McCartney!" Linda was making her way up the stairs with one of her daughters.

Perry implored me to introduce him to Linda, and in his eagerness created quite a scene at the table. I decided to stand at the foot of the stairs in anticipation of Linda's return. As soon as she spotted me, she smiled.

"Sid Bernstein! What are you doing here . . . Stella, I want you to meet Daddy's friend from New York."

I introduced Perry, who happened to be one of the Beatles' greatest fans.

"Where are you sitting, Sid?" Linda asked. I pointed to our table in the back.

"Oh, no. Come with me. You must say hello to Paul." She led me through the labyrinth of tightly packed tables until we reached the front of the ballroom, where I could see Paul and his young son, Jamie.

"Sid, what are you doing here?" He jumped up and gave me a hug.

"I'm in London working on a project."

Everyone was staring at me, trying to figure out who I was. Nearby, I recognized Elton John and Cliff Richard. The producer of the event, a fellow from Capitol Records, walked to the table and took my arm.

"Sid, I want to take you over to meet George Martin."

Martin greeted me warmly. "Sid, I just want you to know that my son, Greg, raves about you. I can't tell you how much I appreciate the fine treatment he received from you when he worked in Lennon. I feel like I know you so well!"

"George is your son? I hadn't a clue. What a wonderful young man. Small world!"

"Indeed it is, Sid."

We talked for a while longer, and it was wonderful to meet this man after all these years. It was also ironic that I had been instrumental in the career of yet another of his boys—first the Beatles, then his son. Through our association I discovered George Martin to be a gentleman and one of the most talented people I have ever met. If Brian Epstein was the fifth Beatle, then George Martin is the sixth. A brilliant record producer, he was an integral member of the team that carried the Beatles to their huge success.

THOUGH "THERE'S NO BUSINESS LIKE SHOW BUSINESS," Gerry had just about had it. The Rascals had self-destructed, my efforts on behalf of Laura Branigan had been for naught, and my once-promising venture at Radio City had turned out to be unprofitable. While I thoroughly enjoyed my consulting jobs, the work was not steady. The precipitous drop in our income frightened her. Under the weight of all these events, Gerry felt ready for a major change. The financial pressures were enormous, and she desperately wanted out of New York and the entertainment industry.

At that time, a self-actualization program known as Ehrhard Seminar Training, or est, popularized by Werner Ehrhard, was all the rage. People from all walks of life were signing up in an effort to find a new purpose to their lives and a new way of living. Gerry decided to try it. The program heavily espoused feminism, and I began seeing changes in Gerry's thinking. I needed to find out firsthand how much est was responsible for my wife's new attitude, so I spent two weekends taking the course.

To me, it all seemed like a lot of bunk. I didn't get "it," and getting "it" was the essence of the philosophy. More important, est was disrupting my family life. All of a sudden, I had to deal with a woman completely different from the one I'd married.

With her new sense of enlightenment, she suggested that we move to Hawaii and leave the insanity of New York behind. We had taken many family trips to the islands, and everybody loved the perfect weather, magnificent vistas, and warm and friendly people. Gerry's idea was made even more compelling because ever since

Rascal Felix Cavaliere and I "groovin'" in Hawaii. 'Twas was "a beautiful morning."

the Rascals had hit it big there, we, too, were treated like royalty. Over the years, we had developed many good friends in Hawaii, one being Fred Williams, vice president of a real estate company. We had stayed in close contact with Fred, so I informed him that I might be ready for a big change in my life.

Fred was in charge of building a mall behind the renowned Royal Hawaiian Hotel. One day, he called: "Sid, you know so much about chocolate. Maybe you'd like to open a chocolate shop here in Hawaii. I would see to it that you get the absolute number-one location in the mall, the space right off the escalator at the entrance. Everybody who comes in will have to pass your shop. It's a can't-miss location."

Gerry was enthusiastic about Fred's proposition, but I was reluctant to pick up the entire family and move to Hawaii. So Gerry and I devised a plan. She would go to Hawaii to open the chocolate shop and the kids would stay with me in New York. If the shop became successful, the entire family would relocate.

When Gerry arrived in Hawaii, she found that the slower pace of the Hawaiian lifestyle caused delay after delay in constructing the mall. She had gone there with a budget and a carefully measured time line. Soon, the money was running low, the months were passing by and still no chocolate gelt.

Meanwhile, I took care of the kids. Etienne, our youngest, was eight, and Adam, our eldest, was seventeen. It wasn't always easy to coordinate activities, but we managed. One way of making sure things got done was to hold periodic family meetings to assign responsibilities: who would wash the floors, who would clean the kitchen, who would do the considerable laundry, and so on.

One day, my friend Lou Levy was visiting and practically fell down laughing listening to me supervise all six kids. He mentioned my situation to a writer friend, and she immediately thought that it would be a great story for The New York Times. The writer interviewed me, and several weeks later an article about a Manhattan father raising six kids by himself appeared in the paper. Shortly after that, the president of Warner Television called.

"Mr. Bernstein, someone here at Warner read the feature about you and your kids going it alone. We wonder if you would consider giving us an option on your story. It would make a great TV series."

Warner paid for an option on the story, but the project never went forward. The market for family-oriented shows had dried up, they explained.

AFTER EIGHT MONTHS IN HAWAII, Gerry finally had run out of money and patience. She called. "Sid, I'm coming home. Fred says it might be another year before the mall is completed, and I just don't have the staying power."

"Okay, Ger. Come home. We all miss you." It had been a long and lonely time.

We planned that she would return to New York on the day we were having a joint birthday celebration for our daughters, Denise and Casey, at Benihana, a Japanese restaurant the kids loved. What a present that would be!

On the day of the celebration, the seven of us went to Benihana. The kids were having a great time and didn't notice that I kept glancing at my watch and the door. Finally, I saw Gerry make her way to our table, and I started to cry. The kids spotted her and jumped all over her. It was a wonderful reunion. We were thrilled that she was home.

One morning soon after Gerry's return, I was leaving the bank when I heard a voice behind me.

"Hey, mate!" I kept walking.

"Hey, mate!"

Then I heard a woman's voice call my name.

I turned and saw Paul and Linda McCartney with two of their children walking toward me. When they reached me, we threw our arms around each other. Pointing to me, Paul said to his son, "You know, Jamie, nobody knows about pizza like Mr. Bernstein. Isn't that right, Sid?"

"I guess so, Paul. Do you really like good pizza?" I asked young Jamie.

"Yeah, yeah!"

"Me too, Jamie. I love it, and I have the size to prove it!"

Paul and Linda laughed.

"Listen, Sid," Paul said, "we're playing the Boston Garden tonight. We'll be back late, but tomorrow I'll give you a call. Maybe we can take all the kids, yours and mine, for pizza."

"That would be great, Paul, but I'm going out of town for a few days. I'd love to do it when I get back. Let's speak soon and arrange something."

After all this time, Paul and I have not yet shared a pie. Maybe one day . . .

THROUGH ALL THE UPS AND DOWNS, Abe Margolies and I continued to spend a lot of time together. Early one Sunday morning, he and I went to Barney Greengrass, a West Side restaurant that attracts people from all walks of life. A New York institution, Greengrass is famous for its lox, eggs and onions, a dish that held childhood memories for us both.

As we were walking home through Central Park after a leisurely breakfast, Abe was chewing on a toothpick, as he habitually did following a meal. All of a sudden, he started to choke and fell to his knees.

"Abe, what's wrong?"

"Sid, I swallowed the toothpick," he managed to say.

I tried not to panic. Almost no one was around at that early hour. I helped Abe up, and we struggled out of the park to his apartment building at Seventy-seventh Street and Fifth Avenue. The doorman rang up to Abe's apartment, but there was no answer, so I rushed to a corner phone booth and called Dr. Ezra Greenspan, Abe's doctor. Greenspan was a good friend of Abe's and a pioneer in the field of chemotherapy, and over the years Abe had been instrumental in raising large sums of money to help fund the doctor's research. Fortunately, Dr. Greenspan was at home.

"Sid, I live nearby. Jump in a cab and bring Abe right over to me."

When we reached his building, the doctor was waiting for us in the lobby. He took one look at Abe and told us to go straight to Mount Sinai Hospital.

"I'll phone ahead. They'll be expecting you."

We cabbed it over to Mount Sinai and were rushed into the emergency room. As Abe lay there being examined, countless thoughts rushed through my mind. I realized how dear Abe was to me. How he had always been there for me. I thought how devastating it would be to lose him. I was afraid.

The doctors dislodged the toothpick and, back to himself, Abe jumped up, thanked everyone and whistled his way out of the hospital. Relief replaced my anxiety, and thoughts of the uncertainty of life rushed through me.

ONE AFTERNOON, DONALD C. FARBER, an ebullient theatrical attorney who was then teaching a course in theater law and business down at the New School for Social Research, contacted me. Don was one of the forces behind the creation of the longest-running off-Broadway musical, The Fantasticks, and he loves show business and the people in it. I accepted his invitation to speak to his students as a guest lecturer.

After class, a gentleman approached me.

"Mr. Bernstein, I am the assistant dean of the New School, and I thoroughly enjoyed listening to you this evening. I was wondering if you would consider teaching a course here."

"That's very flattering, and I thank you for your kind words. I owe the New School a lot."

"How's that?"

"Many years ago, I took a course here on democracy, given by Dr. Max Lerner. It was because of that class that I began reading English newspapers, and that's how I learned about the Beatles."

"How interesting. So you owe us?" laughed the dean.

"Yes, I do! But I must tell you, I'm really not into reading lists, tests, papers and the like, so what kind of a professor would I make?"

"You wouldn't have to. We would just want you to come and tell your stories like you did tonight. Just show up and talk for an hour or so. That's it. We'll pay you for the number of lectures that you do each term. You can do as many as twelve or as few as eight."

"Pay me to tell stories?"

"Certainly. And you don't have to get bogged down with paper-work. There is none. Just share your experiences with the students and answer questions. Why not give it a try?"

"Okay, you've convinced me. When do we start?"

Shortly after my conversation with the dean, I began my teaching career at the New School, and as he had instructed, each evening I simply spoke about a different topic. As Don Farber had with me, I would occasionally bring in guest lecturers with varying expertise in the entertainment industry. Bert Padell, one of the most widely known business managers in entertainment, came in on a regular basis. Bert is a dynamic speaker, and he and I have shared the teaching load at the New School for some years now.

One day after class, Bert and I were shooting the breeze.

"You know what I'd love to do, Sid? Speak to the Music Department at Harvard. I'd like to be able to say that I lectured at Harvard."

A client of mine was a Wall Street broker and a Harvard alumnus, so I asked if he could arrange for us to lecture there.

Two months later, Bert and I flew to Boston and appeared before a large assembly of students and faculty. We had a great time, and I think that those who heard us that day did as well. It took me five years to graduate from high school, but now my resume can proudly state that I have lectured at Harvard!

IN THE SPRING OF 1988, Abe Margolies decided to host a fundraiser for then-Senator Al Gore of Tennessee, who was campaigning for the Democratic presidential nomination. Abe invited sixty or seventy people to Abe's Steak House for a thousand-dollar-a-plate luncheon. When I walked into the restaurant, I noticed that on the right side of the room was a rather large banquet table on a raised platform, where Senator Gore, no doubt, would address the group. I was looking forward to hearing him.

Following cocktail hour, we were asked to take our seats. As I sat down, a young man approached.

"You're Sid Bernstein, aren't you?"

"Yes, I am. How can I help you?"

"Mr. Bernstein, I'm an aide to Senator Gore, and I don't know if you're aware that the senator loves music and is a huge Beatles fan. Would it be okay if I brought him over?"

"Why don't you take me over to his table?"

We walked over to the senator.

"Senator Gore," the aide began, "this is Sid Bernstein, the man who brought the Beatles to America."

Al Gore jumped up, shook my hand vigorously and proceeded to pepper me with questions about how I had come to discover the Beatles, what made me want to present them at Carnegie Hall and how I conceived of the Shea Stadium concert. Over the course of our fifteen-minute-plus conversation, a large crowd gathered around. Had I not reminded the senator about the purpose of his appearance, we might still be there chatting about his favorite group. "I hope we meet again, Sid," he finally said.

"I'll look forward to that, senator," I replied and returned to my table.

I liked what he stood for—and his taste in music!

IN 1988, ALL FOUR OF MY SONS were working at Camp Chipinaw, in Bethel, New York. Bethel is the home of Max Yasgur's farm, where the Woodstock Music Festival had taken place in August 1969.

Gerry and I went to see our boys on visiting day. The camp electrician, Evan Bloom, found out that I was at the camp and introduced himself.

"You're Sid Bernstein, the music man. Would you mind if I asked you a question?"

"Not at all, Evan. What would you like to know?"

"Were you at Woodstock in 1969, Mr. Bernstein?"

"No, I wasn't. My wife was pregnant at the time, and my band, the Young Rascals, had another booking, so I couldn't be there."

"Have you ever seen the site? It's only two miles from here."

"No, I haven't."

"Would you like to?"

"I'm visiting my boys, Evan. I don't think I want to leave them."

"We'll take them with us. I'll get permission."

Evan made the arrangements, and we drove the short distance to Yasgur's Farm. Evan escorted us to the monument that commemorates the historic event—a big rock engraved with all the names of the performers that appeared at the festival. I stood before it and read the names: John Sebastian, Canned Heat, the Butterfield Blues Band, Santana, Joe Cocker, Richie Havens, Country Joe McDonald, Joan Baez, Sha-Na-Na, Arlo Guthrie, Ten Years After, Sly & the Family Stone, Jimi Hendrix, Jefferson Airplane, The Who, and Crosby, Stills, Nash & Young.

As I looked at that large, open field, I could sense the vast crowd that was there nearly twenty summers before. I could visualize the people sitting there for three days and nights in the rain and mud, enjoying the music, each other and the experience. It gave me the chills. I could hear it, see it, feel it.

"Evan, I saw the movie, but it's hard to imagine four hundred thousand people fitting into this space."

"Yes, sir, Mr. Bernstein. I was fourteen at the time and saw it with my own eyes. There were four hundred thousand people here."

Just then, a car started to come up the road.

"Mr. Bernstein, I'll bet you that car has an out-of-state license plate," Evan said. "Every day, without fail, people from around the country come here to see this place and the monument."

An automobile with Montana plates drove up the road. Inside were a man, his wife and two kids.

"Uh, excuse please," Evan said. "May I ask what brings you here?"

"I was here in '69," he answered, "and I wanted my wife and kids to see this place."

"Mr. Bernstein," Evan said, "next year is the twentieth anniversary of Woodstock. People have proposed an anniversary concert, and the original group of producers has tried to put it together, but the town is adamantly opposed. They will not issue a permit."

"Of course they're opposed. You saw what happened in 1969. The roads were paralyzed; there wasn't enough food or water. It's a miracle there wasn't a catastrophe here."

"True enough, but it was an incredible experience anyway! I think you might just be the person who could get a permit."

Gerry and I drove back to camp, dropped off the boys and headed home.

That night, I couldn't sleep. I kept thinking about what I had felt standing in front of the monument. The next morning, excited and exhausted, I picked up the phone.

"Evan, who do I make arrangements with?"

"Are you interested?"

"Yes, I am."

"Oh, my God!" he exclaimed. "Tell me, who do you want to reach? I know everybody!"

"Let's start with the key person. Let's start at the beginning."

"The first person we need to talk to is the Sullivan County supervisor."

"Okay, set it up."

The supervisor explained the local people's attitude. "We've turned down several parties, including the original producers, Sid. Everyone is afraid of a recurrence of what happened at the first one. It took us months to recover from Woodstock. Just take a look at our roads. We can't handle it!"

Rock promoter unveils 'Woodstock '94'

Site is near original festival

By TRISTRAM KORTEN
Staff Writer

WHITE LAKE — Veteran rock 'n' roll promoter Sid Bernstein went public yesterday with his plans to hold a concert near, but not on, the site of the original 1969 Woodstock festival.

Bernstein's plans come on the heels of failed negotiations this month between landowner June Gelish and the Multiple Sclerosis Society. The two parties had been working out an agreement for the non-profit group to have a concert on the original site.

The MS Society still plans to hold a concert in Bethel, but not on Gelish's land. Robert Gersch, MS executive director for southern New York, said the concert will be held on a portion of the original Max Yasgur farm that Gelish doesn't own.

He said earlier that the deal was called off because the society didn't want the sole liability for throwing a public event.

Bernstein, who made a name for himself as a promoter in the 1960s when he first introduced the Beatles to this country, was contacted by Gelish's lawyer, Stephen Davis, two weekends ago. Davis explained that the deal with the society was off, Bernstein said, and asked if he was interested.

At yesterday's news conference in Andy's Place diner in White Lake, Bernstein, partners Driscoll and Bob Morgan, said they had moved $100,000 into an escrow account

His background

Bethel '94 would be the first major music promotion project for Sid Bernstein in about nine years.

He stopped promoting bands and became a music consultant — helping organizers plan events, and consulting with musicians on their careers. In 1983 he produced the off-Broadway play "Lennon" and in 1988 the off-Broadway play "Mayor."

Last summer, he worked in Mexico City putting on a tribute to Elvis Presley.

held by Davis and that they have signed options to buy the land.

Morgan added that any money transactions were contingent upon the town and county approving the plans for a concert.

The partners, who say they have the backing of private firms such as International Management Group, plan to approach the town to secure permission to hold a concert on about 170 acres just west of the corner of Hurd Road and West Shore Drive, the site of the stage in 1969. There's a monument there now.

Morgan said that site wasn't used because the parcels they are negotiating to buy better suit their purposes.

Bernstein's proposal, called "Bethel '94,"

FRANCIS SPECKER/The Record

Music promoter Sid Bernstein yesterday announced plans for a concert next year in Bethel.

begins with a two-day concert on a permanent stage. Future plans include a performance center, a music school and a museum.

Bernstein said he doesn't want to compete with the society or another Woodstock-inspired event in Saugerties on the anniversary weekend Aug. 15, 16 and 17 by promoter John Roberts.

"I would say at the moment that it would be the mid or third weekend in July," Bernstein said. "Definitely not the weekend the boys from Saugerties are doing their thing."

"I'm aware of that, but I'm thinking of something much smaller than the original festival. I'd make absolutely certain that there is sufficient security to handle the traffic. I'm not interested in creating havoc."

"You're not going to bring the Beatles here. Are you, Sid?"

"I only wish!" I said.

"Okay, what you need to do now is talk to some of the town managers. They'll have to sign off on this. There are town and county ordinances that we've passed as a result of Woodstock. You cannot have a mass assembly of over ten thousand people. It's the law."

"Is there any flexibility there? We'll need to sell at least twenty thousand tickets to amortize the costs."

"You'll have to take that up with the town managers."

The first thing I did was talk to June Gelish, owner of Yasgur's Farm.

She agreed that for two hundred and fifty thousand dollars we could use the property for an anniversary festival.

"But, Sid, I don't think you can get the necessary permits," she cautioned.

I had a feeling that I could somehow get the venue, so I contacted

Alan Scott, the town manager of Bethel. At first, he told us that we needed the support of all the other town managers to repeal the ordinances that forbade a gathering of more than ten thousand. Neither he nor any of the other officials were encouraging.

We then embarked on what turned out to be a five-year campaign to stage the festival. We decided to present our case to local residents. I spoke to virtually anyone who would listen: town meetings, boards, schools, Mason and Kiwanis gatherings, synagogue groups. I turned it into a referendum where the will of the people would carry the day.

We had developed a workable plan, and the people of Bethel knew that we were sincere in our efforts and would keep our word. But after it became evident that we were making headway with the people of Bethel, that the local residents wanted it to happen and wanted me to do it, Alan Scott did everything he could to thwart our efforts. He sabotaged, fought and went so far as to propose his own choice, Robert Gersh, as promoter of the festival.

Finally, at a heated and acrimonious public meeting attended by an overflow crowd of Bethel residents, we prevailed over Scott's candidate by a show of hands.

All the campaigning and negotiations had taken so long that we were now talking about having a twenty-fifth anniversary Woodstock Festival. We were awarded the right to proceed with the festival on Yasgur's original site, subject to approvals from state and local authorities.

I had beaten Scott in the town council, but he kept fighting me. He granted an interview to The New York Times, in which he said that I didn't have the money to produce the festival. He enlisted the sheriff, Joe Wasser, and the district attorney to try to talk me out of the project. He refused to give in to the will of the people.

When the original organizers of Woodstock 1969 heard that I had prevailed at Bethel and was moving ahead in my plans to stage Bethel '94, they decided to respond. They went to the town of Saugerties and secured a permit to stage the twenty-fifth anniversary of Woodstock on Winston Farm. They owned the name Woodstock and got a commitment from Polygram Records and

John Scher, a concert promoter whose company had been bought by Polygram, to put up nineteen million dollars for their anniversary festival. Scher and the original group were upset that I had obtained the right to use the Yasgur property. We tried to partner with them, but after several meetings at which I offered to give up my top billing, we abandoned the idea of a joint promotion. They didn't understand that there was no way the people in Bethel were going to give them permission to do Woodstock on Yasgur's Farm. Having averted disaster back in '69, the wary townsfolk would not tempt the fates again.

Scher was so angry at this development that he tried to buy every act we had. He put down deposits on everyone he knew we wanted but hadn't yet signed. Their Saugerties festival did in fact go forward, and Scher and clan ended up spending close to twenty million dollars. There was looting, arson and violence on the last day of their festival. A veritable mess. People came from Saugerties to our site and told us that the real spirit of Woodstock was in Bethel. How could it not be?

I raised one million dollars from investors in Philadelphia, and a local insurance company promised to put up an additional five million. Notwithstanding the admonitions of the sheriff, who threatened me with arrest, and the D.A., we forged ahead.

We paid Mrs. Gelish the two hundred and fifty thousand dollars for the use of Yasgur's Farm and began planning the festival in earnest. We made a deal with the adjoining farm for use of its road for access. We retained Howard Rubenstein, New York's preeminent PR man, to handle our public relations, and we moved our command center to the Concord Hotel, whose management, the Parker family, graciously assisted in any way they could. We contracted with Ticketron to sell tickets. We fought to get the final approvals and the money that had been promised. As far as I was concerned, our festival was on.

Suddenly, the insurance company reneged on its commitment. We were millions of dollars short, with the festival just a few days away. We knew that tickets had been sold in New York and that people were on their way. We also knew that the acts were en route.

We had no stage, no lights, no sound system and almost no money.

I got a call from the largest local radio station in the area, WPDH, which had a signal that could be picked up hundreds of miles away.

"Sid, we hear that you're short the money to stage the festival," said Bob (The Wolf) Wohlfeld.

"Yes, that's true, but we're still going forward," I told the radio audience.

"Do you have the acts?" The Wolf asked.

"Yes, we booked them a while back and gave them deposits, so we expect they'll be here."

"What about the tickets?"

"We know that tickets have been sold, so we believe that the ticketholders will be here and expect to see a show."

"So what do you need, Sid?"

"I need a generator. I need lights. I need sound and a stage. I need carpenters and electricians."

"You don't have the money and you need all this stuff before you can have the festival. What are you going to do?"

"I'm going to move forward," I said. "I'm going to the farm, and I'll find a way to put on this festival."

"How about your threatened arrest because you don't have all the necessary permits?"

"I guess they'll just have to arrest me. I'm carrying on. People are coming, and I refuse to disappoint them."

"Well, there you have it, ladies and gentlemen," The Wolf concluded. "That was Sid Bernstein, promoter of the Bethel '94 Festival, speaking to you from the Concord Hotel, saying he's going ahead."

As soon as I hung up from the interview, the phones in my room at the Concord started to ring. The people were behind us. They wanted Bethel '94 to happen. They had voted for it, and now they backed up their vote with lights, generators, stages, carpentry, electrical work, food, hotel rooms and accommodations of all sorts.

"Sid, you got your stage," said the first caller. "I have flatbed trucks. We'll put them together in a row, and it'll make a perfect stage. I heard you on the radio, Sid! I'm dispatching the trucks immediately. You'll have your stage in ninety minutes. I know where to send them." Carpenters and electricians began calling. "Count us in, Sid. When do you want us at the farm?"

The support was overwhelming. My son Etienne rode six hundred miles on a motorcycle to offer his assistance. Everything we needed materialized, and we held the festival, but because I didn't want to go through the hassle of being arrested, I decided not to show up until the third day. I realize now that it was an error in judgment, because my arrest would have generated publicity. Even so, the estimate was that during the weekend of the festival, one hundred thousand people filtered in and out of Max Yasgur's historic farm.

The festival had been scheduled to run for three days but lasted for five. It was a lesson in what The People can do. I hadn't intended to speak to the crowd, but several of the acts pulled me onstage to praise me for having the perseverance to move forward despite all the problems. I gave all the credit to the people of Bethel and the surrounding towns. "Without these terrific folks," I said, "these five days of peace, love and cooperation could not have happened. God bless you all."

We had not one untoward incident: no violence, no theft, nothing but fun and music. Richie Havens (who brought along a crew to film the festival), Country Joe & the Fish, Sha-Na-Na, Melanie, the New Rascals, Sarah McLachlan, Joe Walsh from the Eagles, Leslie West, Arlo Guthrie and David Pirner from Soul Asylum showed up at Bethel '94 and gave the people a festival to remember.

The financial reality was somewhat grimmer. Our bottom line showed that we had lost close to a million dollars. But you're never too old to learn, and we all received an education about corruption, greed and the disregard for citizenry by elected officials. Equally important, we had created what we'd set out to—a festival of music for the people made possible by the people.

21

Mr. Ambassador

n November 1991, Carnegie Hall put on a performance of Paul
McCartney's *Liverpool Oratorio*. I was the guest of Benji Greenberg,
a great Beatles fan I had come to know over the years. We sat
with Benji's brother, Billy, in the Diamond Horseshoe, and about
ten boxes from us sat Paul and Linda. The irrepressible Benji kept
holding up his BEATLES9 license plate, and finally Paul saw it and
gave Benji the thumbs-up sign.

The management of Carnegie Hall had heard I was in the house,
and at intermission two officials came to our box.

"Mr. Bernstein, so nice to see you! We didn't know that you would
be in attendance, and we would like to invite you to a reception for
Mr. McCartney after the performance. Please bring your friends."

After the concert, the Greenbergs and I went to a reception room
packed with guests and members of the media. Paul and Linda arrived to a blinding burst of flashbulbs, and the press immediately
pounced on them.

Later, as the crowd began to disperse, Linda saw me.

Benji Greenberg with Sir Paul McCartney.

"Paul," I heard her say. "Sid's here!"

They came over to greet us, and I introduced Benji to his long-time idol. It was a pleasure to do, and Benji was having the time of his life. While he and Linda were talking about her hometown of Scarsdale, I asked Paul if Billy Greenberg could snap a picture of them together. Amenable as always, Paul agreed. As Benji pulled out his BEATLES9 plate for the picture, Paul acknowledged him: "Hey, I saw you at the performance. You were holding up that very license plate!"

If a picture is worth a thousand words, to Benji that snapshot is worth everything.

AFTER THE TOOTHPICK SCARE with Abe, I made sure to spend time with him. We never planned anything particularly exciting—a bite to eat or a stroll. We just wanted to be together. One day, as we were sitting in Central Park, Abe said, "You know, Sid, I haven't been able to eat lately. I've completely lost my appetite."

"What's wrong, Abe? Gert told me you're not eating as you usually do. And if your wife tells me, I listen." I tried to keep the conversation light.

"Sid, don't you know that I'm a respiratory invalid?"

"I don't know what you're talking about, Abe, but you have to start eating. You have to push yourself."

There was a hot-dog cart across the street.

"I'm going to get a hot dog from the vendor over there. Can I get you one?"

"Sure," he said glumly.

I bought two hot dogs and gave one to Abe. He took a bite and threw the rest into the bushes.

"Let's walk, Sid. I want to watch the kids playing softball." Abe loved to watch the youngsters in the park. As we walked, I noticed that Abe was shuffling. This was not the Abe Margolies I knew.

Not long after that meeting, Abe was diagnosed with lung cancer. How ironic that a great benefactor of chemotherapy research was stricken with the disease his money was meant to cure. I went to see him every day, whether he was at home or in the hospital. It's a terrible thing to watch your best friend waste away. I was losing Abe right before my eyes. In the end, he came home from the hospital to die.

Hundreds of people from every walk of life attended the funeral of Abe Margolies. He had touched sinners, saints and everyone in between.

Abe was as giving a man as I ever met, and I loved him dearly.

IN 1993, CYNTHIA LENNON invited me to see her son Julian perform at the Beacon Theatre in New York. Julian had developed a musical career and recorded for the Atlantic label. I brought Beau and Etienne; they sat a few rows behind Cynthia and me. The theater was packed, and when Julian walked onstage, he and his band were greeted enthusiastically.

Prior to that night, I had met Julian at the China Club and found him to be gregarious and engaging, bearing an uncanny resemblance to his father. My affection for John made it almost a given that I would like Julian as well. I admired his musical gifts, but the thing that most impressed me was his close, loving relationship with his mother. That resonated with me.

Every so often, I glanced at Cynthia as she watched her son perform. Her eyes were positively gleaming with pride. As my grandmother would say in Yiddish, Cynthia was getting *nachas*.

Whenever I am in an audience—whether as a promoter, manager, agent or just a ticketholder—I have a habit of periodically surveying the crowd to see what they are experiencing. As I was scanning the faces that night in the Beacon, out of the corner of my eye I saw Yoko Ono and her son, Sean Lennon, quietly enter the theater and take two seats to the immediate left of where Cynthia and I were sitting. Cynthia and Yoko had not seen each other for many years. Midway through his performance, Julian paused, thanked everyone for coming, then added, "I would just like to say that my younger brother is here in the audience." All of a sudden there was a charge of excitement in the air. I turned to my two boys, and they nodded as if to say, "We saw Sean and Yoko come in."

"Sean, would you please come up to the stage?" Julian asked.

Sean walked up the aisle to thunderous applause. The two Lennon boys put their arms around each other and began to sing "Stand By Me." It was an unforgettable moment, both touching and tender. Julian and Sean finished the song to a standing ovation. There they stood side by side: the two sons of a slain father. It was one of the most dramatic scenes I have ever witnessed.

After the show, we all went upstairs to greet Julian. He invited us to a post-concert party that Atlantic was throwing for him at the Hard Rock Café. My boys were itching to go, so I accepted. At the Hard Rock, we sat with Cynthia and Julian for about twenty minutes when Yoko and Sean walked in and came over to our table. I asked Beau and Etienne to change their seats so that Sean and Julian could sit together. Yoko and Cynthia greeted each other, and a photographer snapped a picture of them saying hello that was seen in newspapers all around the world. This was the first time in many years that Yoko Ono and Cynthia Lennon had been in each other's presence. Yoko was cordial to everyone, and told me how handsome and polite my sons were. We were all just parents enjoying our kids.

IN 1995, I RECEIVED AN INVITATION from Kevin McCarthy of the New York Mets organization to join in marking the thirtieth anniversary of the Beatles' first appearance at Shea Stadium, a show considered by many the single most important concert in the history of rock-and-roll. That's because it proved beyond a shadow of a doubt that rock acts could fill such a large venue.

"Mr. Bernstein, my father was head groundskeeper at Shea on August 15, 1965. I was two years old at the time. I've been hearing about you and that incredible night for most of my life. My father will never forget it. I also happen to be a huge Beatles fan, and it's a great pleasure to be talking to you. Mr. Bernstein, this coming August 15 we are planning a program commemorating the thirtieth anniversary of the Beatles concert here at Shea. The Mets will be playing that day, and we would like to give you the honor of throwing out the first ball. Would you consider doing it?"

"How nice. Can I bring my family?"

"Certainly. Bring your family and friends."

On the morning of the fifteenth, I went to Central Park to throw some stones so that I wouldn't thoroughly embarrass myself when it came time to throw the ball from my seat in the stands to the catcher. It had been a very long time since I had cranked the old soup bone.

Later that day, the Bernstein contingent was welcomed at Shea by Kevin McCarthy and the Mets. After lunch at the Diamond Club, I went to a studio in the stadium to videotape remarks about August 15, 1965, to be shown later on the Jumbotron, the large screen in centerfield. I spoke of that amazing night thirty years before when the four boys from Liverpool took New York by storm and made music history.

When it came time to throw out the first pitch, I found that my practice had paid off. It was a beautiful toss. I had scored another home run at Shea!

I finally made it into the majors!

MORE THAN FIFTY YEARS AFTER I first met Red Buttons, the boxing fan enthusiastically rooting for the underdog, I called upon him to be the master of ceremonies at a benefit that I was producing for the twenty-fifth anniversary of Daytop Village. The drug and alcohol rehab center in New York City does fabulous work and is a worthy cause. He accepted my offer and gave an outstanding performance at the benefit. I thought of Red's performance when planning Daytop's thirtieth anniversary gala five years later. Again he accepted, and again he was outstanding. The Bronx has surely turned out some wonderful people, and Red Buttons is high on the list.

IN EARLY 1998, MAYOR BARBARA COOKE and the City Council of Liverpool invited me to speak at a memorial for Brian Epstein. They felt that he hadn't been recognized enough for his accomplishments and contributions to Liverpool, and in his honor the city was planning to rename the Neptune Theatre the Brian Epstein Theatre.

As one of several speakers at the memorial, I was asked to talk for about seven or eight minutes. I felt I had to accept. This was, after all, for Brian.

"I'll be there," I said. "When do you need me?" I did not request airfare or expenses for participating in the memorial, and I was later told that this made a great impression on the organizers of the event.

The day before the ceremony, I flew to Manchester, which is twenty or thirty minutes from Liverpool. Robby Quinn, one of the leading members of the City Council, who has since become a dear friend of mine, picked me up at the airport. We drove to town, stopping to look at the houses where Paul, George, Ringo and John had spent their childhood. It put me in the proper mood. They dropped me at the Moat House, a lovely and quaint hotel. After a brief rest, Robby picked me up again and we ate a late lunch and spent the time talking about Brian and Liverpool. When I returned to the hotel, several members of the City Council stopped by to say hello and welcome me. My relationship with Brian and the Beatles seemed important to the Liverpudlians.

The next day, I went to City Hall for the noon ceremony. I met the mayor, and she asked if I would extend my speech to twenty or twenty-five minutes, since several of the other speakers had emergencies and canceled at the last minute.

"Madame Mayor," I said, not knowing that the proper form of address was Your Lordship. "For Brian Epstein I would stand on my head and speak for twenty-five hours if you asked me."

"Oh, how lovely!" she replied. "You'll not be needing to stand on your head, Mr. Bernstein, and twenty or twenty-five minutes would be perfect."

The program began with Beatles music performed by local talent and was followed by remarks from the president and a member of the City Council. Moving letters from George, Ringo and Paul, who were unable to attend, were read aloud, then the mayor introduced me. As usual, I went to the podium without notes.

I told the audience, which included Clive's son Henry, Brian's nephew, about how I had first come to speak to Brian and how we had started doing business together over thirty-five years ago. I explained to them that Brian and I never had a written contract throughout our business relationship. I spoke from my heart about how I felt about Brian Epstein, and when I finished, the audience gave a standing ovation. Many people came to me afterward to say how much they had enjoyed my remarks and how much it meant to them and Liverpool that I had taken the time to participate.

A buffet followed, and I was enjoying the food and conversation when the mayor, the president of the City Council and two other members of the Council approached. "Mr. Bernstein, could you please excuse yourself for a few minutes? We would like to speak with you in private."

Puzzled, I stood and walked with the group.

"Mr. Bernstein," the mayor said, "we have just had an informal meeting of the City Council and have unanimously selected you as the first-ever ambassador from the City of Liverpool to the United States."

Having addressed the mayor as Madam, Mayor and Mrs. Mayor and having been corrected several times, I said: "Your Lordship, I'm deeply honored. Absolutely honored! Thank you and the City Council."

So, if you ever happen to meet me, please remember to refer to me as Mr. Ambassador!

AFTER ACCEPTING THE AMBASSADORSHIP, I was introduced to Bernie Michelson, owner of a music and record shop called Hessy's.

In their formative years, the Beatles had bought much of their equipment at Hessy's and hung out there with their peers from the Liverpool music scene. "Mr. Bernstein, I would be honored if you would be our guest this evening at our home for the Sabbath meal."

Robby Quinn was able to whisper to me, "You should go there,

Sid. Bernie knew the boys when they were in Liverpool, and his home is only two doors away from where the Epsteins lived."

"It would be a pleasure to join you, Bernie."

Bernie and Sarah Michelson have a beautiful home and a lovely family. During the meal, Bernie brought out an old ledger of accounts and showed me some of the entries. There was George Harrison's name and next to it the make of the guitar he had purchased and a record of the monthly payments. I found another entry for Ringo Starr and his purchase of drumsticks. There was one for John Lennon for the purchase of assorted equipment, what he had paid and the balance. What a big kick I got out of that ledger!

Bernie had been extremely fond of "those four boys." They were real Liverpudlians, ambitious and complete gentlemen. It was a lovely evening.

About four or five weeks after returning home, Robby Quinn called from Liverpool to tell me a plaque naming me ambassador had been delivered to the City Council. Robby needed my address so that it could be mailed to me.

"Robby, don't mail it. I want to pick it up in person." There was an idea I wanted to explore.

I went to Liverpool to collect my plaque, and when I arrived at City Hall, a dozen people—government officials as well as members of the press and a representative from the BBC—were on hand. My friend Stan Satlin had accompanied me. The mayor conducted a brief ceremony and presented me with a plaque officially naming me Liverpool's ambassador to the United States.

In response, I explained how deeply touched I was and that Liverpool and its people meant a great deal to me and had played an important role in my life. I also wished aloud that I could do something to repay the honor bestowed upon me. Certainly, the citizens of Liverpool felt that I had done something for them thirty-five years ago. They were saying thanks.

After the ceremony, several members of the Council, Stan and I went back to the Moat House to enjoy refreshments and speak about the idea I was formulating. We had been sitting there for a short while when a desk clerk summoned me.

"Telephone, sir," he said.

I couldn't imagine who would be calling. I took the phone and heard Joe Flannery's voice. "Sid, I am sorry to have to convey such sad news, but I just heard on the telly that Linda McCartney has succumbed to cancer."

I had seen Linda not long ago and she had looked radiant and full of life. I knew that she had been fighting breast cancer, but I thought she was winning.

"I just saw her a few months ago at Carnegie Hall, Joe. I had been telling people how good she looked. What a terrible tragedy!"

"I'm sorry, Sid."

I hung up the phone and felt a wave of sadness. I took a moment to myself and thought about Linda. I had known her

Receiving the Liverpool ambassadorship was a great honor. I carry it with pride.

since she was a young girl in New York. She had been one of the Young Rascals' earliest and biggest fans. Linda was a talented photographer and had shot many pictures of the Rascals. She was lovely and vivacious, and her marriage to Paul had been both loving and enduring, a tribute to them both. They had a wonderful family. My heart went out to Paul and their children.

I returned to the small gathering. So as not to ruin the party, I didn't mention the phone call. However, several astute people asked me if anything was wrong.

"Some unsettling personal news," I said. No one brought it up again.

I found it ironic that the subject of the meeting at the Moat House was cancer research. I was raising the issue because I had an idea about bringing a worldwide music festival to Liverpool in the millennium year, with all proceeds going to such research. It was my way of trying to repay Liverpool for the honor they had bestowed upon me, and equally important, a way of honoring Abe's memory.

At that time, the Labor Party was in power in Liverpool, and Stan and I had become friendly with some of the Laborites on the City Council. We explored the possibility of staging the music festival. Mark O'Conner, an attorney in Liverpool, and Steve Stewart, an accountant at Ernst & Young, provided me with office space and lots of good advice whenever I was in town. They were encouraging and helpful.

Naturally, having the Beatles perform was on everyone's mind. During my many festival-planning trips, people would often ask whether I thought the remaining Beatles would reunite for the occasion. My response was always the same: "This is not about the Beatles. It's about Liverpool and its people."

I didn't think that we ought to impose our wishes on Paul, George or Ringo. I had learned during the time of the Boat People benefit that any initiatives to perform would have to come directly from them. Still I was persuaded by practically everyone involved to try to talk them into reuniting. So, against my better judgment, I contacted Paul McCartney and he graciously, but unequivocally, declined. There was no point in calling George or Ringo. There would be no Beatles reunion.

When the Labor Party lost the election of 1998 to the Liberal Democrats, it put a damper on our plans. The Liberal Democrats listened, but did not have the same enthusiasm for the project as the Laborites had. The notion of a music festival in Liverpool has been laid to rest. But only temporarily. I still hope to make this dream a reality.

> You may say I'm a dreamer,
> but I'm not the only one.
> I hope some day you'll join us,
> and the world will be as one.

Thanks, John. I couldn't have said it better. . . .

22

What Might Have Been!

W<small>E ALL MAKE MISTAKES.</small> Through the years I've let many opportunities pass me by. There was always a compelling reason. Nonetheless, I often wonder what might have been.

E<small>ARLY IN MY CAREER</small> as a promoter, during a fantastic ten-day run of shows at the Paramount, I was in the lobby greeting fans when this extraordinarily handsome giant of a man walked in alone.

"Hey, mister," he said. "Where's Mr. Sid Bernstein? I want to talk to him."

"I'm Sid Bernstein. How can I help you sir?"

"Look, you got James Brown appearing here; you got Sam Cooke; you got Jackie Wilson; you got the biggest acts in the world. I'm a big act. I want to get up there on that stage of yours. I don't sing, I don't play an instrument, but I will do business for you. I want to be in this show for a couple of days. How long you gonna be here?"

"We have about a week to go."

"I won't cost you much. I just want to be on that stage, and I want to talk and perform for the people, but I don't sing and I don't play, Mr. Bernstein."

"We don't have time in the show to add another act. We'd love to have you, but there's just no room."

"You're missing a good thing, Mr. Bernstein. I'd do a job for you."

"I know," I said. "Let's do it next time. I give you my word, the next time we do this, you're in."

In retrospect, I wonder if I should have let Muhammad Ali just walk onstage and say hello to the crowd.

I have no doubt that he would have electrified the audience.

WORKING ON THE NEWPORT JAZZ FESTIVAL in the summer of 1961, I had to do an enormous amount of planning from my office in New York. I had no time for any other project, especially one that would require lots of energy and focus. In the days and weeks leading up to the festival, Billy Fields, Gerry's roommate Nada Rowand and I were working eighteen hours a day in an office above Howard Johnson's on Forty-sixth and Broadway. The phones were ringing off the hook. We were besieged for tickets. We were also dealing with the logistical nightmare of arranging transportation in and out of Newport for all the acts. The three of us were doing the work of ten people. Right in the middle of this frenetic activity, a young girl came into the office.

"I'm looking for Sid Bernstein," she said in an unmistakable New York accent.

"I'm Sid Bernstein," I answered as the phone rang. "Excuse me, young lady. I've got to take this call. We are trying to put on the Newport Jazz Festival, and it's a little crazy around here. Please bear with me if you will."

When I hung up, she tried to tell me her story again, but the phone kept interrupting. Slowly, and in fragments between the interruptions from Billy and Nada, I learned what she wanted.

"I'm a singer, and I'm looking for a manager. Eddie Blum [the assistant to Richard Rodgers] told me to come see you." Mentioning

Eddie Blum gave her immediate credibility with me, since Eddie was a friend of mine and I respected him highly. I looked at her more closely. She was rail thin and wearing ill-fitting clothes, topped off with a strange hat.

Please forgive me, dear. I can't give you the attention you obviously deserve. I don't want to be discourteous, and I would never short-shrift a friend of Eddie's. Would you please call me when all of this is over?"

"When would that be, Mr. Bernstein?"

"In about six weeks. We are committed to a promotion in Hartford with Brook Benton and Connie Francis right after Newport, so early August would be a good time. I will be happy to talk and listen to you sing then."

She was disappointed, but agreed to call in six weeks. I concentrated on the events in Newport and Hartford and forgot about my brief encounter with the young singer.

A few days after we returned from Hartford, Gerry saw an ad in a local paper that piqued her interest.

"Sid, remember the girl that Eddie Blum sent to see you? The one you were too busy to talk to? Well, it says in this ad that she's at the Bon Soir in the Village. Would you like to listen to her sing?"

"Sure, love. Let's go."

What I saw in the Bon Soir that night was nothing short of mesmerizing. Without the hat, the waif who appeared in my office looked polished and sophisticated. While her singing was fabulous, what I noticed most were her magnificent hands. She had the long, elegant fingers of a concert pianist. Her grace and poise made her a presence to be reckoned with.

When the set ended, Gerry and I went backstage to say hello. As we walked in, I saw my old friend Marty Erlichman, who managed Tommy Makem and the Clancy Brothers, a popular and successful Irish folk group.

"What are you doing here, Marty?"

"I'm signing this girl. I met her when she was on the same bill with Tommy and the Brothers at the Blue Angel, and I liked her so much that I'm going to manage her."

I backed off completely. I would never dream of poaching some-one else's act. Because I had been too busy making arrangements for Newport and Hartford to talk to this girl, Marty Erlichman had seized the opportunity. And so I lost the chance to manage Barbra Streisand.

DURING THE HEIGHT OF THE Rascals' popularity, I established an office at 75 East Fifty-fifth Street, in the same building as well-known agent Bert Block. Also in that building were my friends Albert Grossman and Mort Lewis, who managed the Brothers Four, a hot folk act. One day Frankie Valli called. Frankie and the Four Seasons had had many hits. I had presented the Four Seasons when I pro-duced the Paramount holiday shows, and we had stayed loosely in touch over the years.

"Sid, we broke up with our manager, and I'd like to talk to you about possibly taking us on. I know how busy you are, and I don't want to come to your office because of the tumult I'm sure is going on there. Would you consider coming to my home in New Jersey? I heard you like Italian food, so I promise you the best homemade Italian meatballs you ever ate!" Frankie had evidently done some research.

"Frankie, you're on!" I said. "Who could pass up the best meat-balls ever?"

A few days later, I drove to Frankie's house. We spent a fun few hours together, and the meatballs were indeed fabulous. I also lis-tened to Frankie's tales of woe about the group's former manager. But I had done some research of my own, and had heard stories of how the Four Seasons used to fight amongst themselves. There was even an account of their missing a plane flight as they argued. I didn't want to get in the middle of another squabbling group. The Rascals had been enough for me. I begged off.

VERY OFTEN, FRIENDS AND BUSINESS ASSOCIATES would give my name to aspiring singer-songwriters and bands. One day, a handsome young man walked into my office and introduced himself. I recognized his name and knew that he had written a number-one song for The Monkees.

"How can I help you?" I asked.

"I need a manager."

"I don't think that, as a songwriter, you need a manager."

"That's true, but I want to start performing. I sing and also play the guitar. I think I could use a manager now for guidance in becoming a performer."

"I understand. The first thing you ought to do is go to the Bitter End and ask for Billy Fields and Freddie Weintraub. They run talent showcases, and they can help with your presentation. Billy, in fact, was a vocalist who left a performing career to manage the club. He can be helpful to you. Then, I think you should come back here at your convenience, bring your guitar and you can audition for me."

He stood abruptly, looked at me and said, "I'll call you."

Years later, I learned that my use of the word "audition" had offended Neil Diamond, so much so that he didn't want to have anything to do with me.

"Not in my wildest dreams did I intend to offend such a great talent as Neil Diamond. He was a sensitive kid.

ON ANOTHER OCCASION, a rather short young man came into my office while my secretary, Sherry, was at lunch. I motioned to him to sit down as I was finishing a call. When I hung up, I gave him my full attention.

"Mr. Bernstein," he said, "I would like to talk to you about management."

I looked at this nondescript fellow and asked about his aspirations.

"A friend and I have a record coming out on Columbia in the next week or two, and I'd like to get a manager and an agent; we have neither. Until now, I've been doing the bookings myself."

"Do you have the album or anything I could listen to?"

"No, but the record will be out in a week or two. I should have brought a tape, but I forgot. I saw your name in a directory in one of the industry magazines, so I decided to come to your office. A few other names are listed as having offices in this building, too."

"What do you do?"

"I write and play the guitar, and my friend and I sing."

"Tell me . . . who else do you have on your list?"

He looked down at a paper. "Albert Grossman and Mort Lewis."

"That's a good start you have there," I said. "Both men are friends of mine, and both are terrific managers. In fairness to yourself, you should stop in at both their offices. Also, try to meet Bert Block on this floor; he's a great agent. You can use my name to help you get in the door. After you've seen everybody, come back and let me know how you made out."

"Thank you, Mr. Bernstein. You've been very helpful. Can I drop my album off when it's released?"

"By all means. I look forward to hearing it!"

He left and went on his quest for a manager and an agent. The next day, Mort Lewis called.

"Sid, I want to thank you for sending that kid up to me yesterday. He's an interesting, bright kid. I spent quite a bit of time with him, and I'm going to take him and his buddy on."

"You're welcome, Mort. I remember the kid, but I've forgotten his name."

"His name is Paul Simon. He plays with a guy named Garfunkle."

WHILE STILL WORKING WITH Jerry Weintraub at Management Three, I began to hear talk among industry friends about a musical revue called *Grease* being performed by a theater company in Chicago. The word-of-mouth was great, so I decided to inquire further. I tracked down the name of the theater where *Grease* was playing and called the producer.

He confirmed that the show was generating a lot of buzz in Chicago. I explained my background, and he invited me to Chicago to see the production.

Nothing makes a show successful like good word-of-mouth—not advertising, not hype, not promotions, not even critical acclaim. As it turned out, my friend Dick Clark, of *American Bandstand* fame, also had heard about *Grease*. Dick was based on the West Coast, and he found out that I had been calling the theater in Chicago. So was he.

"Sid, we're old friends and go back a long way," he telephoned to say. "I understand that you're interested in that show *Grease*, in Chicago. Why compete? Why don't we work on this together? It's been a long time coming, don't you think?"

"I agree. I'd love to be partners with you, Dick."

Dick and I discussed a plan to coproduce if we were able to acquire the rights to the show. During our conversation, I got the idea that Dick would fly to Chicago from L.A. to begin negotiations for a Bernstein-Clark production. But Dick had the opposite impression, namely, that I would go to Chicago to handle the negotiations. Each thought the other was going, so nobody went.

Several weeks passed with no word from Dick. I called and asked if he had made any progress with *Grease*. When Dick told me that he was waiting to hear from *me*, we simultaneously moaned: "Uh-oh!" A classic case of miscommunication.

Meanwhile, Maxine and Kenneth Waissman, a young couple from New York, traveled to Chicago and struck a deal to bring *Grease* to the Big Apple. The rest is history. *Grease* went on to become a Broadway blockbuster and earn megabucks as a film starring John Travolta and Olivia Newton-John.

Dick and I can only laugh through our tears.

WHILE I WAS MANAGING Laura Branigan's career, I became a regular at several New York City clubs and got to know some of the owners and managers. As a courtesy, they would let me know when certain performers would be appearing. Rick Newman, whose popular Catch a Rising Star was not far from my home, became a pal. I would often stop by to say hello and see who some of the future stars might be. Even though his was a comedy club, from time to time Rick would present a singer.

On one of my visits, I heard a young vocalist with a killer voice that wouldn't quit. She looked like she weighed less than a hundred pounds but was a vocal powerhouse. Rick made sure that I knew when this young lady would be performing.

One day, Rick called. "Sid, the other night after you left, the A&R guy from Chrysalis Records came in with Barbara Skydell from Premier

Talent, and they flipped over your favorite singer. They are both going to sign her. She's all set. I'm going to be managing her. She's going to record for Chrysalis, and Premier is going to handle her bookings. Here's my problem: I'm a café owner. What the hell do I know about management? I'd love for you to be my partner in this deal, Sid. We'll be co-managers."

"Listen, Rick, I'm so involved with Laura Branigan that I couldn't even think of taking on another responsibility. I can't do this to Laura. I'm sorry, but I just can't."

"Okay, I understand."

When Chrysalis released the record by Rick's singer, it was an immediate hit.

Bert Padell, Rick Newman's business manager and a friend of mine, called me.

"Sid, are you crazy? You don't want to be Rick's partner in this? Are you out of your mind? Her record is a runaway hit! Chrysalis is shipping records as fast as they can press them! I'd like to meet with you so we can discuss this further. Please come to my office as soon as you can."

When I got to Bert's office later that week, Rick Newman was there, too.

Rick spoke first.

"Sid, I'm sorry, but I had to tell Bert about our conversation because I need help. I know you like Laura Branigan and are committed to her career, but why should that interfere with what I proposed? I'll do my share, but I'd rather have you as my partner. This management stuff is really not my thing."

Bert piped in. "You and Rick are good friends; you get along. It'll be great for both of you. C'mon, Sid!"

"I'm sorry. I can't do it to Laura."

"You see, Rick? I told you," said Bert. "The guy is nuts!"

As I walked out of Bert's office, I was somewhat disappointed. I felt a real bond with Rick and would have liked to help him with Pat Benatar.

NOT LONG AFTER THAT, I got a call from a female singer whom I had known and whose work I admired. She invited me to lunch, and I could never turn down the opportunity to have a delicious meal with lovely company.

While we waited for our order, she said: "Sid, I need a manager. My husband has been managing me, but we're getting divorced and I don't want to work with him anymore. My career's doing well, so I feel that I need someone with whom I can feel comfortable and who will take care of me. Would you consider taking me on?"

"I don't have to think about it. I've been working on Laura Branigan's career for quite a while now, and I don't really think it would be fair to sign another female artist. Your career has taken off, and you are going to need lots of attention. You deserve someone who can devote the time and energy necessary to maintain your career. I'm sorry, but I'm not taking on any new female singers right now."

"I appreciate your loyalty, Sid. It's refreshing to see. I can promise you that it wouldn't make a difference to me. You could manage us both."

"I know, but I'm sorry, I just can't do it to Laura." Those were my words to Melissa Manchester.

LIFE IS ABOUT CHOICES. What is the saying? "If I had known then what I know now . . ." But who knew?!

23

Bashert

I HAVE BEEN INCREDIBLY FORTUNATE and blessed in my life. My parents could not have been more loving or nurturing. My friends have been true, loyal and unbelievably supportive. My wife has been my devoted partner and confidant. Together, we have raised six of the nicest people you would ever want to meet.

I have never measured success by accolades, honor or money. I believe my life has been successful because of the love that surrounds me. Some people say I have been very lucky, and that may be true. But I believe that there is something larger, something beyond the ordinary, that has shaped my life. Let me explain by recounting one final incident.

AS I MENTIONED EARLIER, Benji Greenberg is one of the world's most devoted Beatles fans. He is simply crazy about them.

One day Benji called to tell me that Paul McCartney was going to be at the Ed Sullivan Theatre to videotape an introduction to his new album for MTV.

"Sid, could you please get tickets so that we can go?"

"Benji, I'll listen to the album when it comes out, but I really don't want to watch a TV shoot. I've seen enough of them in my life. I will, however, try to get you a ticket."

I started by calling Joe Dera, a longtime friend and Paul McCartney's publicist.

"Sid, I don't have any tickets," Joe said. "I've given all mine to the press. But, if I come across an extra one, it's yours."

Next, I called John Eastman, Linda McCartney's brother.

"Sidley [his nickname for me], not only don't I have any tickets, but Joe Dera's office is calling to see whether I can return the few extra tickets they gave me! I had to disappoint them because I've already given them all away. I'm sorry, I just don't have any tickets."

I relayed the news to Benji, but he was unrelenting: "Sid, please! I have to be there!"

I told him I would keep working on it.

On the day of the taping, Joe Dera called. "Sid, we don't have a ticket, but if your friend will come to the door, my right-hand lady, Rachel, will walk him in."

"Thanks, Joe. I really appreciate it. Benji will be there."

I called Benji, who vowed to make it to the theater from Westchester despite the nor'easter that had hit the area, knocking out train service, flooding highways and causing overall chaos.

"I'll get there, Sid, if I have to run all the way."

On the evening of the taping, Jackie Mason, the great comedian, called.

"Sid, could you meet me at the Edison Hotel this evening? Herman Badillo [a New York politician] is thinking about running for mayor, and he wants my support. You're good at this stuff, and I value your opinion. Would you please come?"

"Jackie, first of all, I'm about to have dinner with my family. Second, have you looked outside lately? It's been raining torrentially all day! I'll never get a cab. I don't think so."

"Sid, the meeting with Herman isn't until 8:30. By then, you'll be finished with dinner, and maybe the weather will let up."

I didn't want to disappoint Jackie, so I thought I'd try to make it

"Mister, I'm talking to you," Jackie Mason won a 1986 Tony Award for his one-man Broadway show, The World According to Me!

downtown to the Edison. After dinner, I grabbed my raincoat and told Gerry and the kids that I was going to make an attempt to hail a cab and meet Jackie, "but don't be surprised if I'm back up here in fifteen minutes."

When I got downstairs, the rain was still coming down in buckets. The visibility was extremely poor and empty taxis kept passing me by. Then a cabbie spotted me from the opposite side of the street and began working his way laterally across the avenue. He pulled up in front of me, and I jumped in.

"The Edison Hotel, please."

"Ed-ee-sun?" The foreign-born driver seemed to be new to New York. I reassured him that I could direct him there.

As we slowly made our way downtown, I opened my coat and got comfortable. I placed my hands down on the seat and touched what felt like a chain lodged between the seat cushion and the back. I pulled at it until it was released and saw that a rectangular plastic card was attached to the chain. I held the laminated card up to the dim light.

I pinched myself. *Was I dreaming?* I looked around for angels. I read and re-read the card to make sure I wasn't mistaken. I was in a state of total wonderment.

"Hold it, driver, our destination has changed."

"Change?"

"Yes, please make a right on Second Avenue and Fifty-third Street and head west until I tell you to stop. When we got to the Ed Sullivan Theatre, I jumped out of the cab and ran to the stage door. Flashing my newly discovered staff pass, I walked over to two security men: "Will this get me in?"

"That will get you anywhere you want to go. Come right in."

Inside the theater, the seating area was dark and Linda and Paul were onstage playing with the band. I spotted an empty aisle seat and slid into it. Joel Siegel, a well-known New York theater, movie and TV critic, was in the next seat. He and I were old friends, and I whispered a hello to him and couldn't help adding: "You wouldn't believe how I got here."

"Sid, who more than you should be here?"

I smiled and let it go. I removed my wet raincoat and settled in to watch the taping.

The music was pure McCartney, and the time flew. When the performance ended, I made my way to the dressing-room area, the memories of that wild night when the Beatles did their first *Sullivan* show racing through my mind. The two security guards looked at the staff pass around my neck, then opened the door for me. I walked toward the elevator that would take me to the dressing rooms, and there stood John Eastman waiting with his family.

"Sidley!" he exclaimed. "How did you get in?"

"John, too long of a story, and you wouldn't believe it anyway. I just want to say a quick hello to Paul and your sister. Would that be okay?"

"Go right ahead. Take the elevator. They're upstairs."

I held up my pass to the elevator attendant and he took me up. When the door opened, there stood Richard Ogden, Paul's manager.

"Hey, Sid! What are you doing here?!"

"Oh, Richard, it's a long and unbelievable story. . . . Where's Paul?"

"Over there, in the first dressing room."

I walked toward the dressing room, where yet another security man stopped me. Paul saw me through the open door. "Sid!" he exclaimed, extending his arms. "Are you alone?"

"I couldn't bring my family, Paul. It was tough enough for me to get in, let alone the whole group. Besides that, the story of how I managed to get here at all is truly amazing."

STEVE SHERMAN

The "long and winding road" brought two old friends together.

"What happened?" Paul asked intently.

I related the entire story, then stopped for a second. "I felt like an angel had put the staff pass there, Paul."

"It was the hand of God," Paul said as he tapped my forearm. "The hand of God."

"In Yiddish, Paul, you would say that it was *bashert*."

"*Bashert*?" Paul liked the word. "What does it mean?"

"Destiny . . . the hand of God."

"How do you spell it?"

"B-A-S-H-E-R-T. *Bashert*." He repeated it a few times.

"Paul, where's Linda? I want to say a quick hello."

"She's in the next dressing room. She'll be surprised to see you."

Linda greeted me warmly, and introduced me to several people in the room.

"This is Sid Bernstein, everyone! The man who introduced Paul to America!"

I planted a kiss on her cheek and made my exit.

As I was walking to the elevator, I saw Paul talking to John Eastman and pointing toward my staff pass. As I got near, I could hear Paul say, "The will of God . . . the hand of God."

"Paul, are you telling John the story?"

"Will I ever forget it, Sid? . . . And what is that Yiddish word you taught me? I want to tell John."

"*Bashert*, Paul. *Bashert*."

Index